THE SCOTCH-IRISH IN NORTHERN IRELAND AND IN THE AMERICAN COLONIES

THE

SCOTCH-IRISH IN NORTHERN IRELAND AND THE AMERICAN COLONIES

Maude Glasgow, M.D.

HERITAGE BOOKS
2008

HERITAGE BOOKS

AN IMPRINT OF HERITAGE BOOKS, INC.

Books, CDs, and more—Worldwide

For our listing of thousands of titles see our website
at
www.HeritageBooks.com

Published 2008 by
HERITAGE BOOKS, INC.
Publishing Division
100 Railroad Ave. #104
Westminster, Maryland 21157

Copyright © 1936 Maude Glasgow, M.D.

International Standard Book Numbers
Paperbound: 978-0-7884-0945-5
Clothbound: 978-0-7884-7003-5

Dedicated

In love and reverence, to the memory of
my sister, Janet M. Glasgow, whose devotion to high ideals and rare unselfishness
endeared her to all those privileged to
come within the sphere of her influence.

PREFACE

THE Scotch-Irish are just a part of the Anglo-Saxon race, always distinguished for its love of free institutions and hatred of tyranny. A part of the same race agonized in Holland for many bleeding years before winning deliverance, and England herself fought for human rights against embattled despotism and was successful.

Small states, however, are less likely to engage the attention of the world than are large ones, even if heroic deeds are just as great, if the inhabitants of the smaller states are doers rather than dreamers and talkers, and great injustices may be perpetrated which leave an indelible imprint on the page of history, without receiving much but local attention; yet surely the descendants of any race which has left great and inspiring records behind it should be as conversant with the checkered history of their own people as with that of Greece or Rome or Mesopotamia.

It is true, busy people cannot always afford the time necessary to delve into ponderous tomes or to obtain treatises on the subject desired, and this is the time when a handbook written on the subject required can be of great service. It may happen that the fancied claims of some to the valiant deeds of ancestors puzzle and confuse by discrepancies, misstatements, and alterations of fact, and a convenient manual may prove serviceable in refuting mythical claims, supplying as it can, not only an authentic text, but the names of reliable historians and records of unimpeachable value.

The history of bygone ages is not always pleasant reading, yet if the undesirable portions are colored or omitted, the work cannot be classed either as fiction or history.

The difficult lives of the Presbyterian Dissenters in Northern Ireland seem scarcely credible to the uninformed, yet the facts are incontrovertible. The colonists were descendants of the same race as the English, yet suffered more for their faith than did the Roman Catholics, and it is a notable fact that in spite of the attempt made to exterminate the northern colonists, the effort to liberate the Roman Catholics from their religious disabilities came from Belfast and with but few dissenting voices was endorsed throughout the colony.

It was the staunch Presbyterians of Ulster whose audacity, dauntless courage, and sagacity became such an overwhelming power in aiding the continuance of the Protestant religion in England, and in seating a new dynasty on the island throne.

The influence of this little far-away corner of the vast British Empire on the United States, and thus indirectly on the world, has also been of far-reaching importance, as shown by the history of the Revolutionary War, and of the country.

In this sketch, the author has consulted leading historians of acknowledged repute, and referred to authentic records for important data, yet, conscious of human frailty, she would ask the kind indulgence of her readers.

CONTENTS

I

IRISH HISTORY TO THE TIME OF JAMES I

Two distinct races in Ireland; practically no intermixture. Opinions on this subject of outstanding authorities. The most reliable early record of the country found in *Annals of the Four Masters*. Ptolemy's opinions. The claim to possession of every invader of Ireland based alike on the law of the strongest. The oldest races found in western Connaught and in remote localities in the south. Condition of country at the time of Scandinavian invasion. Commerce carried on by means of barter. Marriage laws and social customs. Druids and their religion. Instrumentality of captive slaves in introducing the Christian religion. St. Patrick; his birthplace. Only two authentic documents give history of Patrick. His theology and the tenets of his faith. Teachings of early Irish church. Schools Patrick established. The Irish missionary Columba and his work. Education confined to clerical class, the people knew nothing of education. At this time nation consists of aggregations of tribes and there are no cities. The pope not recognized in Ireland until the twelfth century, about the same time that England asserted her claims. Succeeding years register no social advance because of almost constant warfare. The Anglo-Norman invasion. Norman names changed to Irish. Ireland was in practically her old condition when the house of Tudor came to the throne, and supremacy was shared between Irish and Anglo-Normans. Irish still have no corporate existence, and plundering and destruction is the daily occupation. The annals of Lough Ce, and the annals of the Four Masters describe manner of life. The Tudors. Mary issues orders for the burning of heretics in Ireland. Mary establishes a colony. Constant rebellion throughout Elizabeth's reign. The pope tries to weaken and destroy the authority of Elizabeth. She replaces Brehon law by English laws and meets one rebellion after another until at last she is victorious. The Earl of Tyrone and his rebellions. Elizabeth founds the first Irish college, now known as Trinity College. Toleration of religion as practiced on the continent and in Ireland, and the penal laws in Ireland and in France. When James I ascended the throne Cork and Limerick refused to proclaim him on account of his heresy. James pardoned Tyrone and restored his property, but the Earl immediately attempted another conspiracy. The case of the conspiracy was tried by the Grand Jury in Donegal when as a punishment for repeated conspiracies the property of the delinquents escheated to the crown thus leaving a large tract of land in the hands of the English sovereign which at a later period was planted with Scotch and English settlers and known as the Plantation of Ulster.

II

THE PLANTATION AND THE IRISH ST. BARTHOLOMEW

The Plantation—Scottish education—Presbyterian ministers in Ulster—James I—Andrew Melville—Charles I—The Black Oath—Star Chamber established, Presbyterians persecuted and prosecuted, and thrown into prison for their faith—Strength of Catholics before 1641—Rebellion and massacre of 1641—Oliver Cromwell punishes the murderers of 1641, and administers the law in Ireland —Cromwell presents the Engagement to Presbyterians, and prepares for their deportation, but later rescinds order on finding them a law-abiding people 43

Population of Ireland at time of Plantation. Large area of land forfeited to the crown due to rebellion of rebel earls. Country found wasted and undeveloped, with dense forests sheltering wild animals. Agent of government in development of plan was Sir Arthur Chichester. Division of lands and conditions of grant; London corporation receives a grant in Londonderry. Houses quickly built, land cleared and put into cultivation. Towns appear. Scottish character which makes the development rapid and thorough described. Sons of the new settlers obliged to walk to a port in order to reach Glasgow or Edinburgh for a college education. The new settlers in Ulster brought their school system with them which they ran without government aid, but as yet there was no college in Ulster. Influence of the Scotch kirk on the character of the nation; the principles inculcated were markedly republican. James Bryce, ancestor of Ambassador Bryce, settles in Ulster to escape persecution on account of his religion. Other ministers arrive, some of them men of rank; some have been college professors, and practically all university graduates. The colonists bring with them a knowledge of the manufacture of linen. Population increases, crops are good, there is some beginning of trade relations. Colonists obliged to be on guard at all times, vigilance must not be relaxed. Idle young men always trying to prey on the industrious. Articles of Religion adopted in convention (1615) of Episcopalians and Dissenters. The Confession of Faith is largely based on these articles. James I, a despot at heart, disapproves of the independence of his countrymen. The Scotch self-reliance and independence the result of environment. Charles I succeeds his father and shows favor to the Catholics. Sir Thomas Wentworth, afterwards created Earl of Strafford, appointed Viceroy of Ireland; is hostile to the Dissenters and they build the *Eagle's Wing* in order to obtain a peaceful life in America, but unpropitious weather drives the small vessel back after they have wrestled with stormy weather for two months. Persecution of the Dissenters increases; attempt made to force the Black Oath on the colonists. Many flee to the wilds to escape cruelties awaiting them. Scotland threatens to send an army to Ulster to aid her suffering people, and Wentworth plans to exile the colonists from Ulster. A Star Chamber is established in Dublin with will and power to punish; meanwhile Catholics were receiving unusual favor. At last Wentworth is recalled to London and executed because of his shortcomings. Catholics now are very aggressive and threatening. Priests meet at Multifarnum, an abbey in Westmeath, and plan a massacre of Protestants. This insurrection of October, 1641, is known as the Irish St. Bartholomew. The ferocities and slaughters of this massacre are revolting and although Ireland is a small country compared to France the loss of life was more than six times as large as in the great French slaughter. Proofs of this gigantic slaughter are unassailable though efforts are often made to minimize the massacres. Cromwell arrives in Ireland and punishes the guilty and is slandered by those who receive what they have meted out to others, but on a scale infinitely less than they have deserved. Cromwell's character. His challenge to the Catholic prelates to show him one injustice he had committed was never met. Cromwell threatens the Dissenters whom he suspects of favoring the Stuarts, but relents when he finds them peaceable and industrious, though he had planned their exile. Ireland very prosperous under the rule of Cromwell. Sketch of Archbishop Laud, who was responsible for much Irish and English misery.

Contents

III

CONTINUED PERSECUTION OF DISSENTERS AND THE SIEGE OF LONDONDERRY

Charles II regains the crown—Prelacy restored, and
Presbyterians again persecuted—Second Act of
Uniformity introduced and emigration of Presbyterians stimulated by the intolerance shown them
—The Catholic penal laws suspended—Rev. Francis Makemie, Presbyterian minister, emigrates to
Virginia and is followed by other pastors; a Presbytery established (the first)—James II succeeds
his brother; an intolerant, bigoted, stupid, and obstinate man, he rekindles Presbyterian persecution
and favors only Catholics—Prince of Orange arrives in England—Londonderry besieged by
French and Irish Catholic armies—Battle of Newtown-Butler won over greatly superior numbers by
Protestants—William of Orange arrives in Ireland; battle of the Boyne won, Limerick besieged,
battle of Aughrim fought and won—William
grants Regium Donum out of Belfast customs
in spirit of gratitude to northern fighters—Plots
against the life of William discovered resulting
in restraining laws against Catholics, but these are
generally not enforced—The Protestant Episcopal Church, character of its clerics, and their effect
on the country—The woolen manufacture destroyed by English legislation; people reduced to
poverty; emigration receives further stimulation
—Belfast, the northern metropolis; its industries   80

Charles II brought back to England. Prelacy restored.
Catholics to receive special favor. Second Act of Uniformity passed. Presbyterian ministers ordered to use
Prayer Book and to discard League and Covenant, and
promise never to rebel against the king. No pastor to
practice his calling who refuses to subscribe. Attempt to
foist alien ministers on people obstinately refused, and
worship is carried on secretly. Bishops more interested
in the technique of public worship than in character of
officiating ministers. Result of bishops' action seen in
obstruction of Protestant immigration and the flight of Dis-

Anne favors prelacy so Anglicans are unrestrained. Pernicious legislation affecting Dissenters enacted and tolerance of William's reign reversed, while Catholics still receive favor. A retrospect. Execution of penal laws only verbally severe while Dissenters are discriminated against and the Non-Conformist life-blood of Ulster almost drained away by emigration to the American colonies. Anglicans are Jacobites and traitors to the House of Hanover. Unrest prevails in the eighteenth century. Kidnaping of Protestant girls. Anglicans support the forced marriages of the kidnapers. Outrage in Connemara where a Protestant settlement is destroyed and there is a similar occurrence in Killala in the south. Tolerant Catholics are not tolerated by the Irish. Hostile attitude

Contents

XV

shown to Moody and Sankey in 1883 and same attitude
manifested in 1911. The Oakboys and Steelboys and petition of latter to Irish viceroy. Eviction of Ulster colonists
from their homes, who join their relatives in America,
now about to enter upon the Revolutionary War. Catholics take the estates of the evicted colonists and organize
a body known as Defenders. Protestants organize a
defensive body called Orangemen. Penal laws against
Catholics relaxed but not repealed. The constitution of
1782. Battle of the Diamond, and formation of first
Orange Lodge as a league of defense against Catholic
aggression. An occurrence at Wexford illustrates the
credulity and fanaticism of Catholics. Membership in the
Orange Lodge, and the high order of ethics and morality
inculcated.

V

EMIGRATION TO AMERICA

The Presbyterian exodus from Ulster excites alarm in
Parliament which orders an investigation; the emigrants flock to the colonies—William Penn busy
in eastern New Jersey—Laws in New York unfavorable to Catholics—Celtic-Irish emigration—
Celtic-Irish characteristics as noted by eminent
historians—Irish abuse of England—Catholic
Emancipation 154

Protestant settlements in American colonies. The Ulster
exodus claims attention of Irish Parliament. Famine
of 1740-1 gives further impulse to Protestant emigration to the colonies. Loss to Ulster in manufacturing
people and in trading cash from 1728 to 1750. Opinion of
Lecky on these emigrants and statement of Parker. Influence of Scotch-Irish on the new country with respect
to education, etc., and their widespread settlements. Opinion of Arthur Young on emigration with respect to the
Ulster colonists and the Irish Catholics. Mr. Makemie
and Mr. McGregor. Quandary of James Logan in Philadelphia, Pittsburg and its founders. Settlements in the
south. Scotch-Irish not always welcomed in the colonies.
Laws against Catholics in New York and refusal to grant
them political privileges. Purchase of Sam Glass. County
of Linn in Kentucky. Scotch-Irish settle in Canada. The
Celtic-Irish emigration begins a century after the Ulster
exodus and is caused by the famine of 1845-6. Irish
leaders encourage early marriages and large families.
Character of Celtic-Irish emigrant. Opinions of historians
and others on the Celtic-Irish character. Irish denunciation of England. Cause of delay in Catholic Emancipation.

Contents

VI

RELIGIOUS WAR

VII

THE UNION AND HOME RULE

VIII

THE SCOTCH-IRISH IN AMERICA AND THE REVOLUTIONARY WAR

Large numbers of Protestant emigrants to the American colonies had fled from their homes because

America proves a welcome outlet to persecuted European Protestants, which explains why American population
in the colonies at the time of the Revolutionary War was
almost entirely Protestant. In the colonies, Anglicans
expect special favor. Schools and religious sects in New
York. Sects in Jersey, Rhode Island, and New England.
Political privileges withheld from Catholics. Education
in the south and Scotch-Irish settlements there. George
Calvert receives a grant of land in Maryland. James
Logan is secretary to Penn and afterwards Governor of
Pennsylvania. The Quakers. Traits of the Scotch-Irish
people. William Tennant and the "Log College." Other
colleges founded in the east. The Presbyterians of Virginia influence the incorporation of the Virginia Bill of
Rights, and influence Jefferson to write his act for the
establishment of religious liberty. American war of independence receives early and vigorous support from the
Scotch-Irish. English statesmen of this period were of
inferior caliber. English conduct of the war in the
colonies. Character of opposing officers. The Mecklenburg Declaration of Independence. Battles of Saratoga
and King's Mountain. Clark's campaign in the northwest compared to the exploits of Hannibal. The stream
of Scotch-Irish pioneers and their settlements. The race
first to secede from England and first to shed its blood
for American freedom.

IX

THE SCOTCH-IRISH IN AMERICA (*Continued*)
—MANY EMINENT NAMES

Population of country when Revolutionary War began
—Most of early successes due to Scotch-Irish—
Friendly Sons of St. Patrick, organized by Scotch-
Irish with only three Catholics—Organizing for

Population of American colonies preceding the war of
independence. Catholics form about one-twelfth of the
people. Attitude of Celtic Irishmen towards the war, and
opinions of Ulster colonists. Opinions on the subject by
Plowden, Bancroft, Froude, William Grace, Ramsay,
Lecky, General Lee, Mr. Custis, Dr. T. Y. Killen. The
Scotch-Irish colonists in America form the organization
known as the Friendly Sons of St. Patrick, and display
the same spirit of toleration towards Catholics shown at
the meetings in Dungannon, when they elect Stephen Moylan, a Catholic, as president of their organization. Names
of members of the association mentioned. The "Sons"
form a troop known as the Light Horse Cavalry. Names
of members on the roll of troops during the war of independence who belonged to the "Friendly Sons." The
Committee of Safety. The "Sons'" record during the war.
Members taking active part in organizing for war. The
patriots establish a bank to relieve distressing situation
incident to the war. Names of subscribers. The Hibernian Society was organized for the relief of immigrants
by the "Sons" and this organization also was composed
almost entirely of Scotch-Irish. Names of members of the
Hibernian Society. Another organization of Scotch-
Irishmen was the Boston Irish Charitable Society also
organized on St. Patrick's Day as early as 1737. Members almost all Protestants and manifested a very tolerant
spirit. The twenty-six original names here given. Campbell speaks of the "Friendly Sons," pointing out their
liberality in admitting three Catholics to their organization. The staunchest friends of American independence,
and the first to take a determined stand on the question.
The Scotch-Irish of Mecklenburg county and their resolutions. The Presbyterians of New Jersey, New York,
and Pennsylvania. Bancroft on the Presbyterians in the
revolted colonies. Rev. John Witherspoon speaks of the
Presbyterians at the Continental Congress. The Presbyterian church suffers severely because of the war.

Contents

xxi

Names of prominent patriots, some of them elders in the
Presbyterian church. Battles at King's Mountain, at
Huck's Defeat. Influences securing adoption of Bill of
Rights in Virginian legislature, and also supporting establishment of religious freedom. Scotch-Irish in House
of Burgesses deny validity of Stamp Act. Other resolutions. The Declaration of Independence. Daniel Morgan, Henry Knox, John E. Howard Campbell, Pickens,
and others at King's Mountain and Cowpens. Anthony
Wayne, Daniel Boone, Patrick Henry, Rutledge, Blair,
and others. Commodore Oliver Hazard Perry and his
five brothers. Matthew Galbraith Perry. Names of nine
presidents of the United States of Scotch-Irish blood.
Names of famous men of Scotch and Scotch-Irish blood
in America, including the patriotic Livingston family, A. T.
Stewart, Asa Gray, Horace Greeley, Robert Fulton, John
W. Mackay, Cyrus Hall McCormick and there are many
others. Thomas A. Edison was part Dutch, and part
Scotch-Irish. Britain has crowned with honors William
Thompson, Lord Kelvin, James Bryce, Lord Carson,
Robert Hart, Lord Dufferin, Lord Lawrence, Sir Henry
Lawrence, Sir John Gordon, Sir George White, and a
host of others all (except Lord Carson) of Scotch-Irish
blood.

THE SCOTCH-IRISH IN NORTHERN IRELAND
AND IN THE AMERICAN COLONIES

I

IRISH HISTORY TO THE TIME OF JAMES I

Introduction—Early history of Ireland—Patrick, patron saint of Ireland—Anglo-Norman invasion—Elizabeth quells rebellion in Ireland—O'Neill rebels—Irish penal laws—French penal laws.

THE population of Ireland consists of two distinct races, differing widely in their racial characteristics, their ideals, religion, and general behavior. One writer discussing the subject said, "They differ by inherent and ineradicable endowment, and the northerner should be judged by his contribution to public welfare, by his devotion to law and order, and his sympathy with civil and religious liberty."

Writers sometimes, either through carelessness or ignorance, give the impression that they think a person born in Ireland is either of Celtic or mixed ancestry. Such impression or statement is certainly very far from the truth, as every well-informed person knows. Erroneous opinions of this character, however, are apt to lead the reader of careful habits to question statements on other subjects emanating from the same source.

Though it may not be necessary to offer proofs of the contention, yet it is interesting to note the opinions of a few authorities on this question.

The *Manchester Guardian* says: "In Ulster you have two communities facing you; intermarriage is virtually prohibited; the children are educated in separate schools." The paper then goes on to point out that Ulster had "a great superiority of wealth and position."

Mr. Kevin O'Higgins, when Free State Minister of Justice, speaking of Ulster, said on March 19, 1925, "A problem of close to a million people, having different ideals, different traditions and aspirations from the rest of their countrymen."

The famous historian McLennan (*Memoirs of Drummond*, 1867, p. 186) says, "There are in Ireland two distinct nations, interfused yet distinct, with separate traditions, and differing in blood, temperament, and religion."

Sir James O'Connor, barrister, and native Irish Roman Catholic, says: "It is as true today as at any other time to say that, racially, there are two races of people in the country, for there has never been any intermarriage worth mentioning." "There have been few Irish-Irish names in literature—the names of Thomas Moore, George Moore, and James Joyce come to mind, but nearly all Irish literature is written by the Anglo-Irish. . . . It will not do to speak of an alien garrison, and, in the same breath, to speak of George Bernard Shaw as 'Irish.'" (*History of Ireland*, Vol. II, p. 236.) "To aver that northeast Ulster and the rest of Ireland are one, is to sin against the light. . . . There is little or no mixture of blood. . . . The Ulster Presbyterian is as unlike the southern Catholic as if they came from, not merely opposite ends of the same island, but from opposite ends of the globe." (*Ibid.*, p. 115.) "The Catholic and the Protestant current had to run in the same channel, but they never commingled: there was no intermarriage." (*Ibid.*, Vol I, p. 145.)

Proofs of the distinct differences between the two peoples are indeed overwhelming, and certainly unnecessary to any one conversant with conditions existing between the two races in Ireland.

The early history of Ireland is of more or less legendary

character. One of the most reliable records is known as
the Annals of the Four Masters, which begins about the
year 441 A.D. Among the classical writers Ptolemy
stands preëminent, for the information he furnishes on
this hazy subject is of definite character. The Greek and
Roman writers have little to say of the Emerald Isle.
Strabo says, "The inhabitants are savages." Ptolemy
mentions sixteen different races that at one time or another inhabited Ireland. Pictish tribes from the adjacent
coast of Scotland conquered parts of Down and Antrim,
and even found their way as far down as Roscommon.
Mentioned among the invaders were the Milesians, and
although their history is vague some knowledge of them
may be gleaned from the Annals of the Four Masters,
which have been compiled from documents no longer extant, and which are regarded as being of more or less
fictitious character.

It would be futile, therefore, for one race or another
to claim a prior right to possession of the country. The
claim of each and every invader down to the present time
is based on exactly the same right—that of conquest, the
right of the strongest. If long possession may be claimed
as a right, then the descendants of the aborigines in Connaught and Cork have the first claim, but their claims,

The belief that a majority of the Irish people are descended from the Milesians has been assailed, and Mac-
Niel insists that a majority of the tribes of early Ireland
are the descendants of subject races. Thus Ireland, like
the sister islands, is inhabited by those who are a blend
of a number of different races, which at one period or
another successfully invaded the country. Some traces
of the aboriginal inhabitants may be found in the south
and west who fled from their homes to escape the invaders.

although the oldest, are disregarded by later invaders who claim all.

From the ninth century onwards, there are accounts of various races who colonized the island, and five successive invasions are recounted. In the year A.D. 795, Norsemen arrived in the east, and there founded a Scandinavian kingdom which existed until the time of the Norman conquest in 1171.

Until the arrival of the Scandinavians, no cities or large towns had been built, and no bridges existed. The Danes founded Dublin, Waterford, Limerick, and Wexford; and these towns remained peculiarly Danish in blood and in laws and customs for three hundred years, although a chronic state of war existed between them and the native Celts. These towns were therefore Danish for three hundred years.

At this period extensive forests covered large areas, abounding in such wild life as wolves, wild boar, red deer, foxes, and game of various kinds.

Hamlets existed here and there consisting of huts built of wood. There was no coined money, and commerce was carried on by means of barter. Marriage laws were notoriously lax. Polygamy and concubinage prevailed. Incest was practiced, and marriage by purchase was an established custom.

The religion of the Druids prevailed in early Ireland. According to Jacques Chevalier and others, the pagan Celt followed savage customs. Some evidence exists of the worship of the sun and of fire; and human sacrifice was practiced on occasion. A belief in spirits prevailed, and a knowledge of sorcery and divination was claimed by the Druid priests. These priests had charge of such learning as existed, and they dwelt in cells which doubtless were the forerunners of the monastic cells of the early Christians. The priests were under the protection of the chieftains, to whom they were not infrequently related. Christianity, it is believed, first reached Ireland through the medium of captive slaves, and by traders and colonists. St. Patrick, the patron saint of Ireland, is a conspicuous feature in its early history. He was born at Dunbarton in Scotland, near the Firth of Clyde, where his father seems to have been a man of some importance. Patrick has left two authentic documents which tell us something of his history. These are his "Confession," and his "Letter to the Christians." These documents tell us he was born in Britain, and that his father was a deacon and a Roman magistrate. Patrick's father and grandfather were both ecclesiastics, and each was a married man.

The Book of Armagh states that Patrick was captured in a filibustering raid by pirates, sold as a slave, and carried to the north of Ireland, where he was put to herding cattle for a minor chieftain named Milcho, near the Slemish mountains in Antrim. Patrick had been carefully brought up, and communing with himself in his solitary occupation, became filled with pious thoughts and aspirations. After six years of slavery he returned to his father's home in Scotland. Here he had visions and dreams directing him to return to Ireland.

He did return as a missionary, and made evangelistic tours throughout the entire country; and his name is now preserved in the nomenclature of many places, as Templepatrick, Downpatrick, Kirkpatrick, and Portpatrick.

Patrick's theology was very simple, like his dress. In his "Confession" he does not once mention the pope, nor does Leo I, pope from 440 A.D. to 461 A.D., ever mention Patrick; neither does our evangelist even once allude to primate or prelate. Every church Patrick founded had a minister or bishop of its own, and each one of these bishops was a married man.

In Patrick's day Prelacy was conspicuous by its absence; he regarded the Bible as the supreme standard of his faith. There is no trace of the worship of any saint, no mention is made of auricular confession, the dying are not anointed. The rite of extreme unction was not administered until the fifth century. Patrick says nothing of transubstantiation or the glorification of the mass. Purgatory had not been heard of.

In Patrick's time no pictures or images were seen in Hibernian churches, and worship was public and in the Irish tongue. Patrick taught that when a good man died he rested or fell asleep in Christ.

It is believed that the great Irish religious teacher died about March 17, 465 A.D., and is buried at Downpatrick.

The early Irish church taught that at death the saints passed immediately to glory. There was no Book of Common Prayer, and no confirmation. The authority of the Scriptures stood higher in Ireland than at Rome, and when the most famous popes were not ashamed to confess their ignorance of Greek and Hebrew, some Irishmen were acquainted with both, which knowledge they applied to the interpretation of the Scriptures. (See Killen's *Ecclesiastical History*.)

Patrick was educated in the southern part of Scotland, and the monasteries he established were said to resemble the schools of the prophets; these were not the abodes of indolent ease-loving men but centers of missionary effort and seats of earnest, zealous learning. The New Testament was in constant use, and the students, many of whom were married men, were teachers and preachers.

After the death of Patrick there was a lapse back to

paganism, but if the light grew dim it did not entirely go out, and about a century after Patrick's demise, a man named Columba became fired with missionary zeal, and taking twelve companions with him, sailed to the island of Iona in northwest Scotland and became the apostle of north Britain as Patrick had been in Ireland. Here Columba established other centers of missionary activity, and he and his companions became Christian teachers not only in Scotland, but in England, France, Switzerland, Germany and Italy.

Mr. Goldwin Smith says that "during the seventh and eighth centuries and a part of the ninth (a period of over two hundred years) Ireland played a really great part in European history."

Nevertheless, though men were trained for their special work in religious schools, a general education of the people of Ireland was an unknown quantity; they remained completely ignorant, even the upper classes, and for centuries after this period the chieftains themselves were unable to write their own names and made their signatures to agreements or other documents by using the thumb, thus affixing their mark or seal.

At this period there was no national life, and no cities or large towns. The nation consisted of groups or aggregations of tribes, many of these tribes being related to each other.

In the Irish church innovations gradually crept in which the ecclesiastics stubbornly resisted. One pope after another made determined efforts to compel the Irish church to conform to Romish customs; but Celtic Ireland refused to submit to papal authority until the time of Henry II, who assisted in fastening papal bonds upon her. Thus it seems that the submission of Ireland to the Vatican, and the claims of Great Britain upon Ireland, date from very nearly the same period.

The Danish coast cities, however, acknowledged the clerical authority of the British prelates Lanfranc and Anselm; and yet Greene tells us the religious houses looked for ecclesiastical traditions, not to Rome, but to Ireland.

In 1101, a Roman pontiff purchased from the Irish Synod of Rathbreasil Irish religious independence, and in that same century the pope bargained away the country's civil independence to a not very reputable English monarch, thus subjecting the people to a double oppression.

During the Dark Ages, schools disappeared from Ireland, and the light of learning almost disappeared, so that the Reformation received no notice.

In the course of time Adrian IV was elected pope, the only English pope ever seated in the Vatican. He had learned that Henry II wished to annex Ireland; for Henry complained that the country was full of captured Englishmen retained as slaves. The infallible pope of Rome was thus induced to issue a bull conveying the island to the British crown, for certain considerations, such as the receipt of Peter's pence and other contributions and favors.

In 1171 England assumed the sovereignty of the country. The attempt to convey the impression that at this time Ireland was a nation united and happy is entirely without foundation. England, however, was even then an organized state and gradually working her way up from a feudal sovereignty to constitutional freedom. There was not a vestige of anything of the kind in Ireland. The Irish people were found in groups or tribes held together by a sort of loose feudal system. They had what was known as the Brehon laws which permitted a payment in compensation for any crime, even murder.

From the time of Patrick, until the arrival of the Danes,

Irish history is almost a blank. There is a record of never-ceasing warfare among the tribes and their chieftains, without any advance in civilization and that too in spite of the activity of the monks in their cells. In the little monasteries the clan was arranged on a religious basis, and here the monks copied MSS., carved figures, painted and bound books, but appear to have had little influence on the rude warriors outside their own quiet haven.

During the centuries of church growth, the country was exposed to continual plundering, fighting, and incendiarism; the women fighting as well as the men. The major tribal divisions approximated the present partition of provinces. Ignorance and poverty prevailed. All signs of progression had disappeared owing in part to the bands of roving chieftains preying on each other, as well as to the struggle with the Danes.

The Norman invasion was brought about by an Irishman, Dermot Macmorrough, who approached Henry II and asked for his assistance in a warfare against his brother chieftains. Henry authorized a number of Anglo-Norman noblemen and their retainers to enter the country and give the needed assistance to Dermot. Among those who arrived were the Fitzstephens, De Burgs, De Laceys, De Couricies, Blakes, Butlers, Fitzurses, and Fitzgeralds. These men subdued the country to some extent, and enlarged and fortified the old Danish towns, which they governed like their cities at home. They lived in fortified castles, issuing forth with their soldiers as if about to raid a foreign country; notwithstanding, they forced their more civilized habits upon the natives, who at the time of their coming were said to resemble a mob of armed savages.

The natives had no habits of industry, no settled habitation, no conception of property; they had their collection of Brehon laws; and learning was confined to the clerical class.

The Norman invasion was followed by a crowd of Anglo-Normans and Norman-Welsh who filled the country, and who became in time assimilated with the Irish. Following the amalgamation of the two races, the newcomers adopted Irish dress and manners and even altered their names, so that De Burg became Burke, and Fitzurse became McMahon.

The four countries known as the Pale were Dublin, Meath, Kildare, and Louth; but the extent of this strip varied from time to time as England's attention was claimed by her own wars.

As a nation the Irish of that day were still without corporate existence or national life; they were O'Neills, O'Briens, O'Connors, or something else according to location; and they fought each other with great gusto.

When the house of Tudor ascended the throne, Ireland was in her usual turbulent condition. A supremacy there was now participated in by thirty Anglo-Norman Irish, and sixty Celtic Irish chieftains. Incendiarism, plundering, fighting, and killing were the habitual occupations so that progress was not to be expected.

In the latter half of the sixteenth century, cattle and human beings were herded together in the Earl of Desmond's castle. The population of the island was about half a million and they lived the daily life of savages.

The manner of living in Ireland at this period is seen in the Annals of the Four Masters, and in the Annals of Lough Ce. Murder and robbery were considered the only occupations fit for a gentleman. The lower orders of the people were utterly despised, and existed as best they might without protection and without rights of any kind. They were preyed upon by their own countrymen, plundered and killed on the slightest pretext and without provocation. The first four sovereigns of the house of Tudor effected little in Ireland. Henry VIII in 1537 tried to enforce Protestantism, which had the effect of annoying and provoking the people and resulted in the bringing together of those who while of different race practiced the same religion. In 1537 the Irish Parliament cast aside the authority of the pope and proclaimed Henry VIII head of the church in Ireland. The Reformation, however, introduced by means of the King did not progress very far in his day, and his son and successor Edward VI lived but a short time. Mary, daughter of Henry and Catherine of Aragon, who succeeded her half-brother Edward on the throne, manifested very early in her reign that spirit of persecution which earned for her the name of "Bloody Mary."

She issued instructions to the Irish lord deputy and council, "that they should by example, and all means possible, advance the honor of God and the Catholic faith; to set forth the honor and dignity of the pope's holiness, and the see apostolic of Rome; and to be ready to punish and repress all heretics and Lollards," etc.

Another order of the Irish Parliament passed, June, 1556, orders the persons proscribed to be arrested, and if necessary to be burnt for the terror of others (see Irish statutes, ninth of Mary).

It was in the reign of Mary that colonization began in Ireland. The natives of those areas known at present as King's and Queen's counties, well aware of Mary's antagonism to those who professed the Protestant faith, had risen against their fellow-countrymen and destroyed most of them, thus leaving large tracts of land unoccupied, which Mary purposed to colonize with persons from other places. The chief towns in King's and Queen's counties were named Philipstown and Maryborough, names which they still retain.

Mary's reign ended with her death in 1558, when her half-sister Elizabeth ascended the throne. One rebellion succeeded another throughout Elizabeth's reign. The pope, who has always aimed at being a sovereign in politics in addition to being king of the church, sent material and spiritual aid to the natives fighting against their Queen. He excommunicated Elizabeth and absolved the people from their allegiance to her, while his banner waved flauntingly in the British Queen's dominions.

The pope demanded the allegiance of the Irish people for himself, and this they gave willingly; indeed allegiance became in a measure a duty of the good Catholic, who is taught, no matter to what nation he belongs, that he owes his first duty to the pope.

During the reign of Elizabeth, English laws were re-enacted in Ireland, and an attempt was made to replace Brehon law with British law; and in spite of the many rebellions against her domination, the Queen never insisted upon the profession of Protestantism as a condition of the retention of property. When the relative positions were reversed the Catholics never dealt with Protestants in the same lenient way.

The tribal institutions including the Brehon laws which bred anarchy were wiped out; yet the Catholics had private toleration of their religion and they were permitted to have seats in Parliament. Although the penal laws were not repealed, the Catholics were not molested to any extent. Parishes retained their priests openly, while chapels and monasteries multiplied, forming a sharp contrast to the intolerance of Elizabeth's contemporary, Philip of Spain, in the Netherlands, where Alva was hounding the Dutch to death on account of their religion, as well as to the cold-blooded executions in England due to Mary's hatred of "heretics and Lollards" in the preceding reign.

Elizabeth met the Irish rebellions one after another with an unflinching and undaunted front. She fought the rebels separately and she fought them together, and in her armies were always to be found numbers of Irishmen fighting for the Queen. The war against the rebels was prosecuted ruthlessly and unceasingly, until at last the country if not at peace was quiet, and no one dared rebel against British authority.

A prominent rebel against the Queen's authority was O'Neill of Ulster. Shane, an illegitimate O'Neill, was a great fighter, and on one occasion visited the British court to present to the Queen his claims in person. The rebel came with his train of gallowglasses—huge bareheaded men clad in their home-dyed saffron-colored shirts, naked legs, and great hairy mantles dangling close to their heels.

Shane, in clansman fashion, prostrated himself, while the sovereign "checked with a glance the circle's smile." Shane returned to Ireland and was slain subsequently in a drunken squabble.

Hugh O'Neill, the next heir, was the son of the Earl of Dungannon who had been murdered by his half-brother Shane. Hugh had been brought up at the English court in order to save him from a similar fate, and his inheritance, the earldom of Tyrone, was by means of letters patent conferred upon him; and he was admonished to uphold the Protestant faith. He was not at all religious, was indeed more of a courtier than a rude Irish chieftain.

It was not long, however, after his arrival in Ulster that he allied himself with O'Donnel, O'Doherty, and others, adopted the Roman Catholic faith, and formed an alliance with Philip II of Spain, for assistance in the defense of the Catholic church. (See the Earl of Tyrone and Hugh O'Donnel to the king of Spain, September, 1595, calendar Carew MSS., p. 122.)

Elizabeth pardoned the rebel earls but the Earl of Dungannon almost immediately attempted another conspiracy, this time with leaders in the province of Munster. He begged the people to join a confederacy in defense of Christ's Catholic religion. A six years' war followed. Spain landed troops at Kinsale in the south, but O'Neill was defeated.

Prior to the Spanish arrival, a nuncio sent from Rome arrived to encourage the Irish leaders. "No Catholic," the priest proclaimed, "could without sin submit to a heretic sovereign, far less take part against the faithful in arms for Holy Church."

In spite of his repeated rebellions, Hugh O'Neill was reinstated in his lands and possessions.

One of the important acts in Elizabeth's reign was the erection of the first college in Ireland, Trinity College, Dublin, which at a later period developed into a university, and at present ranks immediately after Oxford and Cambridge universities. In March, 1592, was laid the foundation stone of the college; and among its first students were James Ussher, afterwards Archbishop of Armagh, James Fullerton and James Hamilton who were Presbyterians. Fullerton was afterwards knighted. Hamilton became Lord Claneboy, founder of the family afterwards represented by the Earl of Dufferin.

The Queen never enforced the Act of Uniformity (this was the first Act of Uniformity) beyond the Pale, and even here it was said to be honored more in the breach than in the observance.

When the Queen of England passed away the tedious Irish wars had ceased; the situation had been handled sternly, firmly, and unceasingly; the rebels had submitted, and Ireland was at last at peace.

Much has been said of the Irish penal laws, yet these, we are told, were almost identical with the laws passed in France, when the Edict of Nantes was revoked. According to Froude, the laws enacted in Spain and Italy against Protestants were a great deal more cruel than those passed in Ireland against the Catholics, and another difference is pointed out: on the continent such laws when enacted were actually enforced in all their severity, while in Ireland they were frequently ignored, even with the connivance of officials.

According to the same authority, there was no Catholic country anywhere, which had shown so much tolerance to Protestants as had been shown to Catholics in Ireland. Froude also states that in Catholic countries laws against Protestants were more severe than any code which any Protestant country had ever enforced against Catholics.

In France, toleration was withdrawn by the revocation of the Edict of Nantes. Non-conformists were imprisoned, exiled, deprived of their estates, and even put to death. No schools were allowed for them in which to teach their creeds, and not even sufficient ground in which to bury their dead. In 1793 Flood said in the House of Commons that the measures of Louis XIV against the French Protestants, and the English laws after the Revolution against the English Catholics, were more severe than any in Ireland and they had not the same excuse. The French Protestants and the English Catholics were far too weak to be a danger to the state; but the Irish Catholics from their numbers and connections with France and the Stuarts were formidable. The penal code was unavoidable.

The observance of the penal laws in Ireland was never

of that relentless, unceasing, cold-blooded character which was witnessed in continental countries as practiced on the Protestants by the Catholics. Had these penal laws been enforced against the Irish Catholics, as they were against the Protestant Albigenses for instance, Ireland would be a Protestant instead of a Catholic country today. Violence, relentless and cruel, does achieve its purpose when persisted in without cessation or compassion, and has been one of the weapons constantly used by the papal power, although complaints are very loud when the positions are reversed. The St. Bartholomew massacre of the Huguenots when 30,000 persons were slain including Coligni and other Protestant leaders was by the order of Gregory XIII celebrated with great pomp and a Te Deum was sung in joy and thanksgiving at the death of the unsuspecting victims of religious fanaticism. The policy of the papal court has always been the same, tolerance being shown only when expedient, and cast aside as soon as possible.

According to Lecky, in 1724 a new law was made against the Protestants in France. By one clause, all who assembled for the exercise of the Protestant worship, even in their own homes, became liable to servitude for life, perhaps in the galleys, as well as to the confiscation of their properties. Another law condemned to death any Protestant minister exercising any religious function of any kind, and also condemned to the galleys any one cognizant of the breach of law who failed to denounce the author of the religious function.

A third law enjoined all physicians to inform the priest as to the condition of a dying patient, in order that, whether he wished it or not, a Catholic priest should be present at his bedside when death arrived.

A fourth law rendered any Protestant who had strengthened a dying relative in his religious beliefs, liable to the galleys with confiscation of his goods. (Sismondia's Histoire *des Francais,* XIX, 241-244.)

As late as the Peace of Paris a Protestant minister at Nismes wrote to the Duke of Bedford, beseeching the intercession of England in favor of thirty-three men in the galleys at Toulon, and sixteen women imprisoned in Languedoc, for the crime of having attended Protestant assemblies (Bedford's *Correspondence,* III, p. 155).

All over Europe there were similar complaints, in Hungary, Poland, Spain, and Portugal. See Buckle's *History,* I, p. 109; also Carlyle's *Frederick the Great,* Book X, Ch. III, and the lists of Portuguese autos-de-fé in the eighteenth century in the British Museum, which have been quoted by Lecky.

Following the death of Elizabeth, James the First of England and Sixth of Scotland ascended the British throne in 1603 and reigned until 1625.

The counties of Cork and Limerick refused to proclaim a heretic sovereign. In spite of this fact, and notwithstanding his many rebellions, the Earl of Tyrone was reinstated in his possessions. Again he conspired against the English crown, this time entreating aid from Flanders. The conspiracy, however, was discovered, O'Neill and O'Donnel fled to Rome, and some of the rebels were hanged.

It was now considered an act of official justice to give full publicity to the punishment of the allied rebels and its justification. "In order that it might be known the rebels were proceeded against justly." A bill was brought before the grand jury in Donegal, and read publicly in the English and in the Irish language, "so as to discover the evidence to all the heavens." The property of the rebels, according to law, and as a punishment for repeated conspiracies, escheated to the crown. The escheated counties were Donegal, Derry, Tyrone, Fermanagh, and Cavan; with Antrim and Down which had been long occupied by Scots.

II

THE PLANTATION AND THE IRISH ST. BARTHOLOMEW

The Plantation—Scottish education—Presbyterian ministers in Ulster—James I—Andrew Melville—Charles I—The Black Oath—Star Chamber established, Presbyterians persecuted and prosecuted, and thrown into prison for their faith—Strength of Catholics before 1641—Rebellion and massacre of 1641—Oliver Cromwell punishes the murderers of 1641, and administers the law in Ireland—Cromwell presents the Engagement to Presbyterians, and prepares for their deportation, but later rescinds orders on finding them a law-abiding people.

AT the time of what was known as the Plantation of Ulster in 1607 the population of the whole island was about one million. The flight of the rebel earls, and the overthrow of their allies, resulted in a large area of land being forfeited to the crown, and this was now at the disposal of the government.

The project of bringing Anglo-Saxon settlers to Ulster had been for some time in contemplation for it was thought such colonists might develop the resources of the country, which up to the present, never had been attempted; and, at the same time, they could be relied on to act as guards and protectors of the interests of the mother country.

At the period under discussion there was still no national spirit in the country. Ireland was not a nation in the usual interpretation of that term. The country was still in the hands of its chieftains and their retainers; and these were constantly preying upon each other like enemies from a foreign country. The spirit of the country and the habits of the people were similar to what Henry II found in the twelfth century.

There was very little cultivation. Dense forests abounded in the north, which sheltered hungry wolves,[1] and through which wandered deer, wild boar, and other forest animals. Owing to the oft-repeated civil wars, some parts of the country, especially in Down, had been almost cleared of their inhabitants.

After a survey of the forfeited lands, the escheated counties were found to contain one and one half million acres, but one million acres of this area was mostly bog, forest, and mountain. This was restored to the Irish. The half million acres of fertile land were settled by Scotch and English families. The Scotch coming to Ulster at this period were from the lowlands of Scotland, and thus, like their brethren in England, belonged to the Anglo-Saxon race.

Some of the native or Celtic Irish had extensive grants of land bestowed on them for services rendered; others took an oath of fealty to the British government and were allowed to remain on the lands granted to the new colonists; and it may be added that in their new position, they enjoyed a protection and freedom from plunder to which they had been hitherto complete strangers in their own homes and country.

The responsible agent of the government, in carrying out the plan, was Sir Arthur Chichester. The lands were divided into parcels of 1,000, 1,500, and 2,000 acres; these parcels were granted to settlers of repute on conditions. The large occupier was required within four years to build a castle and bawn, or walled enclosure with towers

---

[1] The last wolf in Ireland was killed about the beginning of the eighteenth century at Wolfhill, Belfast.

at the angles, and to plant forty-eight men of Scotch or English extraction on the estate. Demands the other settlers were to meet were that they should build a bawn in addition to the dwelling. All the colonists were required to be well supplied with arms.

A London corporation obtained a grant in Derry, and was required to build and fortify the towns of Londonderry and Coleraine, and to comply with the other conditions. Timber for building was free, obtained from the native forests, so with the encouragement received, houses and bawns were quickly erected replacing the wattled huts, and the holes in the ground, in which former occupants had sought refuge.

The land was soon cleared, drained, and fenced; the ground put in order and crops planted. It was not long before a few houses clustered together became the site of future flourishing towns; the beginning of a famous Londonderry crowned the banks of the river Foyle, and a new Coleraine, replacing the one burned down, soon adorned the mouth of the river Bann.

And just a few fishermen's cabins scattered here and there, marked the place which the future was to see industries of far-reaching importance—Belfast, the metropolis of the north, situated on Belfast Lough, now a clean, well-built, bustling town, thrilling with life, having excellent schools, and its fine Queen's College. Londonderry, not so far away, has also a good college, known as Magee College, a stronghold of Presbyterianism.

The Plantation of Ulster effected a complete transformation in the history of the province of Ulster. Formerly its productions were mainly of the banditti order, and it was one of the most turbulent of the provinces; but now there was a complete transformation. The roving gangsters living by plunder and, too proud or too lazy to work for their bread, were replaced by industrious farmers endeavoring by their unceasing toil to render fertile, fruitful, and pleasant the wasted neglected land.

Northern Ireland does not possess the genial climate of the salubrious south or east. The climate is colder and the land, as shown by the English Premier Mr. Gladstone, not nearly as fertile as in the other provinces, and was offered by him for sale at a considerably lower price.

A few Englishmen settled in Ulster, but the majority of the colonists came from Scotland, that land of harsh, bleak climate and infertile soil. In their struggle for existence with the adverse conditions forced on them by nature, this people has developed certain characteristics which have enabled them not only to survive, but to take a high place in the community of mankind.

As a type they are hardy, tenacious, and unconquerable; an industrious and high-spirited race, with high ideals, an insatiable thirst for knowledge, a strong love of independence, and with decided leaning toward republicanism.

Thomas B. Macaulay says, "In perseverance, in self-command, in forethought, in all the virtues which conduce to success in life, the Scots have never been surpassed," and the Scotch have made their mark in whatever country they have adopted; and he continues, "The Scotch were poor, but their intellectual level was high; while the country was the poorest in Christendom, the people vied in every branch of learning with the most favored peoples; Scots whose dwellings were as wretched as those of an Icelander, wrote Latin verse with more than the delicacy of a Vida, and made discoveries which would have added renown to a Galileo."

The Scottish towns had schools since the thirteenth century; and an elementary school system from 1690, at which time provision was made for a school in every parish. Co-education was the rule, and the schools were undenominational. Loving religious liberty and demanding it for themselves, they have not been slow to grant it to others.

Scotland founded her first university in 1411, another in 1494, a third in 1450, and a fourth in 1582.

The Scottish bursarships brought the advantages of a university education to those excluded from it in England, and Burnett, quoted by Lecky, speaking of Scotland in 1670, comments upon the degree of knowledge and education, even among the lower classes, and says: "In the lowlands of Scotland, the standard of general knowledge among the gentry was perceptibly higher than in England (Burnett, *History of Our Own Times,* II, p. 48, Lockhart Papers).

It is indeed no wonder that in the eighteenth century we find the Scotch professor of astronomy, David Gregory, being asked to fill the astronomical chair in Oxford University in England, nor surprising to learn that he was the first person to make that science popular in the great British center of learning.

It was said that the English universities with their enormous revenues were lethargic and prejudiced, while the Scotch universities were glowing with life and zeal in the quest of knowledge. Trinity College, Dublin, was started under Scotch-Irish Presbyterians, but was soon closed to students of their faith, and the Scotch-Irish lads had to walk to a seaport to get to Glasgow or Edinburgh University, where after some years they obtained the desired degree. Ulster struggled for the right of education, and for religious and civil liberty. The Scotch brought to Ulster their school system and their children were educated in their own schools without government aid.

Most of the nobility of Northern Ireland date the acquisition of their estates from the Plantation. Sir Arthur Chichester who supervised the work of dividing the land was the ancestor of the notorious Lord Donegal who was the cause of so many Ulstermen emigrating to America where they did such telling work in the army of the Revolution. Another nobleman of Ulster was Andrew Stewart, Lord of Ochiltree, who sold his barony in Scotland, and came over to Ireland with his Presbyterian clergyman, and forty-five men. He was created Earl of Castlestewart but was not related to the royal Stuart family of Scotland. He was granted 3,000 acres in county Tyrone where Stuart Hall is situated. The present heir to the earldom is married to an American heiress.

The county of Down was colonized by a laird Montgomery, who founded Newtownards, Donaghadee, Comber, and Greyabbey. James Hamilton founded Bangor, Hollywood, Killaleagh, and Ballywalter. Ballymena, which became a flourishing town, was built in Antrim.

A history of the Scotch in Ulster is almost a history of Presbyterianism, so greatly were the people influenced by their Calvinistic beliefs. The Scotch kirk expressed the spirit of the nation whose child it was, and that spirit was essentially republican in character, and the very antithesis of the teaching of the Anglican Church, and of the Roman Catholic Church, both of which upheld autocracy, and strengthened authority.

Prominent among the Presbyterian ministers of Ulster was James Bryce, a younger son of Bruce, the laird of Auth, and an ancestor of James Bryce, author of *The Holy Roman Empire* and *The American Commonwealth*. The elder Bryce fled from Scotland to Ulster to escape the prelatic persecution raging there. He was born in 1659, studied theology at Edinburgh University, and was ordained. He married Catherine Annan and these two came to Ulster and settled at Aghadoey where Bryce lived for fifty years, dying when nearly ninety years old. Mrs. Bryce did her own housework, visited sick parishioners, and taught her sons Greek and Latin, all of whom became distinguished men.

Another outstanding man was Robert Blair who had been a professor in a Glasgow college. Josias Welch, another minister, was a grandson of John Knox, and a great-grandson of Lord Ochiltree, and thus related to the family of the Earl of Castlestewart.

Among the ministers who came with their flocks to Ulster was John Livingston,[1] a great-grandson of Lord Livingstone. Practically all the ministers who accompanied their flocks to Ulster were university graduates, and some college professors. A number of the ministers who came to Ireland were of noble blood, and many of them had suffered from the opposition of the Scotch prelates to Non-Conformist opinions.

James Hamilton, a nephew of Lord Claneboy, was another of the pioneer pastors, who were ministering to the church in Ulster in 1625.

Sir Arthur Chichester was appointed Lord Deputy of Ireland in 1605, and the work incidental to the settling of the Plantation was mainly in his hands. The colonists were self-denying and industrious, and it was not long before the country showed signs of improvement.

The prudent settlers had brought with them from Scotland, the knowledge of and skill in the manufacture of linen (see the Montgomery MSS.). In the early history of this industry, it was almost exclusively of domestic character. The weaving was done on a hand loom at

---

[1] Livingston accepted a call to the parish of Killinchy in 1630, and proved a notable minister. Killinchy is still a flourishing congregation.

home, in an intermittent sort of way, according to the season of the year, or as other engagements of the worker permitted, and when the web of woven linen was complete, it was taken to one of the market towns to be sold, the colonists in this way adding to their comfort and independence.

Among the trades and industries established by the settlers in the north was that of cotton. It was first introduced to give employment to the inmates of the almshouse, but the cotton-spinning work developed rapidly until it supplanted the linen industry.

By the following year an improvement was noticed throughout the entire island. Efforts in cultivation were proving successful and the first crops were excellent. The pastures, now cleared of brush and underwood, were affording excellent grazing ground for cattle, and a trade was being established with Bristol.

The population, stationary for one thousand years, had increased. In 1580 the estimated number of people was half a million, and just before the rebellion and massacre of 1641 it was a million and a half. Unfortunately, however, there were drawbacks to the picture. The colonists were obliged to remain constantly on guard, not only against the wild beasts, but to protect themselves against human enemies not a whit less cruel and savage. A gun was a constant companion by night as well as by day for the protection of life and property. Numbers of idle young men, known as woodkerne and gallowglasses, without income and disdaining honest work, lived a wild, lawless life, existing by theft and forcing the more honest and self-respecting inhabitants of the country to bear the expense of their drinking, gambling, and generally destructive habits.

At this time war was raging in Scotland, between the Calvinists and the bishops. The prelates were forcing prescribed forms of worship on the people which the latter emphatically refused to accept, and Ulster now became a haven of refuge for the persecuted followers of Calvin, just as at a later period the new country of America afforded a refuge from the intolerance and bigotry of the Anglican bishops in northern Ireland.

In the early history of the colony the Episcopalian Church was very tolerant in its attitude to dissenting creeds, but when Archbishop Laud in Scotland and deputy Wentworth in Dublin discovered their power to persecute with impunity, the situation was radically changed. The early toleration may have been due to the fact that Archbishop Ussher, first primate of the Established Church in Ireland, had received much of his education from Presbyterians, and apparently was not so devoted to ceremonials and forms as his brethren of a somewhat later period.

The Established Church in the time of Ussher was so broad-minded and tolerant in its opinions that it adopted "The Articles of Religion" which had been agreed upon in a convention of archbishops, bishops, and clergy (1615). These Articles ignore the necessity of Episcopal ordination, thus implying the validity of ordination by Presbyters. They do not order the observance of religious fasts, and they do not assume the authority of decreeing rites and ceremonies. The worship of God appears more important than its technique, even if less impressive on the emotional and unthinking mind. Thus the Presbyterian ministers occupying pulpits received tithes, and were recognized as parochial clergy, though not prelatically ordained. They preached their Calvinistic doctrine and proclaimed their dissenting opinions, conducting their services of public worship in their own way.

It is indeed an interesting fact that the Westminster Confession of Faith is largely based on these Articles of 1615.

James I of England had been bred a Presbyterian, but he had inherited through his intrepid mother, Mary Queen of Scots, the arrogance and intolerance of the house of Guise. James was a despot at heart. He disliked, and probably feared, the upright, stiff-necked Presbyterians, so he favored the stealthy introduction of Prelacy, for Prelacy was noted for its deference to "the Lord's anointed" and its support of authority, and James liked fawning and flattery, and could have neither from his democratic countrymen and co-religionists.

When the Scotch Presbyterian, Andrew Melville, met his sovereign face to face and boldly told him that no earthly king was a lord or head of the church in Scotland, that the monarch was merely a member of their great religious body, James was too myopic to grasp the idea of the dignity of the people, and their claim to worship as they thought best, and had the straight-backed Melville committed to prison and confined for four years in the Tower of London.

The spirit of Andrew Melville pervaded the Presbyterian Church. The lowland Scotch had been trained in a hard school. Their lives were insecure. They were accustomed to raids from the south and raids from the north, never knowing safety or peace, but facing danger at all times from highlander or borderer. They knew hunger, thirst, and piercing cold when their houses blazed up in the darkness and their cattle were carried away in a sudden foray. Their lands were picturesque but bleak and barren, giving scanty return for the labor expended, but as one of our historians has pointed out, "Suffering that would have degraded a meaner race hardened and ennobled the Scotchman. It was from these ages of oppression and lawlessness that he drew the rugged fidelity, the dogged endurance, the shrewdness, the caution, the wariness, the rigid thrift, the noble self-dependence, the patience, and the daring which has distinguished him ever since." This spirit of self-respect and self-reliance and devotion to what was right rather than what was expedient, found expression in Presbyterianism and showed itself in the government of its church, which bound the nation together and gave the people a voice in the control of their own destinies.

The delegates, both lay and spiritual, to church conventions founded a parliament of their own, with an orderly administration and organization of activities. If the people conferred authority on their elders they were quick to see the wishes of the members obeyed, and the ministers though apparently clothed with a despotic power were after all responsible for the exercise of the authority delegated to them. In actual practice the church of Scotland has proved the most democratic of all institutions; and is said to have awakened the nation to a consciousness of its power, so that the despotism of monarchy was held responsible to the government of the kirk. Is it any wonder that Bancroft says: "The Presbyterians supported the cause of independence; and indeed the American revolution was but the application of the principles of the Reformation to civil government"?

Charles I succeeded his father in 1625; he was an avowed Protestant, and friendly to Catholicism. The King was married to a Roman Catholic, a descendant of the house of Medici and a French princess, Henrietta Maria. The Roman Catholics in Ireland were favored throughout this reign, and though the laws regarding them enacted in the reign of Elizabeth remained upon the statute books, they were scarcely if at all enforced. New chapels were built, archbishops and bishops were actively functioning, and the number of priests in the realm showed marked increase in breach of the law. Notwithstanding these facts, as in the time of Elizabeth, complaints were made of persecution.

Two thirds of the land remained in the hands of Catholics, and in the Irish House of Commons they returned nearly one half of the members, while in the upper house they had a majority. They forced from Charles a modification of the Oath of Supremacy, when they were reminded that other laws of a restraining character remained upon the statute books, and that the religious liberties granted them depended upon the indulgence of the crown.

Now while the Catholics in England were regarded with more or less leniency, Archbishop Laud in Scotland was forcing his missal on the Scotch Presbyterians, and the Scotch Covenanters were fighting strenuously against Prelacy, and with some success.

Wentworth, afterwards the Earl of Strafford, was appointed viceroy of Ireland, and he was antagonistic to all Dissenters, so the outlook for the Presbyterians was gloomy indeed. Persecution of the Calvinists in Ulster began with Wentworth's appointment in 1633. The ministers were first attacked, and then their people. During the reign of James, Prelacy occupied a more or less subordinate position, but had been growing in strength and gaining confidence in its powers and now was riding on the crest of the wave.

The enmity of Wentworth and the persecuting spirit rendered the lives of the colonists so trying that they came together and appointed a committee of two clergymen to go to America and select a place where they might live in peace and according to their convictions. The committee set out on their quest, but adverse winds and waves compelled their return. The persecution, however, waxed hotter, Presbyterian ministers were tried and deposed, and in desperation the colonists decided to leave at any cost, and to brave the raging ocean and the unknown perils of the strange new land, rather than remain at home and become the football of intolerance and the victims of despotic power.

The settlers to the number of one hundred and forty decided to make what might prove a doubtful experiment. They constructed a small vessel of one hundred and fifty tons, and named the little ship *The Eagle's Wing*. The frail craft set sail on September 9, 1638, but again the weather was unpropitious, and the vessel driven by tempestuous winds returned with its daring passengers in a miserable condition and anchored in the bay of Carrickfergus, with the sails of the ship torn and its rudder broken and disabled, on the 3rd of November, almost two months after they had set out on their venturesome voyage.

The devout people now decided that it had been ordained for them to remain at home. Some of the ministers deprived of their pulpits sought refuge in the old homeland, Scotland, and Wentworth vented his fury on the people left behind. A commission was issued authorizing the Bishop of Down to arrest and imprison any Presbyterian in his diocese, and nothing loath the Anglicans were soon very active in a most unChristian warfare. Peaceable law-abiding citizens were cast into prison like criminals for the dreadful crime of worshiping God in their own way. Many of the people returned to their motherland.

The Anglican or Established Church party now resolved to force upon the colonists what was known as the

Black Oath, which required them to swear allegiance to
Charles, which they were willing to do, but in addition
they were to declare on oath they would never oppose
anything he commanded, and they were to abjure all
covenants, including the National Covenant of Scotland
which that country regarded as her mainstay and life-
preserver.

All persons over sixteen were required to take the oath,
both young and old, but all resolved never to do anything
of the kind. Many of them fled to the woods or sought
shelter in caves and glens, leaving their possessions behind. Upright self-respecting persons were tied and
bound with chains like criminals, and thrown into
prisons and dungeons, there to remain until the exorbitant
fines imposed on them had been paid. A Star Chamber
was established in Dublin, and even respectable women,
expectant mothers, were required to take long journeys in
order to appear at the appointed time before the Chamber
to answer for the crime of their religion. Crowds of
decent women fled to the wilds to escape their persecutors,
who were without mercy for age or for sex.

Scotland was indignant at the treatment her people
were receiving in Ulster and threatened to send an army
to the aid of the colonists, but Wentworth, determined to
overcome the opposition of the Presbyterians to his will,
resolved to exile them to Munster; he raised an army
which he said was to be used in Scotland, but which might
prove useful at home while the Presbyterians were being
subdued. Plans were being put into execution, ships were
provided at the public expense, and every Presbyterian
in the north was to be carried away within a prescribed
time.

Meanwhile how were the Roman Catholics faring?
Charles was an avowed Protestant, but disquieting tidings

from Scotland and from Ulster seemed not to affect him at all, and the Catholics in his realm including Ireland were receiving unusual favor. Priests were wearing their habits publicly in defiance of the law, and the Catholics were worshiping as they saw fit, while Presbyterians were fined and imprisoned, their ministers deposed, and their churches closed.

Sir William Parsons, in a letter to Sir Harry Vane, points out the strong influence of the Catholic priests on public business, "so they are able to guide the Parliament."

It was now Wentworth's turn to encounter difficulties. The uncertain political sky clouded for the viceroy. Britain accused him of crimes far more heinous than that of worshiping God according to his conscience. He was summoned to London, accused of high treason, impeached, and executed. Archbishop Laud, as well as Charles himself, died by the hands of the public executioner.

In England, the exactions and duplicity of Charles had driven the people to revolt. The King had tried to get along without a Parliament, but found himself obliged to assemble one in order to obtain funds to fight the people Laud had antagonized in Scotland. The Parliament revolted, and England was soon in the throes of civil war.

The colonists though now relieved from the despotism of Wentworth were soon to face another calamity more far-reaching in its effects and much more destructive.

Early in the year of 1641, rumors of an insurrection were heard; priests from their pulpits inveighed against heresy, and the people were asked to pray for the success of a great cause. It seemed the encouragement given the Catholics had but whetted their appetites for greater power. Catholics showed some predominance in the Irish Parliament, where they vociferously voiced claims for greater power and for self-government, which action was applauded by the Protestant representatives. The King had privately authorized Lord Glamorgan to promise that the Catholic religion should be reëstablished in Ireland. As the general situation in the country was disturbed Parliament planned to send the soldiers Wentworth had collected, ostensibly for service in Scotland, to Portugal for foreign service, but the Catholic clergy again grew very busy and urged Parliament to allow the soldiers to remain at home, and the request of the priests in this respect carried the day, and the soldiers remained in their own country. Again we find Sir William Parsons commenting in a letter to Sir Harry Vane on the weighty influence of the priests "who are able to guide the Parliament" (MSS., 1641, Record Office).

Indeed so strong were the claims of the Catholics at this period that they erected fifteen religious houses in defiance of the law; if proclamations were made they were ridiculed, and many were determined to force the church claims as well as the cathedrals out of the hands of the Established Church.

The massacre of St. Bartholomew, which left an indelible stain not only on the Guises, Charles IX of France, and his mother Catherine de Medicis, but on the whole French nation, was having its repercussions in Europe.

In the beginning of the month of October, 1641, the leaders among the Catholic clergy had a meeting in an abbey in Westmeath, to discuss religious questions and decide how to get rid of the Protestants. After the discussion, these holy men decided to dispossess and banish or murder them, for, as heretics, they were not entitled to mercy. The priests had actually been preparing for their bloody work the whole summer, and the conspirators included the vicar-general Evor McMahon, afterwards Bishop of Clogher, said to be the brains of the conspiracy.

As the Catholic lords opposed the most violent measures it was decided to act without them.

The program included the seizure of Dublin castle. Phelim O'Neill was to seize Londonderry, Henry O'Neill, Carrickfergus, and Maguire, Newry. The Celtic Irish were expected to rise as one man, and it was not thought necessary to instruct them with regard to killing, for an occupation so thoroughly congenial to them could be left to the discretion of a mob thirsting for, and encouraged by their instructors, to thirst for Protestant blood. Dublin was saved by the vigilance of a Presbyterian elder and the force of the insurrection was spent on Ulster where was found the largest Protestant population.

This insurrection is known as the Irish St. Bartholomew, but the atrocities committed, and the relative number massacred, were greater than in the great French slaughter, and the stain left by this bloody deed on the pages of Celtic Irish history can never be eradicated.[1] The pope contributed liberally to the enterprise, giving his material and moral support, just as he did in the French massacre. The pope also sent a nuncio to Ireland, a man named Rinuccini, who placed the full establishment of the Catholic religion in Ireland above and before all reforms in the political government.

The Catholics, who were not allowed by law to possess arms, had been robbing the Protestants of the arms they legally held. On the morning of October 23, 1641, the carnage began. Gangs of armed and unarmed Celtic Catholics stormed the homes of the defenseless surprised Protestants. Phelim O'Neill, a near savage, invited himself to dine with Lord Caulfield, took his host prisoner, and murdered him in Phelim's own house. The same

[1] Some claim thirty thousand, some one hundred thousand were slaughtered in the St. Bartholomew massacre, but in Ireland, a much smaller country, more than six hundred thousand were slain.

Phelim burned the cathedral of Armagh in breach of a solemn promise he had given. Attempts have been made by partisan writers to minimize the butcheries of 1641, but they are well attested. Forty sworn depositions exist in Trinity College and as if to show the scrupulous exactitude with which the material was collected, in a few of them a line has been drawn through part of the evidence. There are also contemporary accounts from reliable persons, Parliamentary MSS., and Museum reports, all relating a consistent story of the same tragedies. Defenseless families were stripped to the skin, turned out in the cold of an unusually severe northern season, those resisting were killed, and if any sought shelter with what they supposed was a friendly neighbor, they were butchered, for the priests had taught it was a mortal sin to give protection to a heretic. Hundreds of settlers from Armagh who had surrendered were massacred. Helpless, frightened fugitives met with were murdered.

As the attack was so unexpected one town after another was taken by the insurgents. Enniskillen was saved through the energy of Cole, and Coleraine received warning in time and became a refuge for the terror-stricken. Belfast, Carrickfergus, and Lisburn were not taken, but outside these havens the north was a sea of blood. Houses of the rich as well as the poor went up in flames. Groups of hungry, naked people cowered for shelter wherever they could find it. We are told the river Blackwater in Tyrone ran red with Protestant blood.

Some of the atrocities were so dreadful they cannot appear on the printed page, but other savageries are bad enough. Infants were dashed against the wall, some tossed to the pigs or flung into boiling pots. Eyes of men and women were gouged out, their hands were cut off and also their ears. Many were buried alive. Women were stripped and then ripped up with knives. Some of the victims were placed on hot gridirons; slices of flesh were cut from men who were then roasted alive. At Loughhall 3,000 Protestants were driven into a church, and the savage Celts let loose upon them. On the bridge at Portadown 196 Protestants were drowned in one day and one thousand others were dispatched in the same way. Special cruelties were reserved for Protestant ministers, thirty of whom were massacred in one district, one actually crucified with a clerical brother on each side. There are other atrocities before which humanity stands aghast and must go unrecorded. Many perished from cold and hunger, and others died from disease brought on by exposure and lack of proper food. Dead bodies remained unburied, and disease appeared and carried off many victims.

Accounts show that the Roman Catholic clergy of all grades gave their assistance to the tragedies daily enacted. These reputed followers of Christ, who counseled his followers to love even their enemies, followed the practice of anointing the murderers before the latter went out to torture and kill their helpless fellow beings. The priests declared the Protestants were devils and killing them was a meritorious act, and if the slayers should chance to get killed themselves in their glorious work, they should escape purgatory and go immediately to heaven.

In the county of Fermanagh, which was almost entirely Protestant, scarcely twenty escaped (Col. Audley in *Relation of Occurrences*). A council was held at Kilkenny to extinguish the heretics (*Hibernia Anglicana*, Appendix, p. 15). The pope sent not only his blessing, but arms, ammunition, and his nuncio, thus helping to prolong the rebellion and slaughter. Not only did the men and women revel in murder, boys armed with skenes (a skene is a long, thin knife) tortured children, and with the men and women destroyed cattle and sheep, not for food, but because they belonged to Protestants. If the fleeing fugitives found rags with which to cover their bodies, or even a handful of straw, it was torn off or set on fire by their tormentors.

Robert Maxwell, Archdeacon of Down and afterwards Bishop of Kilmore, states in his deposition that by the order of Phelim O'Neill they murdered his brother James Maxwell, and the wife of the latter being in labor she was stripped naked, dragged to the river Blackwater, and drowned.

They cut strips of flesh from each buttock of Mr. Watson, and afterwards roasted him alive.

Flesh was cut from living cattle, because the property of Protestants, to make them die in agony. Maxwell gives evidence of a boy who killed fifteen men held in stocks, with a skene. Women and children rivaled men in their bloody work (see *Hibernia Anglicana*, Appendix, p. 10).

In a true and creditable relation of savage cruelties practiced on the Protestants, a gentleman who was an eyewitness of the scenes he describes, and who with his wife abandoned his estate and other possessions, fled the country, and arrived in London on January 16, 1642, says: "The priests and Jesuits commonly anoint the rebels with their sacrament of the unction, before they go out to murder and rob; assuring them for their meritorious acts, if they should chance to get killed they would reach heaven immediately" (see Temple, pp. 93-94, also Froude).

The Roman Catholic Council at Kilkenny undertook with the pope's blessing "to extirpate and root out from among them the workers of iniquity." One party in this council was willing to accept such terms as Charles would give, but the clergy were the most irreconcilable and would not consent. The pope had sent them not only Rinuccini, but arms, powder, money, and priests. The legate would not consent to terms until his church had all it desired. There is something repulsive in clerics of any rank instigating or encouraging war; it is scarcely to be wondered at that the Bible was torn up in leaves and trampled in the gutter by the rebels; it was not Christ's teaching they wanted or followed.

The brutal cruelties practiced on the Protestants by the Irish Celts naturally led to reprisals. A group of thirty Irish Celtic families living on island Magee, Carrickfergus, were slaughtered in January, 1642. These families had nothing to do with the butcheries of their brethren, but men maddened by terror and grief are not too discriminating. These reprisals occurred some months after the onset of the massacre.

On December 1, 1641, a petition was presented to the English Parliament, signed by the Irish Council, stating there were then 40,000 rebels in the field; and according to this document, "Their tyranny is so great, that they put both man, woman, and child that are Protestants to the sword. They have stripped naked many Protestants and so sent them to the city, men and women. They have ravished maidens, and women before their husbands' faces, and taken their children, and dashed their brains against the walls in the sight of their parents, and at length destroyed them without pity or humanity."

On December 12, 1641, the following letter was read in the English Parliament: "All I can tell you, is the miserable state we continue under, for the rebels daily increase in men and munition in all parts, except in the province of Munster, exercising all manner of cruelties, and striving who can be the most barbarously exquisite in tormenting the poor Protestants; cutting off their ears, fingers, and hands, boiling the hands of little children before their mothers' faces, stripping women naked, and ripping them up," etc.

There is also a letter written by Sir John Temple to the King (MSS. Record Office) December 12, 1641: "But what makes this rebellion more dangerous and formidable, and indeed makes it different from all others that have heretofore happened in this kingdom, is that they have profaned your sacred name, and infused into the belief of the people that what they do is not only by your majesty's avowment, but by commission under your majesty's signature. Besides the cause of their taking arms they pretend to be religion, wherewith their priests and Jesuits have with so great artifice and cunning entertained them, making them believe that the Romish religion was presently to be rooted out here, and cruel massacres to be executed on all professing the same. Thus enraged and armed by these pretenses, they march on furiously, destroying the English, sparing neither age nor sex throughout the kingdom, most barbarously murdering them, and that with greater cruelty, than ever yet was used among Turks or infidels. Many thousands of our nation have already perished under cruel hands, the poor remainder so up and down desolate, naked, and most miserably afflicted with cold and hunger, all inns and other places being prohibited under deep penalties to entertain them, or to give any kind of relief to them."

The paper continues its lamentable account in the same strain, and concludes with the statement that the roads were filled with the naked starving fugitives.

Of the numbers that perished, the Catholic priests said that "200,000 had perished in the first four months." The number killed is mentioned in *Hibernia Anglicana,* Appendix, March 16, 1643. Sir William Petty, in *Political Arithmetic of Ireland,* writing of the blood spilt in 1641, states that out of a population of one and a half million, one half million had been miserably destroyed. Thus the massacre of St. Bartholomew pales both in horror and in the numbers destroyed before the Irish St. Bartholomew of 1641.

Scotland again came to the relief of Ulster. In February, 1642, Major General Monroe landed at Carrickfergus with 10,000 men, and it may be said in passing that many of his men remained as residents of the province. Charles was accused of complicity in the rebellion. He had aided in keeping Wentworth's disbanded men together and tried to add to their number. The duplicities, evasions, and unreliability of Charles reached a point no longer to be ignored or excused. His execution relieved Britain of an incubus which must otherwise have ended in still greater disaster.

The Roman Catholic army at Kilkenny was cut to pieces, and the pope's legate returned to the Vatican.

Sir John Temple writes of the harrowing scenes in Dublin, incident to the crowds of dead and dying people that filled the city (Temple, pp. 93-94). Ulster murderers who had survived the war were brought to Kilkenny for trial. Phelim O'Neill, who had been even above the average in his revolting brutality, with two hundred others were convicted and executed. The surviving population was estimated at about 850,000 of whom 150,000 were Saxons.

The estimated loss of life in the war now closed, compared to the population, *"stands unparalleled in the history of the world."*

After the death of Charles, the Long Parliament deprived the bishops of their seats in the legislature, and both houses declared: "that government by bishops and archbishops was evil and burdensome." In 1643 **Prelacy** was abolished and the Solemn League and Covenant of Scotland approved by Parliament.

In 1649, Cromwell arrived in Dublin bringing aid to the minority still surviving, and prepared to dispense justice to all including the murderers who had made such a large part of their country a field of blood. He did not enter the country with thoughts of vengeance only in his heart for he was relying on God to direct his ways. He said at this time, "It matters not who is our commander-in-chief if God be so." In view of the vilification and abuse heaped on the devoted head of Cromwell by the guilty who were punished for their unspeakable savageries, a sketch of this man's character may not be out of place. Not only Cromwell's father but three of his uncles were members of Parliament in the reign of Elizabeth. He was an M.P. himself in 1628 and represented Cambridge in both the Long and Short Parliaments. He was descended from fine yeoman stock, spoke Latin, was something of a mathematician and had a taste for art. Oliver spent some time at Cambridge University, but did not remain long enough to graduate. His wife, Elizabeth, was the daughter of Sir John Bourchier and the two were tenderly attached throughout their married lives. On the thirtieth anniversary of his wedding he wrote to his wife, "You are dearer to me than any other creature." Oliver was a most affectionate father and suffered agonizingly when a child was removed by death. He deeply loved and respected his mother who was his confidential friend and wise counsellor, influencing her son's life for good until her death in her ninetieth year. This lady was of a deeply

religious turn of mind, and Oliver's life shows the effect
of her pious precepts and example.

Cromwell was a very approachable man, simple in his
tastes and very kindhearted and sympathetic to the needy
and suffering. He refused to allow the so-called sports
of cockfighting and bearbaiting on the ground of cruelty,
and it is said he was full of mercy for all created things
whether human or animal. The poet Marvell was impressed by the softness of his heart, a characteristic shown
in the English wars where he was noted for his attitude
of mercy towards the conquered. Before leaving Ireland
we see Oliver making an effort in behalf of Lord Moore
who had surrendered, which was another example of his
usual attitude of mercy.

Two things Cromwell valued highly, and these were
piety and intelligence; and so far as possible his soldiers
were chosen with these views in mind, and were distinctly
above the average both in manners and morals; they were,
so their commander thought, sober, honest, good Christians. And the men were rigidly disciplined. Drinking
and profanity was prohibited, as well as lying, stealing,
or indeed any offense against person and property.
Though rigidly disciplined the men were well fed, suitably
clad, and as far as lay in the commander's power well-
paid. As might be expected, Oliver's men had unlimited
confidence in their leader, so naturally this command was
regarded as invincible and they were victorious in practically every encounter.

When Cromwell landed in Ireland he was no stripling,
his character was formed, he was regarded as a man of
affairs, esteemed, trusted, and admired, a man of deeds
rather than words. He did not seek place or preferment
and was usually forced into prominence because no other

leader was procurable. Is it possible this well-poised, self-controlled, compassionate man should be transformed by the Irish atmosphere into another Ivan the Terrible? The idea is too fantastic; the outcries of the perpetrators of unspeakable crimes have been so loud and persistent in denunciation that some recorders, so-called, of history have related instead of history, the brazen mendacities of criminals in attempted justification of their unspeakable crimes, which accounts are just as credible as the tales of banshees and leprechauns with which some narrators try to beguile us.

The war had lasted eight years, had cost more than 600,000 lives, and resulted in the destruction of property worth millions of pounds wantonly destroyed.

The savage butcheries, mutilations, and tortures of helpless human beings have doubtless never been surpassed, even by the most depraved and ignorant savage races in the history of the world. Lacking unchallengeable proofs it would be impossible to believe that a people claiming at least some civilization and Christianity could reach such depths of degradation and unmentionable cruelties to humanity. If the Irish Celts quickly forget the injury they do to others they never fail to remember any evil done to themselves.

Cromwell was dispatched to Ireland to punish those guilty of the horrors described, and has been execrated by the Celtic Irish, yet Cromwell's treatment of those who played an active part in the Irish St. Bartholomew was kindness itself compared to the savage brutalities and unspeakable cruelties they had visited on the defenseless men, women, and children who were their victims (see Irish massacres and results illustrated by extracts from unpublished papers, M. Hilkson, London, 1880).

Cromwell was apparently a strong, brave, and just man,

anxious to do what was right, and desirous of tempering justice with mercy. On coming to Ireland he ordered that no violence should be done to any one not in arms with the enemy, and that all goods should be paid for. If any tendency toward dishonesty among his followers showed itself, the culprit was summarily dealt with. Reliable authentic evidence proves that Cromwell's actions in dealing with the rebels were strictly within the letter of the law. There was humane treatment of women and children, and only those proved guilty of the most frightful massacre in recorded history were justly executed.

Reaching the country in rebellion, Cromwell said, "We are come to ask an accounting of the innocent blood shed, and to bring to account all who, by appearing in arms, shall justify the same." Another dispatch reads, "I am persuaded that this is a righteous judgment of God upon these barbarous wretches, who have imbrued their hands in so much innocent blood, and that it will tend to prevent the effusion of much innocent blood in the future."

In the campaign which followed, the rebel garrison at Drogheda, largely composed of rebel Catholic Englishmen, was asked to surrender, which they refused to do. Treatment of the Drogheda garrison has been censured. The garrison was asked to surrender in the usual military way, and according to the laws of war at that period and for a very long time after, when defenders of a garrison were summoned to surrender and they refused, they had no claim to mercy.

The garrison was captured and every tenth man shot; the remainder were sent to the Barbados. Authentic evidence shows there was no massacre, and no destruction of women and children. The garrison was treated according to the strict letter of the law.

The garrison at Wexford was treated in a similar manner. Wexford, as compared to some of the other Irish counties, was more or less enlightened, but here as in other rebel localities the same savage ferocity towards the helpless victims of all ages and both sexes was quite as pronounced, and those possessing some education showed as much malignity towards their victims as did their co-religionists elsewhere.

Execution was ordered for those who had instigated the massacres, and those who had been active in the war were given the choice of exile or banishment to the Barbados.

It may be remembered that about two weeks before the massacre began in the late autumn of 1641 a meeting was held at the abbey of Multifarnum and that a number of priests there present had recommended a general massacre of Protestants as the most effectual method of combating Protestant ascendancy, and that after the massacre began the rebels were anointed by their clergy before they set out on their sanguinary activities. Well, for these priests and Jesuits retributive justice was at hand, and they were exiled to the Barbados. Practically every Roman Catholic landowner had exposed his property to confiscation, and this punishment was considered an appropriate penalty to impose for rebellion, murder, and destruction of property.

Cromwell, a truthful man, believed he had acted justly in Ireland. He wrote to an antagonist commander on October 17th, "Since my coming here I have this witness of myself, that I have endeavored to avoid effusion of blood . . . this being my principle, that the people and places where I come may not suffer except by their own wilfulness."

Cromwell somewhat later, writing to Irish Roman Catholic bishops, points out how Englishmen had made their homes in Ireland and had purchased valuable property from Irish owners; that others had taken out long expensive leases on property; that they had bought stocks, houses, and plantations for goodly sums, and how they had lived peaceably and honestly with the Irish people, and all had the same protection and justice without favor from the English laws. Oliver continues to show that the English had given no provocation, and yet had been subjected to the most barbarous massacre without respect to age or sex that had ever been beheld, and at a time when Ireland was at perfect peace. Oliver continues, pointing out the worthy example the Anglo-Saxons had shown in industry, commerce, and traffic to the country, and then asks, "Is not my assertion true? Is God? Will God be with you? I am confident he will not." He then states to the bishops that he had come to avenge innocent blood, and break the power of lawless rebels who were enemies to human society. Cromwell also challenged the bishops to "Give me one instance of one man since my coming here to Ireland, not in arms, massacred, destroyed, or banished, concerning the massacre or destruction of whom, justice hath not been done or attempted to be done." Needless to say the bishops were never able to dispute the challenge thus given, as they would have been glad to do, had it been possible.

The accusation made of Cromwell ordering the killing of men admitted to quarter at Drogheda is refuted by the fact that no quarter was given to those refusing to surrender, so this accusation of partisan writers also falls to the ground. Oliver was never of a sanguinary turn of mind. The Irish leaders who surrendered were to transfer themselves to foreign service and many did so.

Throughout the reign of Charles I which preceded the rebellion and massacre of 1641, the Roman Catholics had been greatly favored. Many were members of Parliament and of corporations; they practiced as magistrates and appeared before the bar although the penal laws remained on the statute books, and their religion was rarely interfered with. All this was now changed and the Roman Catholic religion was proscribed; the Catholics had abused their privileges and it was felt they could not be trusted. The Irish Parliament was abolished and the country united with England.

Ireland was then three quarters Protestant, with the fractious element shut up in Connaught, but the banished Celt was always ready to assassinate any stray Anglo-Saxon who might venture too far from his home, and the former was so hated and detested that had he been allowed ordinary freedom his life would not have been worth a moment's purchase.

Succeeding Cromwell's victorious campaign he turned his attention to the Presbyterians. The Solemn League and Covenant had found its way to Ulster where it was solemnly and devoutly signed by the northern colonists. The Scotch regiments of Monroe who came to oppose the rebels in 1641 were acting as garrisons in the provinces in 1647, and later on they made permanent residences in Ulster.[1]

---

[1] The chaplains who came from Scotland with Monroe's men established an ecclesiastical organization among their troops and on the tenth of June, 1642, the first regular Presbytery ever held in Ireland came together. It was composed of a group of ministers and five ruling elders. The names of the ministers were Rev. Hugh Cunningham, Rev. Thomas Peebles, Rev. John Scott, Rev. John Aird. The Presbytery exercised a protecting supervision over their people and some of those still alive returned to their farms. Additional ministers were sent from Scotland, and elders were pressed into service at home, so the spiritual needs of the people were adequately cared for, and the almost desolate land began to revive again. In 1647, Scotch regiments were still acting in the north, and Ulster had now thirty ordained Presbyterian ministers in addition to the chaplains acting with their regiments.

In the earlier part of 1649 the Presbyterians had sent a protest from Belfast to the English government. This document, styled a "Representation," had been read in all their churches and it condemned the summary condemnation of Charles I. The poet Milton was commissioned by the English to make a suitable reply. Any consideration Charles had to bestow in Ireland was shown to the Roman Catholics, and not to the Presbyterians, notwithstanding the latter disapproved of the arbitrary proceedings of Parliament, and their attitude on this question led Cromwell to demand from the Irish Dissenters an oath which was termed "The Engagement."

This oath demanded the signer to renounce the whole line of Charles and every person pretending to the government, and to be true and faithful to the government. The Presbyterian ministers refused to sign the document as they did not believe royal rights could be disposed of by any group, nor did they consider the Parliamentary proceedings legal; although no Stuart had ever shown them any favor, the rugged Scotch conscience would have its way.

Again the Presbyterians were to suffer for their independence of thought and conduct. Presbyterian homes were surrounded by dragoons, some were arrested and imprisoned, many hid themselves in the woods, and others escaped to Scotland. Pastors sent from England to the north were not acceptable, for the colonists were devoted to their own ministers, and their tenacity was not easily overcome. Cromwell now decided to banish the leading Presbyterians and the people of Antrim and Down to Munster.

A list of the people to be exiled was made out and a proclamation issued which ordered them within a specified time and under severe penalties to remove to the counties of Kilkenny, Tipperary, and Waterford (this list can be seen in Reid, Vol. II, p. 552).

However, as time passed on Cromwell, now dictator, and with a wider experience of the people, saw they were peaceable, industrious, and not given to strife or agitation. The persecutions ceased, pastors were again allowed to preach in their parish churches, and even received a stipend for doing it. In 1643 the Long Parliament abolished Prelacy and Dissenting citizens were allowed to worship God in their own way without interference.

Cromwell the dictator ruled Ireland wisely and well. The interests of honest labor were cared for. Irish commercial restraints were removed, and Ireland was no longer a victim of the jealousy and cupidity of England. The priests were absent, strife was no longer stirred up, and there was no longer agitation to unsettle the people, so the country prospered as she had never done before in any ten years of her previous history.

The rebellion and massacre of 1641 in Ireland was instituted for the purpose of getting rid of the Protestants by death or otherwise, and the regaining of Irish soil for the Celts, although some rather superficial writers have ascribed the insurrection to events which occurred away back in Elizabeth's reign, whose government has been accused of undue severity in stamping out opposition to her authority.

However, there are two sides to the picture. Although English authority in Ireland dates from nearly the same period as that of the pope, the latter seems to have regarded his authority in Ireland as supreme, and because Elizabeth supported everywhere the reformation in religious observances instituted by her father Henry, the authority of the Vatican was used to its utmost to destroy the Queen or set her at naught and plunge Britain into a destructive war.

His holiness excommunicated Elizabeth, absolved her subjects from rendering her obedience, planted his banner in her dominions, and incited her subjects to rise against her authority. In 1579 a Bull of deposition was issued against the queen, and Roman missionaries urged not only the Irish, but English citizens as well, to revolt against the royal authority. The pope at the same time tried to bring about a Catholic insurrection in Scotland. The papacy was urging Philip II of Spain to war against England and bestowed his blessing on the Armada, besides his material help in the effort to utterly crush the English Queen who declined to recognize the all-powerful Vatican.

Realizing that half measures would avail but little Elizabeth used all the force at her command to reduce her insubordinate Irish subjects to her authority, and the measures adopted, though indeed severe and persistent, were not worse than those advised by Pius V and Gregory XIII for use by the Spanish monarch in the Netherlands.

When Elizabeth died her authority in Ireland was everywhere recognized and rebellion against her government had ceased, but throughout her reign the gentry of the Pale went to mass without question and there was no religious persecution.

Laud, Archbishop of Canterbury, and the arch persecutor of Dissenters, was the architect of his own fortunes. The son of a respectable tailor he reached the position of first man in Britain, dining at the royal table and exercising the utmost despotism. Laud is described as a man of steel, without sympathy, a great organizer and very superstitious. He kept a diary which might well raise doubts of his sanity.

His spies were busy everywhere and when he became Archbishop no person whether his rank was high or low could escape the toils of this priest, if he dared to deviate in any degree from the rites and ceremonials prescribed by my lord of Canterbury. Nothing was too small to escape his notice and throughout the land there was persecution, suffering, and misery of respectable God-fearing people caught in the web of ecclesiastical tyranny.

Laud paid great deference to the externals of worship, catering rather to the emotional and dramatic demands, than to the reason and judgment of the worshiper. He restored the voluminous lawn sleeves and surplices, the gorgeous coloring of stained glass windows, and consecrated vessels, with bowing to the east as well as to the name of Jesus. He did not approve of the Puritan Sunday, which he set apart for games and other enjoyment. In spite of artistic leanings he was an excellent business man and made of his church a good financial investment.

The archbishop insisted on kneeling at communion and bowing to the altar. In the year 1637 he established censorship of the press, the Geneva Bible was suppressed, and forcible suppression of the people's will was advocated. The defunct Star Chamber was revived and used to destroy his opponents. Fines and imprisonment were a commonplace. It was said that the year-books of Laud gave the impression that the chief business of the bishops was running down the Puritans, while force and not persuasion was always the weapon to be used.

Laud's talents did not include those of public speaking; it was said he wrote sermons like a carpenter, and did not impress as a speaker for he was primarily a practical business man. He believed in the absolute supremacy of royal authority, and in government by force, thought

Parliament unnecessary, and believed in bending press and people to his will. Laud's belief in omens and dreams would put to shame the veriest psychopath, yet this unbalanced man by virtue of the authority vested in him preyed on his generation causing widespread misery. When he reached the headsman's block no one was so poor as to give him one word of sympathy; and his death was a relief from the apprehension and dread which was almost universal. Probably he had much to do in creating the sentiment which destroyed his royal master, and drove the Stuart dynasty from a throne they knew not how to fill.

Sir Thomas Wentworth, Laud's right-hand man in Ireland, was created Earl of Strafford when he had proved his usefulness in carrying out the commands of the Archbishop, and was appointed Lord Deputy in Ireland in 1633. While in England he was not unfavorably regarded, and was never accused of peculation or of trying to amass wealth by means of his office, but he had a great desire for power, and although he supported the freedom of the people in his earlier years, while in Ireland he became an enthusiast in upholding Laud's dictatorial desires and plans.

As deputy he raised and trained an army to fight against the liberties of the people, and by means of the Irish Parliament, he gathered money to assist Charles in assailing the rights of the citizens and is also accused of packing juries for his own purposes and of being the means of having the province of Connaught declared royal property, and a stronghold for the despotic Charles. He in fact became the tool of Laud, and displayed the same attitude in ecclesiastical matters as well as in the curtailment of the liberties of the press and the people. Strafford was accused not only of subverting the liberties of the people, but of fining honest men and sending them to prison. He had offended because of his too great efficiency in execution of the Laudian precepts and designs and paid the price of his unethical conduct on the headsman's block on Tower Hill.

The Catholics had brought upon themselves severe restrictive measures by the rebellion of 1641, which was more or less similar to what the Protestants had suffered in France, Spain, and Italy who had not engaged in rebellion or massacre, but in spite of the law in the time of Charles I the priests returned and erected their chapels in defiance of legal statutes. It is evident that the confiscation of property and loss of civic and other privileges was the result of their eight years of rebellion and their massacre of British subjects and destruction of property. They greatly injured their position in addition to the loss of their privileges. Preceding the rebellion and massacre of 1641, the Roman Catholics were pressing their claims for self-government on the Irish Parliament, and these claims were receiving careful consideration.

After the Irish St. Bartholomew they were not allowed to teach school until the year 1781. The year 1673 saw the passage of the Test Act in England, which enacted that all persons holding civil or military offices should take the Oath of Allegiance and Supremacy, receive the Sacrament according to the rites of the Church of England, and subscribe a declaration against transubstantiation. This act found its way to Ireland where it was soon in active operation.

Before 1641, the Roman Catholics had held two thirds of the fee simple property of the country, but after 1641 this land was seized by Cromwell, and Catholic tenants but not the landlords, occupied the land. In 1692, Roman Catholics were prevented from sitting in Parliament, they were no longer allowed to possess the electoral suffrage, and were excluded from corporations, the magistracy, the bench, the bar, from grand juries and vestries, and also from the army and navy.

III

CONTINUED PERSECUTION OF DISSENTERS AND THE SIEGE OF LONDONDERRY

Charles II regains the crown—Prelacy restored, and Presbyterians again persecuted—Second Act of Uniformity introduced and emigration of Presbyterians stimulated by the intolerance shown them—The Catholic penal laws suspended —Rev. Francis Makemie, Presbyterian minister, emigrates to Virginia and is followed by other pastors; a Presbytery established (the first)—James II succeeds his brother; an intolerant, bigoted, stupid, and obstinate man, he rekindles Presbyterian persecution and favors only Catholics—Prince of Orange arrives in England—Londonderry besieged by French and Irish Catholic armies—Battle of Newtown-Butler won over greatly superior numbers by Protestants— William of Orange arrives in Ireland; battle of the Boyne won, Limerick besieged, battle of Aughrim fought and won —William grants Regium Donum out of Belfast customs in spirit of gratitude to northern fighters—Plots against the life of William discovered resulting in restraining laws against Catholics, but these are generally not enforced— The Protestant Episcopal Church, character of its clerics, and their effect on the country—The woolen manufacture destroyed by English legislation; people reduced to poverty; emigration receives further stimulation—Belfast, the northern metropolis; its industries.

THE colonists of Ulster, including General Monroe, favored the return of the second Charles to the throne. Charles indeed was willing to accept the honor, and very glad to make all the promises desired besides giving profuse protestations of his regard for Presbyterianism. At heart he was a decided Catholic.

The Long Parliament had declared Prelacy obnoxious and pernicious and had it abolished; but now Prelacy was to be reëstablished; it could be relied on to hold up the hands of "the Lord's anointed," and countenance despotism, and was therefore valuable and deserving countenance and support. Two new archbishops and ten bishops were added to the list of High Churchmen. The Catholics, though regarded leniently during the administration of Charles I, were to receive special favor throughout the reign of his son.

The new prelates, with Bramhall the primate as leader, carried through Parliament a second Act of Uniformity (the first Act of Uniformity enacted in the reign of Elizabeth restored the Prayer Book of Edward VI and enforced its use on the clergy), which compelled every clergyman to profess before his congregation his acceptance of the Prayer Book. He was also to subscribe on oath that the Scottish League and Covenant was not only illegal but impious as well; and to swear never under any circumstances whatever to take up arms against the king; and no one was to hold a benefice, teach, preach, or administer the Sacraments who refused to subscribe.

The prelates ordered that no minister should officiate without their sanction; the use of the Prayer Book was commanded, and public preachers or those holding a benefice ordered to use it.

The spirit of resistance to religious tyranny was strong; eight ministers out of seventy accepted, and were ordained; the remainder were expelled from their churches and congregations, but numbers of their flock followed their pastors, and the ministers who endeavored to continue their duties were cast into prison.

An attempt made to foist ministers on the people met with pronounced antagonism and utter failure. One irate woman proudly declared she had pulled "the white sark ower his heid." Bishop Leslie of Raphoe excommunicated four Dissenting ministers and then imprisoned them for the crime of their religion; and then these persecuted people, like the early Christians in the Catacombs of Rome, met in wild secluded places, with a sentry on guard, celebrated the rites of their church, and worshiped together.

The bishops, it would seem, were not interested in the private lives of the ministers; a man might be a liar, a thief, or any kind of derelict, but if he consented to use the ordered Prayer Book, he was allowed to preach. The prelates considered it a crime to approach the Supreme Being with a spontaneous expression of heartfelt thanks for a blessing bestowed, or to express in the preacher's own words the desire for continued good, even at the risk of making consecrated men and their families homeless.

This action of the bishops had the effect of obstructing the peaceful Protestant immigration that was taking place which soon ceased altogether. Soldiers who had settled on the land in the time of Cromwell and had brought their holdings to a high state of cultivation, sold out their property and left the country. The children of scattered Protestant families throughout the country refused to accept either the liturgy or the mass and, left without any instruction, gradually became Catholics.

In striking contrast to the attitude displayed toward the Non-Conformists was the favor exhibited towards Catholics, who were granted an even greater measure of liberty and freedom than they enjoyed in the reign of the first Charles.

The penal laws were suspended, but the Catholic clergy had already returned and had even erected new places of worship. The Catholics should have been affected by the new Act of Uniformity, but they were permitted to evade it, and the persecuting fury of the prelates fell on the unprotected Presbyterians only.

About one half of the Roman Catholic gentry were reinstated in their former possessions; and there was a general reëstablishment of the Catholic hierarchy. Catholic prelates were given a quasi recognition by the state, and the Oath of Supremacy was not required from Catholics seeking entrance to government positions. The Catholics had a recognized existence which the Non-Conformists did not; the latter had in fact no legal existence.

Bishop Jeremy Taylor was a notorious persecutor of the Presbyterians, now prohibited from meeting together for worship; if they tried to do so bands of soldiers were sent to disperse them, an experience the Catholics never had in Ireland, and if a minister tried to give instruction to his flock he was subjected to heavy penalties. Taylor closed thirty-six churches in his diocese, and soon appointed men of his own sect to fill the vacant pulpits.

The Episcopalian churches were not popular and the clergy had found it necessary to offer bribes to have men and women come to listen to the sermons of the snowy-banded dilettante, while the meeting houses of the Presbyterians had been crowded to the doors with an eager, devout, and enthusiastic people.

As time passed on, the priestly persecution became less virulent, not because the bishops had tired of persecution, but because the government had been induced to call a halt in this baiting of peaceful subjects. It was believed the Presbyterians had found an advocate in Sir Arthur Forbes of the Granard family. At any rate there appeared some attempt at conciliation. After a conference with the King, a small grant was made to the northern Dissenters which became the origin of an endowment, and although the sum was small—it was but six hundred pounds—it proved most acceptable. Persecution however had not been abolished; the Dissenters were bound by law to attend the Episcopal Church, and those who dared to disobey were summoned before the bishops' courts where fines heavy enough to exhaust slender resources were imposed, and every action was watched by spies. In 1684, the bishops regained their power to injure. Dissenting churches were again closed, their public worship again under ban, and the people forced to meet for prayer and praise together when and where they could. This persecution of peaceful people was owing, not so much to the malevolence of the government, as to the lack of supervision of its powerful servants.

The intolerance of the bishops was to have a far-reaching effect, for it resulted in stimulating that emigration from Ulster which began when the settlers there found themselves prevented by adverse circumstances from leading the peaceful quiet lives they had hoped for and expected. The emigration which now began lasted for a hundred years, the emigrants going to New England, to Virginia, and other colonies in a never-ceasing stream, so they were ready and very willing to enter the armies of the Revolution and fight for that liberty they had learned so well to value. Authentic reports tell us they furnished Washington's best generals and were a powerful influence in pushing the war to a successful close.

It was during this third Stuart reign that the Rev. Francis Makemie, in 1681, sailed to America and settled in Virginia, where he died in 1708. Other young Presbyterian ministers had preceded him, even at that early date. In 1698, a young clergyman was working in Maryland who had arrived from Ulster with many of the families who had abandoned their homes in Northern Ireland for a country that could offer more peace and freedom, and they were having their spiritual necessities cared for by ministers sent them by the Presbytery of Lagan in Ulster.

The Rev. William Traill went to Maryland in 1682, and officiated there for many years. The Rev. Josias Makie arrived about 1690, and the Rev. Samuel Davis was pioneering in Delaware in 1706.

It was Makemie who organized the first American Presbytery, which was the Presbytery of Philadelphia, and about the time of the Revolutionary War one third of the population of Pennsylvania belonged to the Presbyterian denomination.

The infant Presbytery consisted of seven ministers, and the Rev. John Hampton, who arrived in 1705, was added to the list. Subsequently four Irish Presbyterian ministers increased the original number. In 1718, William Tennant, who has been called the father of Presbyterian colleges in America, arrived and added much to the growth and prosperity of the church.

Thus it was upon Ulster Presbyterians the privilege and honor was conferred of laying the foundation of the Presbyterian Church in America (just as Scotland had laid it in Ulster), which is now a strong and powerful body, a staunch upholder of the separation of church and state and of the principles of justice and the square deal for all.

The reign of James II, son of Charles I and brother of Charles II, lasted but four years, but those years were replete with cruelty and injustice on an unprecedented scale, and his administration was notable for detestable and inhuman laws, for merciless punishments and unsurpassed judicial iniquities.

James gloried in the exercise of authority, he was diligent and methodical but despotic, obstinate, and vindictive, besides being narrow-minded, bigoted, and cowardly.

His mental outlook showed but limited range. In his earlier years the King was regarded as truthful, but as a King his statements were found utterly unreliable, and he did not hesitate to make the most solemn promises which he had not the very slightest intention of ever keeping.

An outstanding defect in his character was cruelty. While in Scotland, he enjoyed the torture of the Covenanters, who had their knees beaten in that instrument of torture known as "the boot." More merciful men would hasten away to escape the scene, but not James, who looked on complacently while the victims of religious persecutiou writhed in their torture. After a tumult in Scotland he ordered unsparing use of the boot in punishment of the disturbance. In England the King could not give quite such free rein to his impulses because of legislative enactments which might not entirely be set aside, but in Scotland a ruler was not so much restricted. In North Britain, he engaged himself in obtaining the bloodiest law ever enacted against Dissenters, and the new penal laws he was instrumental in having enacted against the Presbyterians were notorious, even in that bloody age, for their atrocity.

The Scotch Covenanters were given up to the license of the army; quiet, decent, God-fearing men and women were murdered in cold blood without the formality of a trial, by Graham and Claverhouse. Neither age nor sex was spared, and the persecution of these Dissenters reached the limit of the law. Aged women held in high esteem by their friends and neighbors because of their piety and charities, were, for offenses scarcely meriting even a reprimand, beheaded or burnt alive. Women and even young girls were persecuted to the very death for their religion.

James was himself utterly lawless. He attempted to

subvert the constitution of his country and enact such laws as he desired. He turned men out of office in a Protestant country only because they were Protestants, and amended by his own authority a long list of statutes. In Ireland during his jurisdiction there Protestants could obtain no justice either in the courts or out of them. Protestant women were insulted and violated without redress, and Protestant citizens pillaged and punished at will. The fiscal resources of the sovereign were direct and indirect; money was taken from the safe, wine stored in the cellar as well as fuel and clothing, while the soldiers were billeted on the Protestants at free quarters. In addition the currency was depreciated and brass money substituted for sterling, and at the same time other old discarded inferior metals were stamped and used as coin of the realm.

In addition to other characteristics the King was utterly unscrupulous, and although penurious he was willing to spend a sum equal to $15,000 in order to gratify his malice against Bishop Burnet who had offended his majesty. Criminals were hired to kidnap the Bishop, who was in Holland in order that he might be brought to England where the victim might be tortured or murdered at pleasure, and Louis of France pledged all possible aid in the undertaking. When the seven English bishops were imprisoned, the king labored night and day to pack the jury sitting on the case so that he might possess the power to punish the ecclesiastics as desired.

The legislative enactments emanating from James were so provocative of evil that they were criticized emphatically and severely by Ronquillo, the Spanish minister, who informed his court that the English laws against popery might seem severe, but they were so mitigated by prudence and humanity, they caused no annoyance to peaceful people, and he informed the Holy See that what a Roman

Catholic suffered in London was nothing when compared to what a Protestant was forced to endure in Ireland. Ronquillo was a zealous Catholic himself.

In Scotland James ordered Catholic emancipation from all laws imposing penalties or disabilities, but persecution of the Presbyterians was to remain unmitigated, even the Conventicle Act which commanded the punishment of death for attendance at a Conventicle was to remain active.

In the beginning of the reign of this last Stuart, the Irish statute book showed scarcely any enactment which imposed a penalty on Papists, although the English laws against them at that time were at least verbally severe. In Ireland the native Celt might become a public functionary and no law debarred Papists from sitting in either House of Parliament. Many of the laws adverse to the native Celt were enacted against turbulency rather than religion.

Following the orders of the English King, Tyrconnel in Ireland had turned all Protestants out of office even in the Protestant towns, so that James had practically a hand-picked Irish Parliament consisting almost entirely of Catholic Irishmen. It was this Parliament that passed that stupendous Bill of Attainder, unequaled in size and scope in history. This great act contained between two and three thousand names. At the top were members of the Irish peerage, then followed the names of baronets, knights, clergymen, squires, merchants, yeomen, artisans, women, and even children. No investigation had previously been made of any of the proscribed persons. Any Parliamentary member who wished to rid himself of an enemy, a rival, or a creditor, simply gave his name to the clerk, and there was not often an objection made to the entry. The proscribed were to surrender themselves by a certain date, and those who failed to appear at that time were to be hanged, drawn, and quartered. Not one of these proscribed persons had been heard in defense. Plans were made to make pardons difficult as well as expensive, and after a certain date no pardon was possible. At the very time this list of persons was made, Protestants were hazarding their liberty, their lives, and their estates in the cause of their ungrateful sovereign, and the greatest care was exercised to prevent any attainted person learning of his condemnation until it should be too late. Not a single copy of the act was made public, so that thousands of the proscribed heard nothing of their fate until it was too late to obtain a pardon. Certainly the Irish Protestants never reached the depth of infamy in their legislative enactments or in cruel deeds to which the Irish Celt so quickly descended.

While the Irish Act of Attainder, as great as it was infamous, shocked the entire world, James boasted that he had by an act granted liberty of conscience to all sects, and at the same time he was ordering a persecution of Protestants as crushing and destructive as any continental Catholic state had ever instituted in its devastated provinces. Even faithful loyalists risking their all for the ungrateful King, found that no sacrifice could atone for their Protestantism. Those who had so extolled "the Lord's anointed" and inculcated passive obedience found no greater favor in the sight of James than others of their sects, and every week ushered in a new act for plundering and murdering Protestants. So opposed was James to all Puritans that when the large sum of forty thousand pounds was collected from English citizens for the relief of impoverished Huguenots, the King refused to let them have this money, to which he had not contributed, unless the sufferers first communicated according to the rites of the Anglican Church, so that these needy and expectant persons went sorrowfully away in their bitter disappointment.

In spite of his great piety, the King was a libertine and consorted with abandoned women, one of whom, Catherine Sedley, he created a duchess in her own right, in spite of the angry objections of his outraged Queen. It seems, however, the trespasser salved his conscience, to his own satisfaction at least, by punishing himself in private for his misdeeds, and when after the King's death the Queen entered a convent, she carried with her the instrument of torture which the King used on these occasions.

The notorious Judge Jeffries of "Bloody Circuit" fame had the unqualified approval of his sovereign. James believed in the doctrine of expediency and did not hesitate when persons stood in his way to have them removed by assassination. A plot to assassinate William III of England was hatched in the French War Office, receiving the approval of both Louis and James. When the prospective assassin was presented to James and to his Queen, James said, "I have been informed of the business. If you and your companions do me this service you shall never want." The hired murderer failed to achieve his object, and his confession received wide publicity, for it was printed in many languages.

James was devoted to the Jesuits and professed himself a son of the order. He kept one of them, Father Petre, at his court, and appears to have planned his life according to the model they provided.

However devoted he might be to the rites and ordinances of his church, his life certainly affords an example of everything to be avoided. He was a faithless husband, an indifferent father, a faithless friend, cruel, selfish, vindictive, a liar, a perjurer, and an accessory to murder. Whether the life of James was influenced by Jesuitical association it would be hazardous to say. In the opinion of Macaulay the members of this order were sycophants "and owed their influence to the indulgence with which they treated the sins of the great, and the servants of these were shown how they could without sin help themselves to their master's plate"; and again, "Whatever praise those fathers might justly claim, flattery itself could not ascribe to them either wide liberality or strict veracity. They never scrupled when the interests of their order were at stake to call in the aid of the civil sword or to violate the laws of truth and good faith." And these facts, we learn, have been proclaimed to the world "even by men whose virtue and genius were the glory of the church of Rome."

The repudiated English King died of apoplexy at St. Germain after a life filled with deeds of cruelty and injustice. The great historian Hume has said, "The people were justified in their resistance of him."

When James ascended the throne, Ireland was regarded as just a colony, and the new monarch, probably realizing his unpopularity, thought it would be a good plan to establish a residence in Catholic Ireland, to which he could retire in case of necessity. To further his designs, an order was issued in secret to oust the Protestants from all offices in Ireland, and to fill the vacant places with Roman Catholics.

Lord Tyrconnel, also known as "lying Dick Talbot," was designated as the man who should carry out the designs outlined by James. The bench, the bar, and all similar positions were to be filled by Catholics. All religious tests were to be dispensed with, the Oath of Supremacy no longer required. Protestants were dropped from office and Catholics appointed in their places. No Protestant could now fill any place in civil service, army, or navy. Eight thousand veteran soldiers were dismissed and left without support.

The civil administration of the country was handed over to fanatics, mostly ignorant men and some of them criminals and outlaws. A second Act of Settlement ordered lands that had been confiscated restored without recompense for improvements (see Clarendon to Ormond, *Letters*, Vol. I).

There was a reversion of outlawries, and families put in claims; charters of corporations were revoked; Protestants were required to furnish arms and horses to their enemies, their property and lives thus placed at the mercy of the soldiers. Men who had been outlaws and gangsters wore the King's uniform. Tenants of Protestant landlords were ordered not to pay rent. Protestant property was seized, so that in the short space of three months one million pounds in property value had disappeared.

Soldiers were ordered on guard around bakeries, so that no Protestant might buy a loaf of bread (see King's *History of Protestants in Ireland, by an Eyewitness*). The country was now ordered by fanatics, bandits were commissioned officers. Rumors of massacre were in the air, and according to Dr. T. Y. Killen, James wished to rekindle the fires of Smithfield. Lord Clarendon writes to Rochester (*Letters*, Vol. I), "All power is in the hands of the conquered nation, and the English who did conquer are left naked and deprived even of the arms which by the patents of Plantation they are obliged to have in readiness for the King's service."

The Lord Chancellorship was delegated to a man who had been guilty of forgery, with slight, if any legal knowledge, and another, Thomas Nugent, remarkable only for his blunders, was made Chief Justice of the King's Bench, Stephen Rice, a graduate of a Jesuit college, was made chief of the Exchequer and was hostile to the Act of Settlement. Richard Nagle, also a graduate of a Jesuit college, was awarded the attorney generalship, and Keating, a Protestant, was associated with two Catholics and appointed Chief Justice of Common Pleas. The Protestants were voicing complaints because their titles were ignored, while forged documents and false witnesses received recognition.

In the Court of Exchequer, the charters of all the cities and boroughs in the country were declared forfeited, and Protestant towns placed under the government of Catholics. Sheriffs were selected from the Catholics and juries as well. Many men now carrying on the business of the country, were illiterate, and previously had been engaged in menial occupations.

The new Catholic soldiers, long accustomed to hold subordinate positions, swaggered around in their newly found authority, delighting to humiliate the Protestants, especially the Englishmen, even though they were quartered on Protestant householders, without paying for their support.

Meanwhile William of Orange had arrived in England, and the Irish troops received the call to arms. It is said that never in the history of modern Europe was there such a rising of the people as now in Ireland. Not that they were so fond of James, for their leaders hoped to throw themselves into the arms of France. In the new army, the officers were few, but commissions were distributed with a lavish hand. No enticement in the way of adequate remuneration for services was offered, but the intimation that they were free to plunder their Protestant fellow countrymen was irresistible. The whole

Catholic population were arming themselves—the women
were ordered to provide themselves with skenes. (The
skene had been used freely by women and boys on the
helpless Protestants, some of whom had been placed in
stocks prior to the killing, in the massacre of 1641.)

The manufacture of guns and swords was carried on
with alacrity, and if a Protestant workman refused to
assist in the making of death-dealing weapons to be used
on his co-religionists and relatives, he was thrown into
prison.

About 100,000 Irish were now in arms, inclusive of
soldiers and numerous banditti. Protestants were warned
they must deliver up their arms (which they were required
by law to possess), or their houses would be sacked by
soldiers.

Armed banditti carried on a plunder of the country.
Protestants could not obtain justice in the courts and the
destruction of property was enormous. No article of any
value was left behind. The wealthier homes were stripped
bare, and the property carried off or destroyed.

It was not unusual for the cow of a Protestant to be
slaughtered in order to provide material for a pair of
brogues. As many as 100,000 sheep were wantonly destroyed.

The Protestants feared another massacre and began to
fly for their lives. Some of them fled to England and
others to Ulster, where Protestants were more concentrated. People of Leinster started for Londonderry, while
the Munster fugitives and those from Connaught escaped
to Enniskillen.

Meanwhile one of the Irish commanders, with the rab-
ble behind him, left the country he passed through desolate.
His forces were defeated at Dromore and as his followers
ran, they burned the bridges, and destroyed the ferry-

boats and the towns belonging to a Protestant population which were left in ruins, without a single inhabitant.

Omagh destroyed its own buildings in order to leave no shelter for the enemy, while the inhabitants of Cavan, abandoning their homes, fled for shelter to Enniskillen and those of Lisburn sought refuge in Antrim.

James proceeded to the north, but finding the country he passed through desolate soon returned to Dublin where the Parliament was actively engaged in enacting new laws. In order to deceive the people a Toleration Act had been passed which was meant to have no significance. It purported to grant liberty of conscience to all the Christian sects, but in a very short time the King gave evidence he had no such intention. The supremacy of the British Parliament over Ireland was annulled, and then followed those acts of confiscation and proscription of property so notorious, and on a scale the most extensive hitherto known. Tithes were transferred from the ministers of the Established Church to Roman Catholic priests, and another bill repealed the Act of Settlement, thereby transferring thousands of square miles to the descendants of the plunderers and assassins of 1641. This transfer of land to Celtic owners was carried by acclamation. Then, what has been described as "the hugest Bill of Attainder" ever known was prepared and became the law of the land (as before mentioned). Not only men were attainted but also women and even children, who had offended by being born of Protestant parents. The attainted numbered 2,240 persons.

Until this time, the directly penal laws against Catholics were scarcely known. Roman Catholics could sit in either Irish House of Parliament, and could inherit property as well as bequeath it; they could also educate their children as they wished. When the Saxons returned to power, however, their profound distrust of Celtic tactics and opinions were remembered, and found expression in other legislative acts enacted with the return of the Anglo-Saxons to their former offices in the legislature.

Not only did the settlers in the northern province have their estates confiscated, the Protestant clergy were driven out, and Lord Tyrconnel prepared for his warfare against England by efforts to destroy, with the aid of the legislature and the military, the entire Ulster colony through exile.

In spite of the restrictions on the persons and property of the Protestants, the bishops and clergy of the Established Church continued to pray for "the Lord's anointed."

Rumors were heard of further persecution, and perhaps massacre. A letter was received which warned of massacre on a definite date, and coincidently a message was delivered in Londonderry announcing the marching of a Roman Catholic army to attack the Maiden City. The Derry garrison had been withdrawn to London, doubtless by design, and the city left defenseless. Londonderry was not fortified to resist a military attack, such defenses as it had having been prepared to withstand the attacks of an excited, tumultuous Celtic peasantry, and these had proved adequate during the massacres of 1641, when Derry had won the proud title of the "Maiden City." It was not long before the regiment under the command of the Catholic Lord Antrim appeared in sight.

Excitement and anxiety reached the nth degree. After a hurried consultation it was decided "to shut the gates, and keep them out." The Anglican Bishop, Ezkiel Hopkins, objected to shutting the gates in the face of "the Lord's anointed," but the bishop's words made no appeal, and eight or nine young men who were apprentices working in the city rushed to the gate and barred the way to the astonished soldiers, who had expected to effect an easy entrance.

The names of the young men who displayed their initiative and daring in the face of the entering enemy were: Henry Campsie, William Crookshire, Robert and his brother Daniel Sherrard, Alexander Irwin, James Steward, Robert Morrison, Alexander Cunningham, and William Cairns; they were almost all Presbyterians.

The Earl of Tyrconnel had sent a traitor named Lundy, an Episcopalian, to Derry as governor, and Lundy being a Protestant and not suspected, was admitted with two companies of soldiers of his own religion. The new governor had professed his allegiance to William of Orange, but actually was plotting with the adherents of James. He worked strenuously to spread doubt and discouragement throughout the staunch little army of men and women inside the walls of the besieged city. He had prevailed upon every Ulster garrison to retire upon Derry, and now all that the north represented were found inside the walls, and there were there many inhabitants from other countries and towns in the northern land, of the same steadfast, unflinching fiber.

Macaulay's description of the fortifications of the Maiden City paints a very vivid picture of the actual conditions faced by the intrepid little garrison behind the walls. This author says: "The fortifications of the town consisted of a wall overgrown with grass, and without the protection of a ditch in front of it. The draw-bridges had not been used for years, and the chains were rusty and unfit to be used." The historian continues, "Whatever an engineer might think of the ramparts, all that was most intelligent, most courageous, and most high spirited among the Englishry of Northern Ulster and Leinster, was crowded behind them."

Within the walls "seven thousand men were capable of bearing arms, and the whole world could not have furnished seven thousand men better qualified to meet a terrible emergency with clear judgment, dauntless valor, and stubborn patience." Macaulay continues to say, "these people had been enabled by superior civilization, close union, sleepless vigilance, and cool intrepidity to keep in subjection the numerous and hostile population." We are told that the intrepid defenders of Derry spoke English with a remarkable purity and correctness; and that both as militiamen and jurymen they were superior to their kindred in the mother country. (See *The Character of the Protestants of Ireland 1689.*)

The true character of Lundy was discovered, and that he had promised to deliver up the fortress on demand. He was accused of treachery and refused a vote in the arrangements being made for defense.

Realizing the importance of organization and order, a conference met to decide the steps to be taken in defense. Officers were appointed and placed in charge of eight regiments, and the cannon mounted in position. This civilian army numbered seven thousand fighting men, who were to oppose a force more than three times their number, almost all of them French, trained to the highest degree, equipped with the most modern and efficient arms of the period, and ready for any sort of emergency.

The famous siege of Londonderry began in April, 1689. The defenders had found it necessary to tear up the street pavements and pile up the stones on the walls. Shells thrown into the city could not be returned for the city possessed neither mortars nor bombs. The defenders were, however, able to annoy the enemy very effectively by making unexpected sallies, on one of which occasions Captain Adam Murray attacked and killed the French

General Maumont. Such successes were encouraging but no decisive action could be claimed by either side, and the food supplies of the garrison were running very low. The character of the food caused disease to appear which did more towards thinning the ranks than even the cannon balls thrown inside.

During the attack the women in Londonderry might be seen everywhere in spite of menacing cannon balls, and where the fire was thickest, serving out ammunition to the men and carrying water to those who required it. As time passed on, and food grew scarce, the besieged had to content themselves with the meat of starved horses, dogs, rats, mice, and tallow; the people became walking skeletons, the soldiers so weak they had scarcely strength to carry their arms, and yet there was no thought of surrender.

General Rosen, a commander of the opposing army, who thought it would be mere child's play to gain a victory over a few thousand half-starved civilians, grew furious at the continued opposition, and gathering up old men, women, and children he placed them in front of his army and threatened these poor creatures with death, and the defenders with the execution of their relatives, unless there was an immediate surrender. The garrison replied by erecting gallows on the bastions in full view of the enemy and sent a message to Rosen asking him to send a chaplain to prepare some prisoners of rank held inside before their immediate execution.

The prisoners, too, begged to be saved from the death awarded to criminals. The plan succeeded, and the hungry children and their frightened elders were set at liberty and the siege continued.

Yet strangely enough, while the Derry garrison were on the point of starvation, ships were lying in the river

Foyle loaded with provisions, sent from England. The opposing army had thrown a boom across the mouth of the river and the commander apparently lacked initiative and courage to surmount the difficulties facing him, for he had remained at the mouth of the river for seven weeks. He was finally assisted to action, and not without difficulty the huge beam was broken through, and soon the starving people behind the walls of the "Maiden City" were enjoying the generous rations sent them as they listened to joyful peals of bells all over the happy city.

It has been said the siege of Londonderry "exhibited a sublimity of courage and fortitude without parallel in human history since the fall of Jerusalem before the arms of Titus Vespasian." Eight thousand of the enemy were slain, but one half of the garrison died, mostly from disease engendered by lack of proper food; and the deeds of the defenders have been compared to the exploits of Homeric fiction.

The siege of this little town in Northern Ireland is the most memorable one in, the history of Great Britain. It lasted altogether one hundred and five days, and the plucky garrison was reduced from the seven thousand men it started with to three thousand. The losses sustained by the French and Irish armies were large; and the King as well as the fine French army were chagrined and disappointed.

No city in the United Kingdom has played such a decisive part in determining the religion of the British Empire and its throne as the proud "Maiden City," Londonderry.

During the siege, the town of Enniskillen without any kind of fortification was defended by men as steadfast and indomitable as their relatives inside the walls of Derry. They made a number of raids and collected an abundance of food. They also fought an opposing army of five thousand men at Newtown-Butler, although they numbered but three thousand; and they won this important victory three days after the boom over the river Foyle was destroyed.

The Irish Presbyterians claim it was they who bore the brunt of the siege of Londonderry which saved liberty and Protestantism in Ireland. The machinations of the conspirator Lundy, who was not a Presbyterian, were calculated to deliver the city to James. The plotter was discovered before it was too late and he was allowed to leave the city in disguise and make his way to his friends outside. The effigy of this traitor to the cause of liberty still is burnt annually in Northern Ireland.

A report on the defense of Londonderry may be found among the MSS. in the British Museum, which was drawn up in 1705. (Also see Transaction found in the Journals of the House of Commons, 1689.)

The siege was a preliminary to other encounters between the forces of the British monarch and William of Orange, who had been invited to replace the impossible James. William was married to the daughter of the latter, thus his cousin, who had been brought up a Protestant, and therefore found himself opposing his father-in-law. The Prince of Orange was brought up on the Calvinistic beliefs of his motherland and professed the faith of his country. Like his great ancestor, William the Silent, he was noted for his toleration of the honest opinions and principles of others, although the spirit of tolerance at this period received little recognition.

On June 14, 1690, William landed at Carrickfergus in Ireland, and from thence with his suite rode to Belfast where he was enthusiastically and ceremonially received. With his army he reached the river Boyne on the last day of June and on the following day the troops were facing each other across the famous river. James, although he must have realized what winning this battle would mean to his family and all his interests, sought a place of safety where he might view the battle without exposure to danger and kept at a safe distance throughout the engagement.

William had under his command 30,000 men consisting of Scotch, Anglo-Irish and Dutch, besides soldiers of other nationalities, but all were of the Protestant faith. The defenders of the Maiden City were there as well as the dragoons of Enniskillen and the victors of Newtown-Butler.

On the morning of the battle the Prince of Orange was recognized by his foes on the opposite bank of the river, who hoping to destroy their opponent shot a cannon ball in his direction which struck William on the shoulder. The Prince lost some blood but making little of his wound had it bound up by an attendant, and later mounted his horse and with a sword in the unwounded hand led his men into the very thickest of the fight. The faithful Schomberg was killed but the leader went on, and where he led victory followed. A ball struck the cap of his pistol, the heel was shot off his boot, but he seemed invulnerable. The bravery of the commander inspired his men and they were winning on every side. As might have been expected James was overwhelmingly defeated. The Celtic-Irish soldiers ran, flinging away their equipment, and the King too ran to Dublin, berating the Irish soldiers and accusing them of cowardice. In the Irish metropolis the Protestants were confined in their homes afraid to venture on the streets lest they should be murdered. The best of the Celtic-Irish army fell in this battle though the slaughter was not great and the Celtic slain numbered about 1,500. The Prince of Orange issued orders that no unnecessary blood should be shed, and that captives should be treated with consideration. The loss of the victors was relatively small. This famous battle, renowned in song and story, was fought on July 1 (Old Style) or on July 12 (New Style), 1690, and is annually commemorated in Northern Ireland.

The siege of Limerick followed the battle of the Boyne. William returned to England and the siege lagged, but was renewed the following year when the battle of Aughrim was fought, which after a severe contest resulted in a victory for the party of William. The number killed in battle here was greater than in any other battle of the age. The Treaty of Limerick followed but was never ratified by Parliament and was not observed.

Tidings of the wound William had received at the Boyne were carried quickly to Rome and to Paris where Mary of Modena awaited her husband, and it was believed William had been defeated. Melfort, state secretary for James, wrote from Rome: "Herod [Prince of Orange] is gone, there must be a restoration and reestablishment of despotism. The power of the purse must be taken from the Commons. Political offenders must be tried, not by juries but by judges on whom the crown can depend. If the King is forced to pardon let it be as few rogues as he can." This letter is still extant and shows if the power had remained with James that in all probability the country again would have been drenched with blood.

The Anglican bishops continued to pray for the "Lord's anointed" until James in his flight reached Dublin after which event prayers ascended for the victor.

William was lenient towards the Irish Catholics. Officers were taken back into the army and oaths altered so as not to conflict with tender consciences. The abjuration of the pope's pretended right to interfere with the allegiance of the subject was dispensed with in their favor. Schools were provided for Catholic children who were forbidden to have schools of their own or to go abroad for educational purposes.

When the army of James scattered through the country, there were renewed the old familiar acts of plundering, burning, houghing the poor helpless cattle, and assassination.

The Calvinists had proved to the world their loyalty and courage and William was sensible of what he owed to them, but the Dissenters were still fettered by the Act of Uniformity, their religion was still under ban, and they could be compelled to worship in the chapels of their persecutor and enemy, the Established Church. It was true, they were now eligible as magistrates, and for commissions in the army, could sit in Parliament, or be members of a corporation, but they still felt fettered by the chains the Established Church had been allowed to fasten on them.

The King as a mark of his appreciation to the Presbyterians had granted the Regium Donum from the Belfast customs to the pastors of the denomination mentioned, for which just favor the beneficiaries were duly grateful. William had noticed the petty spitefulness of the Anglican brotherhood when dealing with Dissenters. He therefore submitted to the Irish council the draft of a Toleration Bill which should free the Non-Conformists from the perpetual irritation in which the godly men of the Anglican Church desired to restrain them. The Anglican prelates, however, had a very decided numerical strength in the Irish Parliament, and were supported by landowners, also now High Church men, who owed their estates to Cromwell, but who were ashamed to be associated with Cromwellians, so that the alliance of the prelates with the

Cromwellian and other Irish peers was wellnigh invincible. The bishops endeavored to have the Regium Donum discontinued, and eventually they were successful. They even went so far as to attempt to force William to establish the Test Act, which forbade any one to hold office, unless he was a communicant in the Episcopal Church.

An archdeacon, named Lemuel Matthews, had a young Presbyterian minister committed to prison for conducting his religious service without using the Episcopal Book of Common Prayer. The same Lemuel was subsequently arrested himself, not for the crime of making extempore prayers, but for irregular practices unbecoming one of his profession.

The prelates obtained a vote in the Irish House of Commons that there should be no toleration of Presbyterians unless the Test Act were enforced.

William III was a constitutional monarch and was besides a stranger in England, with many jealous enemies. He was compelled to be true to his oath of office, and as the Dissenters were still without legal recognition the force of circumstances was strong enough to prevent the king compelling the narrow, bigoted churchmen to cease their persecutions, and it was only possible to prevent some of the most outrageous statutes from being enforced against the former. When "the Lord's anointed" happened to be a Calvinist the sacred oil had no effect on the prelates.

At Cookstown, in Tyrone, the rector had the Presbyterian church torn down in the year 1701.

The Toleration Bill of William was opposed with the utmost virulence by the High Church party, although they formed but a third of the Protestant party and about one eleventh of the whole population. The High Church men wished to keep the army, navy, the learned professions, and the civil service as their own exclusive preserve and although they had rendered far less assistance to the new sovereigns than had the Non-Conformists, still they wished to bar the latter from all the privileges their valor and steadfastness had won; and they were able to have the Regium Donum suspended and to defeat the Toleration Bill.

As the late rebellion had been promoted by the Catholic clergy, it was believed that public safety was threatened by their presence. Consequently the whole staff of priests and friars were ordered within a prescribed time to leave the country or be held guilty of high treason.

As it happened there was a discovery of a Catholic plot to murder the King in 1695, and a letter appeared on the table of the House of Commons which was found among the papers of the Catholic Bishop Tyrrell setting forth a plan for the destruction and death of all the Protestants in Ireland. The public feeling caused by the discovery of these plots led to the enactment of more stringent laws against Catholics, and they were now excluded from voting at election for members of Parliament, and oaths of certain kinds were to be exacted from them.

A Catholic bishop or priest was not allowed to teach school, he must take oaths of allegiance and abjuration, and was not allowed to purchase lands.

This spirit of intolerance did not emanate from William himself, who was very tolerant in an intolerant age. The Catholics themselves were never tolerant save when the force of circumstances compelled them, and the disabilities suffered by them in Great Britain were not greater than the Protestants suffered in Spain, France, and Italy at the same time, at the hands of the Catholics. Indeed the disabilities of Catholics in Britain were probably less, as shown by the Catholic disregard of these menacing enactments. And in Ireland the state of the country was such that Protestants did not dare to take farms beyond the borders of the towns where their numbers served as protection. That these laws were more menacing on paper than anywhere else is evidenced by the fact of the Catholic clergy disregarding the bill for their expulsion and building new chapels in the very face of the law.

William's Parliament wished to keep Ireland a dependent country and acts of commercial restraint were enacted which will be discussed elsewhere.

Although the King had rescued Protestant Britain from civil and religious tyranny, he was not a favorite. Eight of the bishops and many of the clergy refused to take the new oaths of allegiance, and were known as non-jurors. The King died in 1702.

William III of England was a descendant of the famous William the Silent of Holland and a son of William II, Prince of Orange, and Mary, daughter of Charles I of England. The blood of the famous Coligni ran in the veins of William Henry, and the family of Nassau, to which he belonged, was said to be "singularly fertile in great men." The Nassau family held an exalted position in their homeland, though exercising a somewhat indefinite authority.

William was left an orphan at an early age and was thus deprived of the domestic interest and affection which would have been his in happier circumstances. Although the physical body of the Prince was frail—he had weak lungs and was subject to attacks of asthma—he showed a marked ability at an early age, was ambitious, resourceful, and possessed an indomitable will, which never acknowledged defeat. He also displayed a marked diplomatic ability.

In appearance he was slender and of rather frail appearance with a wide forehead and a nose curved like an eagle's beak. His eyes were keen and his mouth showed strength and decision.

Cast upon his own resources in a sense, he became self-reliant and independent, so that the endowments of nature were developed by training and environment. But his manners, perhaps because of his early domestic life, were not prepossessing; he was reserved and inclined to bluntness, lacking the suavity and graciousness of the perhaps less honest courtier. He was nevertheless very steadfast in his friendships and attachments and while affectionate was not demonstrative. He appeared at his best on the battlefield; here he was gracious, kind, and sympathetic, perhaps his natural self. He was brave, and daring to a fault, exposing himself on the battlefield as if he bore a charmed life and was found in the very thickest of the fight, often leading his men to victory. He was not reckless, however, for he possessed sound sense, but was a strong believer in predestination and was very determined and very tenacious of purpose. When William was twenty-eight years old he married his cousin Mary of England, the daughter of James, Duke of York, afterwards James II. Mary was then but sixteen years old, and was a strong, healthy, and beautiful girl, who honored her taciturn husband with a love and devotion rarely equaled and seldom surpassed; and in all truth it must be allowed that her husband requited his wife's devotion with a loving trust and confidence which lasted until death,

Owing to the misrule of James II, William was invited to England as the husband of the eldest daughter of James, who finding himself deserted on all sides skulked off to France leaving everything in confusion.

It was decided that Mary and William should reign conjointly with most of the executive work in the hands of William. The latter possessed the qualities of a great leader though his talents were not appreciated in England as they were on the continent, partly due to his habitual coldness and reserve. On the Continent, however, his genius effected a transformation in the relative position of the European powers.

James II had made England a dependency of France and of little relative importance; in the hands of William, England resumed her position as one of the great European powers.

France at this time was very powerful and very despotic; she had trampled on the rights of other European states, made many enemies and persecuted cruelly the Protestants in her dominions. William determined to humble the great Louis and to protect the Protestants who had suffered unmeasured agonies for some hundreds of years.

A coalition against Louis was effected between England, Holland, Austria, the duke of Savoy, and the empire of Germany, and Roman Catholic princes were thus induced to give their protection to the reformed faith. Through the influence of the English King, Waldensian captives were returned to their homes, and their children, forcibly removed from those homes to be subjected to instruction in Catholic schools, were returned to their parents. William was constantly using his influence to protect the victims of the Reformation.

The English law courts under William were conducted humanely and as far as possible justly, forming a marked contrast to the perversions of justice and cruelties of the previous reign. William had selected his ministers with impartiality and had nominated Tories as well as Whigs, although the former were regarded as his enemies, but the King had made his selections according to merit rather

than party. The plans of government put into effect
have been compared to those of Richelieu in ability and
boldness. Few could equal the King as a negotiator,
and this was acknowledged even in England, where as a
foreigner he was not popular. But on the Continent he
was regarded with admiration and honored even in the
Catholic states as chief of the confederacy against the
Bourbons, even though that admiration was sometimes
mingled with hatred.

In every country on the Continent churches of the
Reformation were giving fervent thanks to God for the
assistance received as the effect of William's negotiations
with their rulers, and the letters of the British sovereign
are said to prove he was one of the greatest of European
statesmen.

Many difficulties faced the soverign in England. The
treasury was depleted, with insufficient funds to carry on
the work of government, so that the King borrowed money
on the security of his own word. He was disliked by his
own party because he would not be vindictive and punish
his enemies now they were in his power, so he received
no thanks from either party because he would not descend
to the malicious and partisan acts of his predecessor.

Born and bred in a country honoring the Calvinist religion, William desired to remove the handicaps which the
Dissenters had suffered for four centuries in Britain, and
to give them relief, but the Anglicans, in spite of their
treatment in the previous reign, were still opposed to religious freedom for others, so long as they enjoyed it
themselves, and the non-jurors as they were called, mostly
men of inferior intellectual capacity, made all the trouble
their small minds were capable of.

There were plots against the life of the King which
happily failed, but the most dreadful blow he received was

the death after a few days' illness of his wife from a malignant variety of smallpox. The husband remained night and day at the side of his suffering wife, and was so prostrated by her death that his friends were alarmed at his condition.

A monument was erected to the memory of the beloved Queen, which took the form of a retreat for seamen on the banks of the Thames. The palace at Greenwich was converted to form this monument, and is the finest of its kind ever erected to any sovereign.

William reigned in England from 1689 to 1702. Before his death he had achieved the two great objects which he had constantly in mind since his accession to the throne. The insolent pride of Louis XIV had been humbled and the persecuted members of the reformed faith had received much-needed protection. Due to the vigor of his intellect in spite of his frail body, his power and ability were widely recognized and he was acknowledged both as a great man and a great king. He had raised England from the position of a pensioner on the bounty of France and of just as much importance in world affairs as a duchy capable of bringing a few thousand men into the field, to that of a first-rate European power.

His death was accelerated by an accident received while riding and from which in his weakened condition he was unable to recover. He died as he had lived, nobly, and in full possession of his faculties. Near his deathbed were his lifetime friends who had served him long and faithfully and who had more than once placed their own lives in jeopardy to save his.

After death a small packet tied with black silk ribbon was found on his body which contained a gold ring and a lock of hair, the last cherished remembrance of one who had preceded her husband.

The Protestant Episcopal Church was the Established Church in Ireland by ukase of the government, and has had an important bearing on the history of Ulster.

This branch of the Protestant fraternity owes its existence to the dominating judgment of Henry VIII, who in order to carry out his own demands made himself the head of the church. According to Buckle, the new creation was "from the first a schematic establishment owning its own defense against heresy, and defending itself from that accusation through its appeal to private opinion, to which it owed its existence," and Buckle goes on to say that "if private judgment was not supreme, then the church was guilty of apostasy."

However a church that is fortunate enough to have a powerful backing, feels strong enough to set up many claims which might be difficult to explain or justify. The Established Church in Ireland claimed its descent from the church of Patrick because of some fancied resemblance in the forms of worship adopted, while the Presbyterians were convinced that the absence of Prelacy and of certain ceremonies in their church and their belief in the spirit rather than in stereotyped forms of expression or of devotional attitudes showed that their religious organization was in the closest conformity with that established by the founder of Christianity in Ireland.

Whichever view is taken or whatever the value of such claims it is certain the Established Church claimed a divine right for its existence, a claim resting on mere superstition, and which like all such unprovable assertions has long gone to the discard except where the weak-minded or ignorant are concerned. Yet though today we may smile indulgently or derisively at such views, in the early history of Ulster, the Anglican Church was powerful enough to punish drastically those who derided its mythical claims. Consequently the Anglican prelates with the authority vested in them by the royal "Lord's anointed" attempted to subjugate the consciences of the people, and force them to accept machine-made rites and ceremonies.

The Established Church also showed a domineering and persecuting spirit, which, according to Lecky, kept the country on the verge of civil war. The Anglican establishment was supported by tithes exacted from Presbyterians and Roman Catholics to whom they rendered no service as well as from their own small body of people. The crown stood back of this creature of its own creation, and showered gifts and preferments upon it, with the result to be expected from such favoritism. The Dissenters, on the other hand, had no legal existence and as a result no legal recognition, although the Catholics had, and the latter were regarded by the Episcopalians with more or less tolerance as a closer relation than the far-away Calvinist whom they looked upon with hate and some anxiety.

Although we have long been familiar with the tribulations of the Irish Celt not every one is aware that in addition to occupying the least fertile and perhaps the bleakest province in the country, the northern Dissenter had more handicaps than the Roman Catholic, and while the latter was able by connivance to evade many of these handicaps the Presbyterian was not so fortunate. We read in Lecky (Vol. II, p. 216), "The religious establishment in Ireland was one of the most powerful of all agencies in demoralizing the people," and the measures employed for the suppression of Dissenters were said to be the most tyrannical enacted in the eighteenth century. This legislation provided that no Dissenter on pain of three months' imprisonment should keep either a public or private school, or should act as tutor or usher unless he had obtained a license from the bishops, and had engaged to conform to the Anglican liturgy. If a teacher so qualified were present at any other form of worship he was liable to imprisonment for three months, and was also incapacitated for the rest of his life from acting as a schoolmaster or tutor. The Dissenting bodies petitioned to be heard by counsel against this destructive bill, but their petitions were disregarded.

The laws under discussion were enacted during the reign of Anne, who permitted the bishops many abuses of power; but before the reign of Anne, the Test Act and the Corporation Act enacted in the reign of Charles II excluded Dissenters from offices of trust and power unless they took the Sacrament according to the rites of the Established Church. The bishops fought to keep the Test Act on the statute books and for about seventy years they were successful. Thus no Presbyterian could hold any office in army, navy, customs, or courts of law. The powerful bishops forbade Presbyterians to be married by their own lawfully ordained ministers, prosecuted them in ecclesiastical courts if they disobeyed, and pronounced the offspring of the Presbyterian marriage a bastard. Bishops introduced clauses into their leases which banned a Presbyterian church from being erected on their land. They charged Presbyterians a higher rent for their farms and induced others to do likewise. They were instrumental in enacting the Schism Act (1714), destined to sweep the Dissenting church out of existence, and this dénouement was only prevented by the death of the reigning sovereign. The Dissenters were handicapped by having no representation in the British Parliament. In the Irish House of Commons they had but ten or twelve members, while in the House of Lords there were not infrequently twenty-two bishops present in a house of forty-four members.

These powerful prelates received a setback during the period of the Commonwealth when the bishops were deprived of their seats in the legislature and declared an impediment to reformation, and prejudicial to the civil government. The British Houses of Parliament passed a bill for the utter abolishment of Prelacy in 1643.

The bishops so opposed to Presbyterianism were by no means puritanically minded. They sold clerical preferments, and provided for their curates salaries on which these men could scarcely exist. The Anglican ministers were derelict in such duties as administration of Sacraments and visiting the sick, so that the number of their parishioners began to fall off, and the people had to be bribed to come to church and listen to a sermon.

Indeed the character of a number of the prelates was not conducive to respect for the cloth. One of them, Bishop Hackel, was convicted of "flagrant simony," and non-residence; he had also admitted Roman Catholics to church livings, and furnished them with false certificates. Wade, dean of Connor, was accused of adultery, and for this cause was deprived of his living. Milne, a prebendary of Kilrush, was accused of habitual drunkenness. The attorney general for Ireland, Lord Clare, through a parliamentary speech, drew attention to the appointment of a young man to a vacant bishopric who was of notoriously infamous character, and objected to for that reason by the Bishop of Armagh. The man in question owed his appointment to the Tories. Digby, Bishop of Elphin (1691-1720), was generally an absentee and owed his appointment to the bishopric because of the skill he displayed painting in water colors, which delighted his powerful friends. Fitzgerald, Bishop of Clonfert, was for over thirty years in a more or less imbecile condition and depended for the management of his diocese on a young girl he had married. Another prelate named Power had been a deer stealer but was saved from the gallows by turning informer; his appointment was made by Archbishop Boulter on recommendation of Lord Townshend (British Museum MSS., 20-22). These citations do not by any means exhaust the list of derelicts, but serve to show the character of many of the prelates who became so ardent in the persecution of Dissenters from their own denomination.

It was not unusual for one curate to be asked to care for as many as a "dozen cures of souls" for which duty he was paid about one hundred pounds per annum (see the primate to the Duke of Newcastle, March 7, 1728, MSS. Record Office). That the members of this opulent hierarchy were not indifferent to their material interests is evidenced by the letters of Swift, who wrote, "However indifferent men may be in religion they know if latitude were allowed to Dissenters the few such employments in cities and corporations would soon find other hands lay hold on them" (Address to both Houses of Parliament by the Draper Works quoted by Froude).

The Anglican prelates had so much influence with the press and the leading gentry, not to mention their parliamentary strength, that they were able to perpetuate the disabilities of the Dissenters, and secure such legislation as favored themselves, which placed their competitors at a disadvantage. George Doddington, secretary to Lord Pembroke, writes, "The bishops in the House are as high as Laud with great influence over the temporal lords, most of whom have but little sense. Believe me the country is priest-ridden as much as Portugal or Spain" (Sept. 2, MSS. Record Office).

While Archbishop Laud was putting his views in practice in Scotland, bishops Echler and Leslie in the sees of Raphoe and Derry were vigorously enforcing the Act of Uniformity against the Dissenters, though allowing it to remain a dead letter where the Catholics were concerned. When the former refused obedience to their persecutors they were deprived of their charges. A Court of High Commission viewed the charges and passed canons prohibiting Dissent, and causing the offending Dissenters to be thrown into prison. Emigration of the Presbyterians again received vigorous stimulation, but the incarcerated Presbyterians remained in prison until after the Earl of Strafford's execution.

Each fresh outburst of persecution had the effect of stimulating the Presbyterian exodus to America which drained the country of its men and women, industrious, self-respecting, and staunch in belief and dauntless in character. The Presbyterians finally won from the bishops —at least for a time—the connivance enjoyed from the first by the Catholics.

The inconsistencies of the prelates is illustrated by their views on the respective legality of Presbyterian and Catholic marriages.

In the disturbed eighteenth century there were many instances of young Catholic gentlemen carrying off the daughters of well-to-do Protestants, ravishing the captives, and then by the aid of renegade priests marrying the victims. These bishops who had declared marriage by an ordained Presbyterian minister illegal unless performed according to the Anglican technique, declared the forced marriage performed by derelict clergymen and priests according to law, and that such marriage could not be dissolved except by their own spiritual authority. The question was discussed in the Irish Parliament where it was shown that by these criminal marriages Protestant settlements were broken up, family ties dissolved, and the worst specimens of the Catholic priesthood supported. (See MSS. Record Office on rape and forced marriage, also see Record Office, Carey to Secretary Delafoyle, Jan. 2, 1732.)   It was said and believed the violators here mentioned were punctual in attendance at church.

By an act of 1665 the Presbyterian ministers who administered the Sacrament of the Lord's Supper to a member of their flock were liable to a fine of $500, but resistance to tyranny is obedience to God, and persecution of religion fans the flame of resistance.   In 1668 the Presbyterians were erecting their plain little meeting houses, mostly in obscure localities as far as possible from unwanted observation.   They had no splendid cathedrals to make appeal, or stained-glass windows, nor the pealing music of majestic organs.   The delicate-handed priest might intone his manufactured prayers elsewhere, but here the earnest pastor appealed to the heart and to the conscience of his dearly loved people whose joys and sorrows were his own.   In 1684 the Dissenting churches were again forcibly closed and the people worshiping in glens and secluded places with a sentry on guard.

"The state of the church is very miserable," writes Lord Clarendon to the Archbishop of Canterbury, after the persecution of the Presbyterians.   "Most of the fabrics are in ruins, very few of the clergy reside in their cures but employ pitiful curates"; and he continues, "the cures are supplied by those who will do it cheapest."

The Established Church numbered half a million yet was possessed of power and privilege to an unprecedented extent.   In the Irish House of Commons it claimed 176 seats out of the whole number of 300, so with other backing it was practically omnipotent.

It must be admitted that material welfare was omnipresent and at times seemed to take precedence of spiritual responsibilities. One learns with astonishment that the bishops were willing to degrade the Sacrament of the Lord's Supper, making it a "key to office," for any candidate for a government position, no matter what his antecedents or reputation, must first partake of this Sacrament before being eligible to the position, and he must communicate according to the rites of the Anglican Church. The bishops ignored the criticisms of this procedure, which indeed was consistent, for they contended refusal to observe the rites of their church was a more heinous crime than actual wrongdoing.

Was the attitude of the hierarchy of the Anglican Church towards rites and ceremonies, and towards other religions, explained by its origin and history? When Henry VIII brought the Anglican Church into being his idea was to have the church of his creation differ from the church of Rome only on the point of supremacy. He simply substituted himself for the pope. Succeeding years found other changes necessary as it was essential to obtain the aid of Protestants, most of whom condemned Roman dogmas and practices. Bishop Hooper, for instance, who died for his opinions, refused to wear the episcopal vestments. Bishop Ridley ordered the Eucharist administered in the middle of the church. Bishop Jewel compared the clerical gown to a stage dress and a fool's coat. Archbishop Grindal regarded the miter as the mummery of consecration. Bishop Parkhurst desired the Church of England to model herself on the plan practiced at Zurich, and so on with other clergymen. It was found necessary for the reformers to meet the party devoted to rites and ceremonies and special clerical garb halfway, and the result was the Anglican Church. Archbishop Cranmer played a leading part in meeting objections advanced and reconciling those of different religious views, and was considered well fitted for the task because he was unscrupulous and a courtier as well as a divine.

The Anglican Church was thus the child of compromise and occupies a position between the churches of Geneva and of Rome; even Cranmer himself, however, believed there was no distinction between bishops and priests, and that the laying on of hands was unnecessary.

In spite of religious difficulties, Ireland had built up a prosperous woolen industry. England, too, was engaged in the manufacture of woolen goods and dreaded a rival in this field.[1] Parent countries at this period were accustomed to regard their own interests as of much greater importance than those of their colonists, and acted accordingly.

Consequently, the British legislature in its wisdom saw fit to impose certain restrictions upon Ireland, and in 1666 tolls were imposed on Irish cattle imported into England and finally such importations were entirely prohibited.

Another statute forbade the importation of corn except under certain conditions; then came the Navigation Acts of 1670 and 1671 which refused to Ireland the privilege of importing from the Plantations commodities which were to her of great importance, such as wool, cotton, tobacco, sugar, and coffee, unless these were first landed in England, where a tax could be collected.

According to the customs of the time, Great Britain had a legal if not a moral right to take such action, but she decided to go still further. When Irish shipping interests had been destroyed, and cattle could be no longer exported, the land had been turned into sheep farms which produced wool of a very fine quality.

---

[1] England's manufacture of woolen goods dated as far back as the reign of Stephen.

Northern Ireland had taken advantage of this fact, had established factories for the manufacture of wool into fabrics of various kinds, and the factories were almost entirely in the hands of Protestants who according to a very reliable authority on Irish commercial questions, Miss Murray, were almost exclusively Presbyterians. This woolen industry gave employment to as many as 12,000 persons in the north, and to fifty thousand others scattered all over the country, and was thus advantageous to the whole people.

England, fearing her commercial interests might suffer from Irish competition in the woolen trade, although the industry was in the hands of her own colonists, persons of her own race and blood, colonists she had planted in the north for her own protection and upon whom she relied as guardians of her interests, resolved to strike a blow at her friends and gather in all she could for herself. The British Parliament then passed another legislative act, which had an absolutely ruinous effect upon the woolen industry in Ulster; and it was Northern Ireland to whom England gave this knock-out blow, although from the frequent allusions made to this legislation it would be natural to suppose that Celtic Ireland was the greatest sufferer. The legislation in question abolished the very successful and remunerative woolen manufactures. (See Hely Hutchinson, *On Commercial Restraints in Ireland in 1777.*)

After the destruction of the woolen trade, we learn from Lecky that sixteen thousand pounds yearly was struck off the Irish pension list which the people now were unable to furnish. The country was reduced to an appalling condition of misery and poverty, and in consequence every poor year following this misfortune produced a famine for as long as fifty years after.

When England wiped the woolen trade out of existence, she had pledged herself to assist the linen manufacture; her aid, however, was negligible. According to O'Connor, England's "aid was tardy and slight" to the linen trade, and the bounties she bestowed on her own Lancaster, she refused to extend to Belfast.

Protestant emigration after the destruction of the woolen trade was again stimulated, and continued with increasing volume for three quarters of a century. Although she had no linen trade herself, the mother country gave direct encouragement to the manufacturing rivals of the Irish linen manufacturers and workers, so that the Protestant artisans decided to leave the country for lack of work; and instead of the compensating help which was promised, duties were levied on the coarser varieties of linen fabrics, which was a direct violation of the agreement made when the woolen industry was destroyed. The case is thus presented in the Commons' Journal, Dec. 15, 1773:

"They had been confined by law to the manufacture of flax and hemp. They had submitted to this condition, and had manufactured those supplies to such good purpose, that at one time they had supplied the whole British navy. Their English rivals had now crippled them by laying a disabling duty on sail-cloths, in hopes of taking the trade out of their hands, but they had injured Ireland without benefiting themselves. The British market was now supplied by Holland, Germany, and Russia, while to the empire, the result was only the ruin of Ulster, and the flight of the Protestant population to America. If Great Britain reaped the fruit of this policy, the Commons of Ireland would behold it without repining or complaining, but it aggravates the sense of their misfortunes, to see the rivals if not the enemies of Great Britain, in possession of those advantages to which they think themselves entitled by every principle of policy and justice."

The result of the policy practiced by the mother country on this question was an unceasing tide of emigration to New England, to Virginia and other colonies (see Burke's *Settlements in America,* pp. 174-75).

The hempen manufacture was so utterly discouraged that it completely disappeared.

It had been proposed to repeal a prohibitory duty excluding English cotton yarn made in Ireland, and to admit Irish sail-cloth and cordage free of duty (see Annual Register, pp. 173-186), but such a volume of protest was heard from British towns against the participation of the Irish manufacturers in English trade, or even allowing them to dispose of their commodities in a foreign market, that the project was necessarily abandoned.

When the colonists came to Ulster, they carried with them their implements for use in the linen trade and a knowledge of the spinning and weaving of linen. The work, however, was not confined to Ulster, but was spread all over the country. During the Wentworth administration when the Irish woolen industry was annihilated, the deputy, perhaps in compensation to Ulster for the blow dealt her woolen trade, at his own expense, imported flax from Holland, and skilled workers from France and the Low Countries to stimulate the spinning and weaving of linen.

In the reign of William III, Louis Crommelin and his brother William were brought from France to give attention to the Huguenots who had fled from their own country. Louis established himself in the north, at Lisburn, and William going south opened centers of linen industry in Cork, Waterford, Kilkenny, and Dublin. When the Irish House of Parliament distributed bounties to the industry through the linen board, the seat of that board was in Dublin, and its operations included every county in the country.

When the Union took place between the two countries at the beginning of the nineteenth century, the linen manufacture, as such, was scarcely known in Belfast. We learn from Benn's history of the town of Belfast, published in the early part of the nineteenth century, that at this period the cotton manufacture in all its branches was the principal manufacture of Belfast, and that the work employed 27,000 persons. In 1814 they were employing steam and driving 99,000 spindles, but very little linen cloth was at that time woven in the town.

The remarkable development of cotton spinning and weaving was due to the fact that cotton was spun by machinery, while the linen weaver was forced to depend on the local spinning wheel.

The puzzling problem was solved by Andrew Mulholland, the owner of a cotton mill on York Street, Belfast. This manufacturer saw that the linen work could not be carried on to any great extent, while linen yarn was obtainable only in very small quantities, and he was stimulated to greater effort by the fact that flax grown on Ulster fields was shipped to Manchester to be spun, and then returned to Belfast as yarn.

It was not long before this Scotch-Irish man, with true Yankee initiative and dispatch, was producing linen yarn in his cotton mill in York Street (1830). Linen yarn could now be spun in Belfast instead of Manchester. Other manufacturers quickly followed the example set by Mulholland, and secured for themselves a place in the growing industry, now known throughout the civilized world.

Those who read and know the history of the linen industry in Ulster, know it was not bounties, or legislative favor from England, that established the famous manufacture. Ulster succeeded in spite of destructive handicaps thrust upon her. Initiative, energy, foresight, and industry placed her where she is today. Meanwhile the linen industrial centers established by William Crommelin in the south and east gradually dwindled away, although they enjoyed exactly the same advantages and opportunities so energetically and ably used by their countrymen in Northern Ireland.

Mulholland was not the only Yankee in Belfast; doubtless there are many of them. The Barbour & Sons Linen Co. is known around the world. It manufactures linen thread, and hemp as well as linen, and is one of the largest concerns in the United Kingdom. It also has branches in America. Sir William Ewart started life as a hand-loom weaver and is now one of the leading manufacturers of Ulster.

The statement made by the Rt. Hon. Sir James O'Connor regarding Ulster is uncontrovertible. He said: "There is no part of Ireland that owes less of its prosperity to the government than Ulster. While in the rest of Ireland, public money has most properly gone to the making of harbors, of drainage works, and other works of public utility, the northeast has had little, if any, government assistance. I should not like to pledge myself to the statement, that not a sixpence has been spent in Protestant Ulster, but such a statement would not be far from the mark. Ulster owes her prosperity, in the main, to the sturdy character of her inhabitants, their comparative freedom from land and political agitation, and their capacity for hard work."

Sir James O'Connor is a Roman Catholic Irishman.

In 1839, the linen industry employed 9,017 workers,

and in 1917, 90,000 (see Jordan, *Modern Irish Trade and Industry*).

Belfast stands abreast of the leading manufacturing centers of Great Britain. It contains the foremost establishments in Europe "in respect of such activities as linen manufacturing, shipbuilding, ropemaking, etc. It is the fourth port in the kingdom in respect of revenue from customs, its contributions thereto in 1910 being 2,207,000 pounds as compared to 1,065,000 from the rest of Ireland." (From *Position of Ulster*, by Rt. Hon. Thomas S. Sinclair.)

In 1791 there was no place in Belfast for the laying down and building shipping vessels of any type, and in 1858 Edward Harland, a young Scotchman, came to Ireland with the purpose of starting this industry in Dublin, but his proposition was turned down in that city and the young man resolved to try his luck in Belfast, and here he started his industry with a capital of five hundred pounds. A young Dutchman named Wolff subsequently joined the venture and advanced Harland three hundred pounds. Thus was established one of the greatest shipbuilding industries in the world with a wage bill between fifty and one hundred thousand pounds per week. This shipbuilding industry is still carried on under the name of Harland and Wolff and has a world-wide reputation.

In 1934, there was an increase in the trade of the port of Belfast, the tonnage cleared being 3,709,529 tons. The goods traffic also showed increase, being 3,110,264, an increase of over 13 per cent from the previous year. In the world's shipbuilding statistics for 1934, Messrs. Harland & Wolff's combined yards occupy second place in the output figures.

IV

OAKBOYS, STEELBOYS, DEFENDERS AND ORANGEMEN

Anne, the Queen—Full rein given to Prelacy; Schism Act enacted, designed to wipe out Presbyterianism; act passed designed to throw Irish property into the hands of the Anglican
Church and reduce the Catholics to beggary—Unceasing and
virulent persecution of Presbyterians while Catholics are
practically unmolested—Emigration of Presbyterians fostered by the unremitting persecution—Menace of the Pretender—Rape and forced marriage—Protestant settlement
wiped out in Connemara—Same kind of occurrence at Killala
—Tolerant Catholic punished by Catholics—Evangelists
Moody and Sankey incur wrath of Catholics—Whiteboy Association, its atrocious acts—Ulster landlords turn tenants out
of their homes and many go to America—Hearts of Steel
Association, formed to prevent their legal robbery—The Defenders organize and are guilty of many criminal acts—Peep
of Day Boys, an association to prevent Catholics procuring
arms they have no legal right to possess.

ANNE, the second daughter of James II, succeeded
her brother-in-law William in 1702, and reigned
until 1714. The Queen was not of strong character and depended much on favorites. A member of the
Anglican persuasion herself, she apparently had a great
deal of confidence in the prelates of the Established
Church, who were very powerful throughout her reign,
and who, when the restraining hand of William was removed by death, gave full play to the intolerance and
hatred so frequently manifested towards the Presbyterians,
still without legal toleration. The good bishops without
delay took steps to have the Regium Donum which William

ordered paid from the Belfast customs taken away. The prelates of the Established Church were denying the validity of Presbyterian marriage and were using every effort to have the Test Act introduced into Ireland. Success crowned their efforts in 1704 and now a body of peaceful, loyal, and law-abiding people who had well served the state in her darkest hours, who had more than any other body of people worked to keep the British interests intact, and who in their service had suffered the heaviest losses themselves, were to be subjected to a law as insulting as it was unjust.

The prelates of the Established Church doubtless were of the opinion that by means of this act they would add to their own stationary numbers and win members from the overflowing Presbyterian churches whose members, rather than lose position, preferment, and opportunities for further advancement, would feel compelled to accept what was offered, and that the Scotch-Irish colonists would conform to the tyrannical laws. The bishops, however, proved poor psychologists; the stubborn Scotch conscience was quite beyond their analysis. Presbyterianism, in spite of obstacles of various kinds, had been growing, so their Presbyteries now numbered nine, and the act threatened them with degradation and loss, if fidelity to their ideals remained unshaken.

According to this law, already referred to, all persons holding any public appointment must take the communion according to the form of the Episcopal Church or lose their positions, while any person who communicated according to the prescribed formula, was, whatever his previous character, eligible for appointment.

Expediency, however, was a practice receiving no recognition from the Dissenting colonists although the sword of Damocles hung threateningly over their heads.

When it fell, even in the Maiden City where they had done so much to give the town a never-dying fame, ten out of twelve aldermen were thrown out of office; fourteen burgesses out of twenty-four were likewise expelled. This in a town where they had starved and suffered and many of them had died fighting for their homes and the British crown. In Belfast and all over the country similar occurrences were enacted. Magistrates, town councilors, postmasters and postmistresses were pushed out of office. These proud, self-reliant and self-respecting people could not have one of themselves occupy even the most humble public office in a country they had enriched by their intelligent labor and effort. Their pitiful pittance of the Ragium Donum was after repeated effort on the part of the Episcopal churchman finally denied.

The Toleration Act passed in the previous reign was annulled. It became a penal offense for a Presbyterian to teach a school. Pressure was brought on landlords to charge Presbyterians higher rents, or to refuse them outright. Certain clauses were inserted in leases prohibiting the erection of Presbyterian churches, farms and homes were not to be rented to Presbyterian tenants. The press was induced to publish abusive pamphlets against them. Dean Swift and Vicar Tisdall of Belfast were as vituperative in this warfare as if they had been fishwives. Some Presbyterian ministers were thrown into prison for public preaching until they were relieved by the lord's justices, who interfered and protected the preachers from their ministerial foes. In some towns the doors of Dissenting churches were nailed up by order of the warring clericals.

Notwithstanding the persecuted church continued to grow, and the literary misrepresentations of the bullying clergy were met by vigorous and illuminating replies.

In order to reënforce the Test Act the Schism Act was

passed. The men who helped to make this law were notoriously unscrupulous, and they were Lord Bolingbroke in the Lords and Mr. Windham of the Commons. This bill provided: "That no one under pain of three months' imprisonment should keep either a public or a private school, or should act as tutor or usher unless he had obtained a license from the bishop, and had engaged to conform to the Anglican liturgy. If a teacher so qualified were present at any other form of worship he should at once become liable to three months' imprisonment, and should be incapacitated for the rest of his life from acting as schoolmaster or tutor."

The Dissenters were also excluded from the University.

Thus as late as the reign of Anne the Presbyterians were more restrained in their religious observances than were the Roman Catholics in the reign of Elizabeth, two hundred years earlier. It is not surprising to find a letter from Dodding to Sunderland (Sept. 2, MSS. Record Office) which says, "Romish priests are authorized to exercise their religion, while the Dissenting ministers are made liable to very severe penalties for acting according to their persuasion."

A bill for the further regulation of the penal law was also receiving attention, and a code was enacted designed to transfer the entire land of Ireland to the Established Church and reduce the Celtic Irish to landless dependency. By the new law conveyance of property by Catholics since 1704 by which a Protestant was injured was declared null and void, and Catholics who had pretended conversion in order to qualify for holding a position, must bring up their children as Protestants. Unregistered Catholic clergymen were to be fined.

And now with regard to legislative double dealing, in order to escape the penalties which refusal to take the oath

would entail, instructions were issued in private for ab-
solving those who had complied with the law. The bishops
continued their harassing tactics toward Dissenters, and
the Ulster emigration showed enormous increase. It was
noticeable while the Presbyterians were subjected to
numerous disabilities by the High Church party the
Catholics were regarded differently. The venomous attitude of the Anglicans toward Calvinists was absent where
Catholics were concerned. Catholic schools remained open
when the schools of the Presbyterians were nailed up: the
prelates were too busy harassing the Dissenters to interfere
with the Catholics. The penal laws, it is true, were unrepealed, but were more honored in the breach than in the
observance. Catholic lawyers practiced in the courts,
priests came and went without registration, chapels were
erected, prelates performed their usual functions. When,
however, the Catholics mistook mildness for meekness,
and destroyed Protestant life and property, they invariably
made their position in the country many times more difficult.

When the country was threatened by an invasion of the
Pretender, Jacobitism was so prevalent in the Established
Church that the Presbyterian body was the only one in
the country upon which the crown could place reliance
should an invasion of the Pretender become a fact.

The Pretender was preparing an expedition in Scotland,
and the Irish aborigines of the west were proffering assistance. If an emergency arose there was no adequate force
to resist him with the exception of the Ulster militia,
and that body had been practically annihilated by the Test
Act, for the Non-Conformists could not have a single military officer of their own co-religionists, and when they
were asked to enlist they declined. All classes were dis-
contented, and the country was without protection, with

a French army in the offing, and still in spite of the unsatisfactory situation, the bishops continued to oppose legislative relief being extended to Presbyterians.

Anne died on the very day the Schism Act was to have become active, which was designed to wipe out Presbyterianism, deprive Catholics of their lands and hand their property over to the Established Church. It is a fact that all through the eighteenth century discontent, disorder, and violence prevailed.

A retrospective view of colonial Ulster shows clearly that the body of people who suffered most oppression, hardship, who were violently persecuted, and who received least help and encouragement from any source were not the Roman Catholics but the industrious and peaceable Presbyterians. Three times they found themselves in imminent danger of exile from Ulster, and only chance prevented their forced transportation, and this too, without rebellion or disloyalty on their part.

Wentworth, Earl of Strafford, the Irish deputy and tool of Laud, was prevented from exiling the northern Dissenters only by his own impeachment and execution.

Cromwell, fearing the support of Ulster might be given to the house of Stuart because the Presbyterians disapproved of the violent death of Charles I by his subjects, had planned to transport the whole colony from Ulster. In fact they were to go within a specified time: Cromwell changed his mind when he discovered the Presbyterians were really peaceable and industrious and could be let alone, but the list of names of those to be exiled was prepared and ready for use.

The northern Dissenters again faced transportation when "lying Dick Talbot" planned to make Ireland a safe place for James II and believed it would be impossible to do so, unless the Presbyterians were compelled to evacuate

Ulster. On this occasion they were saved by the victory won by William at the Boyne.

The Presbyterians, Independents, Huguenots and Quakers had no protection in their public worship as the English Dissenters had, owing to the high-handed opposition of the Anglican Church in Ireland, and the sects mentioned were also denied entrance to all civil and military positions. The Presbyterians alone were one-half of the Protestant population, yet out of three hundred seats in the House of Commons they occupied but ten.

With regard to the execution of the penal laws against Catholics, they were only verbally severe. The Catholic priests were obliged to register their names and take out licenses and no foreign priest was supposed to enter the country, but the laws were rarely observed, and a pension of $100 afterwards raised to $150 per annum was set apart for every priest who would enter the Established Church.

According to the bill for the repression of popery "papists" were disqualified from acting in the courts as solicitors, yet the courts were full of Catholic attorneys who assisted in determining the descent of properties. Catholic bishops held ordinations as usual and met with no interference. Priests seemed to regard the Registration Act as a great joke and performed their various offices without any thought of obtaining a license. Catholic schools remained open and other restraining laws were but food for amusement. Not so were observed the penal laws against Dissenters. The Presbyterian magistrate was deposed, and one with no recommendation other than that of appearing occasionally in the Established Church was appointed. Persons of stainless reputation were prosecuted in court for living with their lawfully wedded wives, and the children of such couples were denounced as bastards. The Anglican ministers desired to celebrate all marriages themselves where Non-Conformists were concerned as it afforded them both prestige as well as material benefit and at the same time allowed them gratuitously to insult their rivals the Dissenters who were really revered by their people.

An effort was made in the Irish Parliament by justice loving statesmen to remove the Test Act from the statute book, but the bishops could not be prevailed upon to relinquish an instrument of torture so readily wielded and so powerful.

The rancor of the bishops astonished even the laymen, and it is recorded, "To the spiritual peers a Catholic was but an erring brother while a Dissenter was a detested enemy."

The divine-right bishops continued to harass the Non-Conformists, and the Presbyterian emigration to the American colonies increased with gathering volume so they were on hand to fight for those human liberties they had well learned to value, when imperial tyranny threatened the rights of a free people.

In Ulster, prelatic persecution had lasted so long that the province was almost drained of its dauntless Protestant blood. The injury done to this religious body was irretrievable. For the greater part of its stay in the north the Established Church had acted more like a corrupt political machine than a religious body. Its selfishness and cupidity had been colossal. While paying its curates a starvation salary, the prelates rolled around in splendor gratifying their material and animal tastes at the expense of their spiritual interests. They hated the Presbyterians for their higher ethical standards, and their greater success as pastors of their people. The lives of the prelates are a commentary on the bestowal of power on the unfit, on those unable to exercise control even over themselves.

With the accession of the house of Hanover, the powerful bishops found their former large power to injure at will, considerably curtailed. The Regium Donum of which the malevolence of the bishops had deprived the Dissenting clergy, was restored, and increased by 800 pounds per annum. In 1719 was passed a Toleration Act in spite of the opposition of the bishops, which exempted Presbyterians from the penalties hereto suffered for the celebration of their acts of public worship. The bishops were still powerful enough to retain the Test Act, and they also opposed a bill exempting Presbyterians from penalties for serving in the militia of their country before they had partaken of the communion in the Episcopal Church.

As the eighteenth century neared its end the political rights of the Presbyterians improved. In 1745, with the Pretender at the head of an army in Scotland they could not have the Test Act removed from the statute book, even though they had enrolled in the militia for the defense of the kingdom, although they had reasons which would have excused them from doing so. Because of opposition, nothing could be done for them then save the enactment of an Act of Indemnity which only secured them from punishment for their loyalty. In 1780, the Test Act, which had defaced the statute book for seventy years, was at last repealed. Another triumph over the steadfast enemies of the Dissenters followed in 1782, in spite of the most obstinate and persistent opposition of the bishops, thirteen of whom registered their opposition on the Journals of the Irish House of Commons, when an act was passed declaring the perfect validity of the Presbyterian marriage rite, and the pettiness and spitefulness of the clericals could no longer injure in this particular way.

Strange indeed that of two enemies that one which is

the most powerful and has wrought the greatest injury to the other, is the most implacable and unforgiving, apparently only because it has wrought the greatest evil, and scarcely even deserves forgiveness.

Why all this persecution of a devout and pious people? Perhaps the suffering inferiority complex of the near-great demanded compensation for the injured ego which would not be satisfied until some kind of satisfaction was obtained.

In the reign of the first George the Roman Catholic religion was proscribed, but it was not restrained, for the penal laws were not regarded. New chapels were built, and mass celebrated without interference (see the primate to the Duke of Newcastle, March 7, 1728, MSS. Record Office). The primate said, "The papists by law are allowed a priest in every parish, which are registered in pursuance of an act made ten years ago . . . yet for want of due execution of the law, many are come in from foreign parts, and there are in the country popish bishops concealed that ordain many."

When the country was in imminent danger from an invasion of the Pretender the Established Church was so tainted with Jacobitism that reliance could be placed on the Non-Conformists only, and yet because of the political strength of the prelates in Parliament, it was impossible to have the Test Act repealed. The situation was so critical, however, the Commons thought it wise to insert a clause in a bill indemnifying the Presbyterians who had been commissioned in the army, declaring that Non-Conformists might in future hold rank in the army or navy without danger of persecution.

This measure, so necessary for the safety of the country, became law in spite of the most violent opposition of the Anglican bishops and clergy, although the knowledge was common property that these gentlemen were traitors to the new monarch and his family, and actually Jacobites themselves.

The bishops went so far as to declare they were not desirous of prosecuting the Dissenters for defending their country when called to the colors but they fought to confine Presbyterian services to the militia and refuse them admittance to the regular army; and indeed it is a matter of record that the proposal to grant commissions to Non-Conformists in the regular army during the war was carried by a majority of just one person.

Because of their numerical strength in the Parliament the hierarchy of the Established Church could prevent concessions to Dissenters, even of the most meager character, and even these were opposed (we learn from Records), as if Christianity itself, rather than their own petty, personal interests were in danger of being destroyed. (See the Duke of Bolton to Secretary Scragge, July, 1718, MSS., Ireland Record Office.)

As the colonists of the north were a larger and stronger body than were the other groups of Anglo-Saxon Protestants scattered throughout the country, the young women of the north were not subjected in the same way to the kidnaping outrages perpetrated on their sex in other parts of the country.

The kidnaped victim was allowed no legal escape from the marital bonds forced on her by the aid of degraded priests and clergymen, and the evil reached such proportions that Parliament at last recognized the grave character of the offense and enacted legislation imposing very severe penalties on the ecclesiastics guilty of aiding in the crime. The law however seemed to have little effect, and the outcry against the wrong continued. The kidnapers, it became evident, were men with influential connections and were not often convicted, or if they were, a pardon was usually obtained for the heroes.

The castle government was feeble and the outrages continued and were the means of breaking up Protestant settlements. Elizabeth Squibb, the daughter of a Quaker merchant of the city of Cork, was kidnaped by the son of Sir James Cotter, a man said to be a great favorite of the southern Catholics. The kidnaper was arrested, convicted, and sentenced; and the young man was eventually hanged. The whole south of Ireland rose in furious rage. Young Quaker girls were mobbed on the streets of Cork and received threats of being "Cottered." No Quaker could appear on the streets without endangering his life. The mayor of Cork appealed to the Roman Catholic clergy to use their influence to appease the people, but without effect. The flame spread through Catholic Ireland. Quakers were waylaid and beaten. In Cork a girl mistaken for Elizabeth Squibb would have been torn to pieces but for the arrival of forcible assistance just in time to avert a tragedy. This frenzy reached its acme five years later and the following story is related by an eyewitness, Paul Lydy, who turned informer.

The tragedy occurred on February 22, 1725. The house of a Quaker named Johnstone of Carroe was broken into by eleven men; the gang robbed the house, set Johnstone on a hot griddle, and poured burning coals over him, then kicked and beat the poor man, who soon afterwards died. The wife was also unmercifully beaten. (See Exam. of Paul Lydy, King's County depositions, 1726, MSS. Dublin Castle.) After the murderers had completed their work they set themselves down to an uninvited supper, which consisted of bread and cheese; on being informed that meat was obtainable, they said they would not eat meat in time of Lent.

The Irish apparently are very readily stirred up to a pitch of ungovernable rage as shown by a number of other incidents.

A certain Lord St. George owned some land in Connemara, which he determined to plant with thrifty Protestant families who should make the most of their opportunities and increase the value of their holdings. Decent homes were provided for the newcomers but care was taken that no Catholic family should be removed or interfered with in any way. The men of the vicinity, however, many of them houghers of cattle, rose to the occasion, leveled the houses to the ground, and destroyed the settlement. The priests told the people they were contending for Holy Church and the Holy Catholic religion. (See Anthony Miles to the Earl of Kildare, July 30, (?) Church MSS. Dublin Castle.)

An incident of similar character occurred in 1798 at Killala, where the Earl of Arran had planted a colony of Presbyterian weavers which had grown to one thousand members. When the rebellion of that year occurred they were denounced as Orangemen, their homes plundered and robbed of everything of value, their houses then wrecked, and the victims sent as prisoners to Ballina.

This spirit of intolerance and savagery was general; the crime so common in the south and west of houghing helpless cattle again manifested itself especially in Mayo and Galway. If the injured man dared to prosecute the offender, he paid the penalty of his boldness with his life, and the magistrate who convicted the criminal, the witness who gave testimony, and every assisting juryman was as certainly murdered.

A Catholic who betrayed a breadth of mind and a tolerance for the opinions of others which his fellows were unable to understand, was bound to suffer. We are informed that a Catholic servant who attended family prayers in the home of a Protestant, when those prayers contained nothing whatever unfriendly or hostile to the Catholic belief, was excommunicated and his life and prospects in the Catholic community ruined; even a Roman Catholic who entered a Protestant church, listened to a Protestant sermon, or received moral training from a Protestant minister was dealt with in the same autocratic and tyrannical fashion.

A Protestant bishop draws attention to a case of this kind occurring in his own family, and related by Lecky: The Catholic sometimes read the English Bible, on which the Christian religion is founded, and occasionally attended the Protestant church in his vicinity. He was excommunicated for this heinous offense and lost all his work as a house-painter. Being advised to sue for damages against the priest who had injured him, he, knowing his life would be in danger if he did so, fled the country. The carelessly enforced or not enforced at all penal laws, were far less to be dreaded than the tyrannies of priests enraged at what they considered any encroachment of their privileges.

The chronic attitude of the Celtic Irish towards any Protestant denomination was manifested towards the world-renowned evangelists Moody and Sankey in the year 1883. The peaceful, friendly evangelists were mobbed in Wexford, a town far ahead in civilization and education of other localities in the south and west. The theater in which they had hoped to address the Protestant or any willing part of the population was wrecked and destroyed.

Perhaps this attitude may not seem surprising when we remember what Lecky has said, that "the Catholic priests wherever they were in the ascendent were ever a persecuting body." Surely we cannot expect the water to rise higher than its source, and if the people are bred in and taught intolerance practically from their birth, would it not be vain to expect them to be magnanimous or to follow the example of Christ who said, "Let brotherly love continue"? There is no doubt the influence of the priest on the Celtic Irish population is very great, for education is in the hands of the clerics from childhood.

In the year 1893 a delegation of English workingmen interested in the Home Rule question arrived in Belfast. One named S. J. Field from Scotswood-on-Tyne wrote to the *Times* May 5, 1894: "I was not aware the priest commanded the people of the flock under pain of excommunication to vote for particular candidates. To talk of intolerance and influence is a mild way of putting it. The will of the peasantry of Ireland means simply the will of the priests. These statements cannot be contradicted."

In the *Spectator* March, 1911 (p. 12), Miss A. W. Richardson of the Society of Friends writes: "This afternoon I happened to have a conversation with a young Salvation Army captain, a Scotswoman, who was collecting for self-denial work. She had three years before been quartered at Waterford (Redmond's constituency) and tells me that no Salvation Army officer dared to walk through the streets of that town in uniform. The first officer stationed there—not very long ago—was soon after he arrived knocked down while quietly walking in the public street, and savagely beaten. He would have been killed but for the intervention of two sailors. She herself had always to be met when she arrived at the railway station by special police sent for that purpose, and the open-air service held over in the week was only made possible by a street guard of police. Such protection, she said, restricted assault on Salvation Army girls to spitting and cursing which were freely indulged in. Two Catholics who ventured to join the Army while she was there had to leave town as they were fiercely boycotted and could get no work. But Waterford was not worse than other towns down there. I could not have believed it had I been told of the state of things in Ireland. English people ought to go and see what the south of Ireland is like; for unless you have been there you cannot judge."

The pope himself acknowledges his immutability and his intolerance, he does not change with a changing, progressive, and civilizing world. To think for oneself is an error, and error is worse than crime. Tolerance for the opinions of others is allowed only when the power to prevent it is lacking and it must be endured.

Whiteboy disturbances were a very serious cause of disquiet and alarm in the eighteenth century, beginning about 1711, and were specially troublesome in the south and west. In the south the agitation was said to be caused by lands becoming the property of graziers. The Whiteboys wore a white shirt over their clothes, hence their name. The Whiteboy gangs practiced the most revolting cruelties. Cattle were houghed, and men had their hamstrings cut like the cattle and were left in helpless agony. A common practice was to tear out the tongue of the offender by the roots, and to throw him into a pit lined with thorns, then earth would be thrown into the pit and the victim left to die, suffering and alone.

The following was written by Edward Crowe to the bishop of Cloyne on this matter, "All night long we heard the roaring of helpless cattle as they fell under the knife: with wild cries and volleys of shots from bogs and mountains, and the huzzas of the houghers" (quoted from Macaulay). The people were obliged to carry their guns constantly to protect their lives; and it has been said that the principal leaders of the Whiteboy movement were the religious teachers and leaders of the people.

The Whiteboy Association spread to the west and other Roman Catholic neighborhoods. It was said to have originated in a Catholic chapel and spread among the Catholics by means of chapels. When soldiers were on the track of the Whiteboy, he fled for sanctuary to the chapel altar. They plundered and robbed, tortured and maimed. The pitiful cries of tortured cattle could be heard through the night while the loud huzzas of the human beasts resounded over bog and swamp, as the criminal gangs rushed to the performance of other deeds of torture or death.

While Whiteboy disturbances were spreading in the south and west an association of Protestants appeared in the north. They wore a sprig of oak in their caps and their particular grievance was a Road Act which compelled them, that is the house-owners, to keep the roads in repair at their own expense. The roads to be repaired were not actually public, being kept for the convenience of private property holders, but these landed proprietors sat on grand juries and ordered the house-owner to render this work for them gratuitously. The Oakboys were also dissatisfied with an advance in the tithe rate, an increase of rent and enclosing the commons. Captain Erskine, sent to investigate, found grand juries were supporting the interests of leading men at the expense of the householders, who were required to pay fifty thousand pounds a year of county cess, and that one infamous job after another had been created in the interests of the great men, at the expense of the people. The five counties affected were Derry, Armagh, Tyrone, Down, and Antrim. The matter was easily adjusted and a new Road Act removed the cause of complaints. The Oakboys had annoyed and insulted those who had disagreed with them, but they were never guilty of the atrocities, cruelties, and crimes of the Whiteboys.   Peace was restored in 1763.

The cupidity of the landlords, their desire to get rich overnight at the expense of their industrious tenants, was causing another serious grievance.   The tenant farmers had taken their farms when in a wild, uncultivated condition; they had expended much time and labor on the land; they had plowed and drained, cultivated, and fenced it, enormously increasing its value.   Now when the tenant's lease expired, if he still wished to retain his land, no concession was made to him for his improvements and he was actually required to pay a much larger rent for land which owed its increased value entirely to his own labor and expense.   As much as one hundred thousand pounds was the price demanded by the capitalists, which of course the farmers were unable to pay.   The lands were taken over by jobbers, sublet, and the tenants were turned out of their homes.   The Marquis of Donegal, a descendant of Sir Arthur Chichester, turned a whole countryside out of their holdings in this way.   A certain Mr. Upton and other landlords followed the example set by the Marquis of Donegal, and over a wide area the people were forced from homes they had made in a howling wilderness, which in five generations they had turned into attractive cultivated lands.

England had so little regard for these people of her own race, the protectors of her interests in a hostile country, who were thus left homeless, that she created Lord Donegal a marquis, and made Mr. Upton a viscount, for their services in making it possible for Ulstermen to give most valuable aid in defeating the British army in America, for these injured colonists were her indomitable foes in the American Revolutionary War.

The consternation and distress created by these tyrannies in addition to their religious handicaps, paved the way for the formation of an organization known as the Steel-boys, who were almost entirely Presbyterians. These men administered illegal oaths and even destroyed property. They searched offices for deeds of land, but were never accused of theft or murder. The object they had in view was to protect themselves from a legal robbery causing their ruin. They felt they were resisting their despoilers rather than the government, which passively permitted their destruction.

They presented the following petition to the viceroy in Dublin castle: "Petition of those persons known by the name of Hearts of Steel." "That we are all Protestants and Protestant Dissenters and bear unfeigned loyalty to his present majesty and the Hanoverian Succession. That we are all groaning under oppression and having no other possible way of redress, are forced to join ourselves together to resist. By oversetting ourselves we are reduced to poverty and distress, and by our rising we mean no more but to have our lands, that we should live thereon, and procure necessaries of life for ourselves and our starving families.

"That some of us refusing to pay the extravagant rent demanded by our landlords, have been turned out, and our land given to Papists who will promise any rent.

"That we are sorely aggrieved with the County Cesses, which though heavy in themselves, are rendered more so by being applied to private purposes. Yet lest it should be said that by refusing to pay the cess, we fly in the face of the law, which we do not intend, we will pay the present cess, and we hope the gentlemen of the county of Down, will in future have pity on the distressed inhabitants.

"That it is not wanton folly that prompts us to be Hearts of Steel, but the weight of oppression. Were the cause removed the effects would cease and our landlords, as heretofore, live in the affection of their tenants.

"May it please you to inquire into the cause of our grievances and lend your hand to eschew the evils which seem to threaten the Protestants of the north: and let not false suggestions of men partial to their own cause inflame your wrath against innocent and injured persons who are far removed from the ear of government, and any other possible means of redress," etc. "By the Hearts of Steel." (Irish MSS., 1772, S.P.O.)

Ulster was the only province affected in this peculiar way, the only one that had been taken as a wild uncultivated country and made a pleasant cultivated land. The Hearts of Steel destroyed the property of the intruders on their farms and searched houses for deeds of property and leases but were never accused of theft.

The Presbyterian clergy believed the people were right and the Viceroy, Townshend, realized the provocation given to the colonists, but the patriotic House of Commons had sympathy for the greedy landlords only, and recommended sending soldiers to the north to overawe the distressed people. General Grisborne arrived in Ulster and was invited in a friendly way to remove the evils from which they suffered and restore peace.

Conditions became more quiet but the evicted people abandoned the ungrateful country they had long faithfully served and sought a new home in the land where so many of their countrymen had found a refuge from religious persecution. The Hearts of Steel and their families reached America, now on the verge of rebellion against the mother country, where they swelled the army of American patriots fighting for the right to own the works of their own hands and own themselves; and these Ulstermen did much, very much, to help win liberty for the coming republic. According to Gordon, the Hearts of Steel boys "contributed powerfully, by their zeal and valor, to the separation of the American colonies from Great Britain."

At an earlier period the Dissenting colonists had fled from the persecution of the bishops of the Established Church, and when the woolen trade was destroyed and the linen trade entered on a period of stagnation, a steady stream of Ulster families poured into America and were there in time to assist in the architecture of the new republic.

Ulster remained in an unsettled condition for some time after the Protestant families had been expelled from their homes, and their property sold to the highest bidder. The colonists resented the intrusion of Catholics into the homes built by their toil and the lands made valuable by their unceasing toil. Formerly Ulster had been almost entirely Protestant, now the Catholics had increased in numbers and were providing themselves with arms in spite of the law. To make matters look more threatening, news came from the south that the Catholics there had disarmed the Protestants. An association was then formed by the northern colonists, named the Peep of Day Boys, whose main object was to search the Catholic houses for the arms it was believed they illegally held. The Catholics were vociferous in their complaints and the matter was brought to the attention of Parliament. Here the legislators who had nothing to say when the Whiteboys disarmed the Protestants in the south, were filled with wrath against the northern Protestants who had deprived Catholics of the arms they had no right to possess. The northern Celts then organized themselves into a body which became known as Defenders; they were all Catholics and later became United Irishmen. Most of the Peep of Day Boys were Presbyterians and became Orangemen.

The Defenders formed branches or lodges in every county, and made members of a large number of the Catholic peasantry. They entered Protestant houses, which they robbed of the arms they were required by law to possess, and waylaid and murdered nine men in Roscommon (see Pelham to Portland, May, 1795). The minority naturally became alarmed at the accounts of assassinations, remembering the dread 1641, and in Armagh the farmers dreading what might happen resolved to disarm, before it was too late, the Catholics settled among them and to force them out of Ulster. The alarm among the Protestant settlers and its consequences must be laid squarely on the shoulders of an unscrupulous Parliament without initiative, normal judgment, common sense, or ethical perception.

The destructive industrial laws had driven large numbers of Protestants from the country and caused much unemployment, and in spite of an unrepealed Disarming Act it was decided to allow the Catholics to provide themselves with arms. The Protestants regarded this measure as a very dangerous one for them, and wished to have the Disarming Act observed. The vacillating Parliament asked the Celtic people to ask for the repeal of their disabilities, and then wavered back to a policy of coercion. This occurred in 1739, and at that time Parliament passed a bill to prevent whiskey distillation; England, however, interfered to prevent the bill from becoming law which would have caused her the loss of the whiskey tax.

The Catholics in speeches from the throne were called enemies, and the Irish viceroys officially would urge Parliament to enforce the penal laws and privately forbid the same laws to be enforced, lest the Catholic allies of England should become alarmed.

Irish misery because of its tyrannical purblind government was increasing; the French war had occurred and 50,000 Irish Celts were ready to render aid to France. Thurot, the French commander, entered the bay of Carrickfergus and after plundering the town had threatened to attack Belfast.

Ulster had been left not only without arms but without any protection whatsoever, and England, it was felt, deserved the most severe criticism thus to leave the country without any protection.

The penal laws against the Roman Catholics while not repealed had been greatly relaxed, and Catholics who called themselves Protestants were practicing in courts of law, and Catholic juries were in active service; yet the favors shown had excited no gratitude but seemed rather to have increased antagonism, so that the gentry had armed themselves for self-defense. The Irish Parliament had extorted from the mother country the Constitution of 1782 and the Sacramental Test finally after seventy years of service was wiped out in 1780; it had owed its life to the Anglican bishops, now unable to keep it alive, and the Presbyterians were at last placed on an equal footing politically with other sects. The commercial restrictions also were removed and England, now at war with her American colonies, had again left Ireland without protection. It was at this juncture that the northern colonists decided to organize for their own protection and volunteer associations sprang up overnight as it were, and soon numbered 40,000 men.

England had previously placed an embargo on the exportation of food products from Ireland so that her troops on American soil might be provisioned more cheaply, and in so doing had almost ruined Irish farmers. When the voluntary movement sprang into life the despotic attitude of the mother country became more conciliatory and the removal of some long-time prohibitions resulted.

The Peep of Day Boys decided to try peaceful conclusions with the Defenders and met for this purpose at Portadown. One of the former, however, named Atkinson was shot at on that day by an overenthusiastic Defender, and on the succeeding day a party of Protestants were waylaid and beaten. On Sept. 21, 1795, the antagonistic associations met at a village called the Diamond in Armagh, where mediators from each party worked for peace and had almost concluded it when a fresh body of Defenders appeared and excited fresh hostilities. The Defenders were now the most numerous but their opponents were better organized, and the Catholics were defeated, leaving forty-eight of their number dead on the field of battle.

It was on the evening of this day that the first Orange Lodge was formed. The many concessions granted Catholics, far from placating them, had merely brought to the surface those feelings they formerly had thought wise to conceal, at least to some extent; now many were swaggering and boasting in their newly acquired liberties of the ultimate fate awaiting the Protestants. Riots were reported at different places and an organization was planned for the better protection of Protestants against the authors of repeated attacks.

The Orange Lodge was established as a league of mutual defense, and bound its members to maintain the laws, and the peace of the country as well as the Protestant constitution. No Roman Catholic could become a member, and each individual was bound by a solemn oath not to reveal any of its secrets. The oath of the Orangeman bound him to defend the king and his heirs so long as they upheld the Protestant ascendancy. (See *Orangism, Constitution and Objects,* by Richard Lilburn, 1866.) Alexander Boragh says the Orangemen are almost entirely members of the Established Church, and in his opinion their aggressions were due to the jealousies produced by the associations, conspiracies, language, and conduct of the Defenders.

Defender movements were increasing in number, and members were accused of the murders of informers of their evil deeds. During the preceding twenty years, the Celtic Irish had been conceded an equality with the Protestants, including equal property rights and almost the same privilege. These concessions, however, had served to make them more unruly, and more difficult. A magistrate of Dromore in Antrim said, "The Protestants dare not go to bed at night without a watch, because they feared they might be murdered." It was said these persons had formed an Assassination Club.

The Orange Association hoped to combat the anarchy about them. According to Knox, chief secretary and brigadier general, each member was to have a sincere love and veneration for his maker; he was to be humane and courteous and an enemy to cruelty and brutality. He was to be zealous to promote the honor of his king and country; was not to use profane language and must carefully observe the seventh day of the week. Loyalty to the king was inculcated, and the support of Protestantism. Only Protestants could become members. Secret signs and passwords were agreed on in order to guard against spies and traitors. Members of this association were permitted to enlist in the district corps, and some were incorporated in the yeomanry.

The Orangemen were dreaded and hated by those whose

actions merited punishment, and they were dreaded more in localities they had never entered than in the districts where they were known.   False stories regarding them were circulated, and believed in by the credulous who were taught to believe the Orangemen were out to murder and kill like so many of their own co-religionists.

This credulity and blind unreasoning rage and hate is well illustrated by an occurrence in Wexford in the rebellion of 1798.   The Roman Catholics were murdering their Protestant fellow countrymen as fast as time and strength would permit.   They had invaded and were plundering the home of a Protestant gentleman, known as Colonel Le Haute.   The drawing room here contained some orange-colored furniture, and there were two fire-screens decorated with ribbon of the same shade.   The screens displayed mythological figures, including Hope with an anchor, Minerva and her spear, also a blindfolded Justice, the Cyclops, Ganymede, and the eagle.

These screens were exhibited on the streets of Wexford as the Orange insignia.   They were said to be found in an Orange meeting place, and the figures decorating the screen represented the torture and death designed for Catholic men, women, and children.   Soon an ungovernable mob was raging through the streets of Wexford, and the innocent owner of the screens would have paid with his life for his ownership of the decorated fire-screens, but for two Catholic men who interfered at the risk of their own lives, and had the offender safely committed to prison for trial.   The mob was so incensed at the loss of their prey that the whole town committee were for some time in danger of losing their lives.   (See Hay, pp. 197, 198, also Gordon, pp. 148-9, and Plowden, Vol. III, pp. 741-2.)

The Orangemen became a volunteer police force, for the

executive was inefficient and timid. They aided in the execution of laws designed to hold murderers in check, and curtailed the raids of roving bands of assassins who terrorized the country, so they earned the detestation of the antagonists whose plots they thwarted. The Orange lodges multiplied and in the early part of 1797 numbered 20,000 men, who were the terror of evildoers. In 1798 they filled the ranks of the yeomanry and were an obstruction to the United Irishmen.

The Orange Society included men of rank and standing in the community, men of high character who would never countenance the degrading pledges a fiercely partisan and Catholic people circulated as the Orangeman's oath. Among the members of the Orange Society were the Marquis of Hertford, Marquis of Abercorn, Lord Northland, the Earl of Londonderry, Mr. Cope, Messrs. Brownlow and Richardson, and other possessors of great landed estates in Ireland. A goodly number of Presbyterians were also members of the society.

The existence of a pledge to destroy their enemies was only one of the many falsehoods circulated by mendacious fanatics anxious to goad others to greater acts of rapine and cruelty. The Orangemen have repudiated always with the most profound emphasis and solemnity, the existence of any such oath. No such oath has ever been found on the body of an Orangeman whether living or dead, while the so-called Ribbonman's oath has been found on the bodies of Ribbonmen, dead in battle, in localities far apart, and what is significant this oath displays exactly the same phraseology in all cases. Besides it is undeniable that the admonition contained in the oath is in conformity with the action displayed by the Ribbonman when opportunity offers. Hugh Boyd Wray, testifying before the House of Commons Committee in 1832, also Miles O'Reilly, Colonel Verner, and Mr. Cassidy testified to the identical phraseology in the Ribbonman's oath though found in widely different parts of the country; this oath contained the promise to wade deep in Protestant blood.

V

EMIGRATION TO AMERICA

The Presbyterian exodus from Ulster excites alarm in Parliament
which orders an investigation; the emigrants flock to the
colonies—William Penn busy in eastern New Jersey—Laws
in New York unfavorable to Catholics—Celtic-Irish emigration—Celtic-Irish characteristics as noted by eminent
historians—Irish abuse of England—Catholic Emancipation.

PROTESTANT emigration from Ulster began near
the beginning of the seventeenth century, for the
amity of the Established Church toward Dissenters proved short-lived, and the persecutions of the
favored church were persistent, despotic, and cruel. At
first individuals or small groups relinquished their homes
to seek a better land, then the tide of Protestant emigration
which began with religious persecution was aided by the
artificial poverty of the people induced by the deliberate
action of the parent government on the other side of St.
George's Channel. The stimulation of Protestant emigration by the destruction of the woolen manufacture lasted
for three quarters of a century; this tragedy was followed
by the virtual expulsion of the farmers and landholders
over a wide area from the lands their labor and other ex-
penditures had made valuable, without any compensation
to them for the reclaiming of a wilderness to a fertile,
smiling expanse of cultivated country. Thus occurred a
stream varying in volume from time to time but continuing steadily from Ulster to the American colonies.
These emigrants founded the linen trade in New England

(see Burke's *Settlement in America*). The thrifty people carried with them not only the implements of their trade, but capital as well. They are not to be classed with the destitute emigrants who left Ireland a century later after the famine of 1846.

The exodus from Ulster became so great that Parliament became alarmed and ordered an investigation of the cause (see report on causes of emigration from Ulster, June 6, 1729). The magnitude of this torrent of emigration from Ulster caused many friends of the colonists to fear the removal of the entire Presbyterian population from Ulster (see Woodrow's MSS., Letters, XX, No. 129) Six thousand persons arrived in America in 1729, and before the middle of the century 12,000 were arriving annually for several years (see Proud's *History of Pennsylvania*, Vol. II, pp. 273-4). It was said the "prelatists trampled upon them as a stiff-necked generation, because the Presbyterians refused to recognize the lawfulness of their power, and the civil rulers subjected them to penalties because they protested against tyranny, and demanded the exercise of constitutional power in the state. The spirit of the intrepid colonists is shown by their daring assertion in their Assembly in 1649, when they declared "that a boundless and unlimited power is to be acknowledged in no king or magistrate, and that there is a mutual obligation between the king and his people."

These Anglo-Saxons of Ulster, like their ancestors in the lowlands of Scotland, were always staunch upholders of education, and wherever they went in the new land of adoption they founded schools and colleges that their families might be trained to discharge creditably and faithfully all the duties of life. The famine of 1740-1 gave immense impetus to Presbyterian emigration (see Killen's *Ecclesiastical History*).

This large number of Ulster families entered America with a consuming sense of injustice and an overwhelming indignation against the mother country who had used them to defend her interests, often at the expense of their lives, who had allowed them to be defrauded of their property and subjected them to humiliation, injustice, and tyranny, and who had thus replaced their ready friendship with a bitter enmity.

It was computed that from 1728 to 1750 Ulster lost by emigration one quarter of her trading cash and the like proportion of her manufacturing population (see History Collections relative to the town of Belfast). The Scotch-Irish emigration was a heavy blow to trade as well as to land cultivation, for in a number of instances the jobbers who had bought the cultivated lands of the Ulster emigrants proved harsh landlords to their own people, the Celtic Irish.

The Ulster emigrants found themselves preceded by a number of their own Presbyterian clergymen. From 1670 to 1680 many families settled in Maryland and according to Macaulay during the first half of the eighteenth century, the Irish counties of Down, Antrim, Tyrone, Armagh, and Derry were almost emptied of their Protestant inhabitants.

England held the opinion common to most states of the period, that colonies existed for the sole benefit of the mother country, and chose to ignore the fact that they were for the most part established by subjects fleeing from her jurisdiction to escape tyranny, robbery, and persecution.

Lecky says: "After the English Revolution of 1688, a steady stream of Scotch-Irish Presbyterians poured into America," and according to the historian Parker, "During the period of twenty-five years preceding the [American]

Revolution, ten distinct settlements were made by emigrants from Londonderry [Ireland], all of which have become towns of influence and importance."

The Ulster colonists exercised a profound influence in the building up of the country of their adoption, for they left their mark on legislation, education, and theology, as well as in the army and navy. They have taken a high place, sometimes a leading place, in questions relating to commerce and agriculture, for they have displayed initiative, daring, resourcefulness, and sound common sense. They were the first to reach the other side of the Alleghanies, were among the first settlers in Tennessee, and as we can learn from Marmion's *Maritime Ports of Ireland,* there sailed from Lough Foyle in Northern Ireland in 1718, about one hundred families who founded a colony in New Hampshire, which has become famous in the history of America, for it is said "the Derry emigrants of New Hampshire were of as much importance to their adopted country as were those of Plymouth, and from them are descended equally if not more distinguished men." In the year 1727, 3,000 persons sailed from Belfast, Lough, and 1,000 more arrived in the following year to be succeeded by 4,000 in the succeeding three years, and between 1720 and 1742 the stream from Presbyterian Ulster was rarely interrupted.

Arthur Young, whose descriptive tours in Ireland are regarded as a classic, discussing the unusual outpouring from Ulster in the eighteenth century says: "The spirit of emigrating in Ireland appeared to be confined to two circumstances, the Presbyterian religion and the linen manufacture. I heard of very few emigrants except among manufacturers of that persuasion. The Catholics never went; they seem not only tied to the country, but almost to the parish in which their ancestors lived." Young goes on to say, "The Protestant emigration had subsisted perhaps forty years, insomuch that at the ports of Belfast and Derry, etc., the passage trade, as it was called, had long been a regular branch of commerce, which employed several ships, and consisted in carrying people to America. The increasing population of the country made it an increasing trade, and when the linen trade was low the passage trade was high."

It was Mr. Makemie who organized the Presbytery of Philadelphia, the first in the new country, and his coadjutors were all Scotch-Irishmen from Ulster. The Rev. Mr. McGregor was pastor of the flock locating in New Hampshire and who founded the new city of Londonderry, named after the far-away Maiden City.

As early as 1682, William Penn, a Quaker, interested a number of Scotchmen in a scheme of colonizing the eastern section of New Jersey. It was these emigrants who founded the College of New Jersey, afterwards Princeton College.

The Scotch-Irish came in such numbers to the city of brotherly love that James Logan, the Scotch-Irish Quaker, secretary of William Penn, was puzzled what to do with them. Logan was Governor of Pennsylvania in 1699-1748.

The thriving city of Pittsburgh was also founded by the Scotch-Irish from Ulster so that it has been said "to be Scotch-Irish in complexion and history as well as in the countenances of the living and the records of the dead."

In the south Atlantic states many of the people are also of Scotch-Irish extraction, for during the eighteenth century they swarmed into North and South Carolina and Georgia, as well as Virginia and Maryland. In 1738 these people settled both east and west of the Blue Ridge Mountains, except in the lower portion of this area, which was being settled by Germans.

In the year 1736 Henry McCullock from Northern Ireland succeeded in obtaining a grant of 64,000 acres in Duplin County, North Carolina, and was instrumental in bringing there about 4,000 of his Scotch-Irish friends.

Other emigrants also came to Charleston and other ports along the southern seaboard. W. W. Henry says according to S. S. Green, "So great was the population of the race in North Carolina before the Revolution that they may be said to have given direction to its history," and with their advent began the educational history of the state. Matthew Thornton speaks of the influx of Scotch-Irish families to Charleston and of 1,000 emigrants who came in a single year to South Carolina, from Pennsylvania and Virginia, driving their stock before them. These people, Thornton says, were Scotch-Irish and showed prominently the traits of economy and industry, and the part of the country in which they settled became the most populous part of the province. Another author, Ramsey, states that it was to this element of the population that South Carolina is indebted for much of its early literature. He says further that a great proportion of its physicians, clergymen, lawyers, and schoolmasters were from North Britain. The early settlers of South Carolina showed many Huguenots as well as Scotch-Irish, and the prosperity of Georgia is said to be largely owing to the latter race. The pioneering people of Kentucky were largely Scotch-Irish who pushed their way into new territory, going on to Mississippi, Arkansas, Alabama, and Florida.

The conqueror of Texas was a Scotch-Irishman who

had been one of the fighters in the famous siege of Londonderry, and later arrived in Pennsylvania.

This prolific race gave children to the states of Ohio, Iowa, Minnesota, and California, distinguished as they were by initiative, enterprise, and love of adventure as well as a desire to improve their condition.

The Rev. Thomas Craighead led the way to Bristol County, Mass.; in 1715 he settled at Freetown. Cotton Mather writes to another Presbyterian pastor in New England, the Rev. James Woodside, Dec. 3, 1718, " 'Tis more than time that your brethren should bid you welcome to the western side of the Atlantic and make you a tender of all the brotherly assistance that we are capable of giving you," etc. (Mather MSS., p. 189, American Antiquarian Society). Nevertheless the Scotch-Irish emigrants were not received with friendly greetings everywhere. Dissenters in England were not regarded with too friendly eyes and the reputation of the Irish Celt, his turbulence and vindictiveness towards those of different race and creed, did not predispose in his favor, and many doubtless made the mistake—made by many even today—of classing all persons from Ireland as belonging to the Celtic race.

During the reign of William III (1689-1702) Roman Catholics were not welcomed in New York. William III was a Presbyterian himself, and in that age of more or less violence, a Catholic plot was brought to light (1695) for the murder of the King and another plot for the extirpation of Protestantism. The result was penalties imposed on Catholics for the violation of the law.

A law was enacted against Catholics in New York, and no priest or Jesuit had permission to enter there under pain of heavy punishment. In 1643, however, the first

Catholic missionary who penetrated the colony of New York, the Jesuit Father Jogues, in a letter dated August 30, 1643, mentions that he heard the confessions of a Portuguese woman and a young Irishman on the island of Manhattan.

The puritans of New England refused to grant political privileges to Roman Catholics and the Continental Congress was permeated with the same spirit of hostility towards Catholics.

A number of the Scotch immigrants who went to Boston in 1718 proceeded to Worcester, Mass., and Prof. Arthur L. Perry, who was himself of Scotch-Irish extraction, believed that at least two hundred went to Worcester in 1718, and some of these later were found acting as officers (according to town records) although there was a prejudice against Irishmen.

A Scotch-Irishman named Sam. Glass purchased from Joist Hite, a Hollander, a large tract of land in the year 1732, and gave to his pastor, the Rev. John Hodge, five acres of ground on which to build a Presbyterian church, with a graveyard attached. The donor and his pastor are both buried in this cemetery. Two sons of the owner of the large tract of land, with a son-in-law named James Vance, and Becket, another son-in-law, were settled in the same vicinity. (See Foote's Sketches.)

William Linn, one of the famous Londonderry garrison, has been honored by having one of the counties in the state of Kentucky named after him. Townships named Donegal, Londonderry, Tyrone, and Coleraine were in Pennsylvania in 1732.

A spirit of enterprise and investigation prompted a number of the Scotch-Irish in New Hampshire to penetrate still farther north, until they reached Nova Scotia, and at Truro they established a settlement. Some of these new settlers came from the town of Londonderry in New England. Included in the party reaching Truro were the Archibalds, afterwards so distinguished, also Captain William Blair from Worcester, and a defender of Londonderry. Others of the same race and religion followed. Many of the Canadians are of Scotch-Irish descent, and they may be found in every province, some centers entirely peopled by them; and it may be added that wherever they have settled in the new country, these forward-looking people have been leaders in education, ethics, and in those qualities which promote a higher civilization.

The tide of Celtic Irish Roman Catholic emigration began one hundred years after the Protestants of Ulster had sought refuge from religious persecution, legal robbery, and the handicap of commercial restrictions in what afterwards would be known as the United States of America.

The religious and political Celtic Irish leaders had been strongly opposed to emigration in any form for their people. Doubtless a few adventurous souls, refusing to be trammeled by religious or other bonds, followed the urge to see new sights and new countries, but the number was exceedingly small, so that at the time of the American Revolutionary War the number of Celtic Irish in the country was relatively insignificant.

The Catholic priests not only banned emigration but encouraged early marriages and large families, so that it was not at all unusual for girls to become brides at the age of fourteen and at the age of sixteen a young mother might have two or more children in her family.

We find in the Reflections and Resolutions of Maddeus, a criticism of these early marriages and the resulting large families, who also says, "Our Protestants do not marry young." The *Journal des Debats* observes that "other countries would be as bad as Ireland if there existed the same reckless increase of population and the same aversion to emigration." Notwithstanding a poor-law inquiry of 1830 said, "The poorer classes of the Irish are better off than those of the same class in France and Italy."

O'Connor, Roman Catholic Irish barrister, says (Vol. I, p. 275), "For the cause of nine tenths of the terrible sufferings which the people endured, culminating in the famine, was that they multiplied very rapidly, and would not be allowed to emigrate." The same author says, "The priesthood favored early marriages," and "The Irish policy was opposed to emigration. Emigration was a crime against the nation. From Kerry to Antrim, the rocks, the stones, the lakes, the rivers, the bogs, the very sods of turf shrieked to heaven for vengeance against it, or against any Irishman who advocated it." So the people multiplied and Ireland being an agricultural country was unable to support the teeming population. The increase of the population of Ireland during the eighteenth century exceeded that of any other country in Europe. In 1700 it was 1,250,000, in 1800, it was 4,500,000. In 1840 the Irish population was 8,000,000 and but five years later was nearly 9,000,000, and between two and three millions of these were supported by charity. Naturally there was great economic distress for which undoubtedly the teaching of the priests was mainly responsible, but of course no one thought of censuring the priests; the blame for all the Irish misery was laid as usual on the British government.

Great Britain favored emigration for the Irish population, but that fact counted for less than nothing in Ireland.

On the other hand few of the Celtic Irish peasant class could afford to emigrate. The north had industries and a better knowledge of land cultivation, and preferred emigration to the conditions facing them at home, and besides there was no spiritual authority interfering with northern emigration.

With the failure of the potato crop in 1845-6 and the consequent famine, emigration became compulsory, for the great bulk of the people relied for their subsistence almost entirely on the potato, and now they were deprived of that succulent vegetable. The potato blight which caused such widespread distress is a disease which in a day or two destroys the healthy plants. It first appeared in the United States in 1844 and reached Europe the following year, spreading over a large part of the country. England and Scotland suffered very severely from the potato disease as well as Ireland, and Great Britain certainly did everything in her power to relieve the situation, although her efforts won her no gratitude from a large part of the country.

When Celtic Irish emigration became inevitable in 1847, it lasted for years, and the emigrant ships were filled to overflowing with young men and women from Celtic Ireland. One of their countrymen and co-religionists describes these people as "ignorant and pliable peasants, near to destitution, many of them with frames enfeebled by want." The next two decades brought to America close on two millions who had neither education, nor training of any kind, and so took their place among the lowest in the large cities. Such people were fitted for nothing but manual labor, and it is well known their main contribution has been mainly in that field. They were taught to think of themselves as exiles from their own country by the evil treatment of England and because of her cruelty to them. They were trained in hatred against her and encouraged to visit upon her all the vituperation and abuse of which they were capable.

From 1847 to 1854 more than one and a half million of Celtic Irish people emigrated to the United States, where they found occupation in the very lowest ranks of labor.

During the period of famine, the British government extended unlimited sympathy and help towards the suffering people. This government purchased one hundred thousand pounds' worth of indian corn for porridge, and established public works of various kinds, such as road-making, and about 100,000 men were given employment. Relief committees were also established, and over three millions received separate rations. Cooking utensils were provided, for many of the needy held very primitive ideas with regard to the preparation of food, and so the famine was relieved. Partisan Irish writers say with an accustomed lack of veracity, that this was an artificial famine, caused by England, and ignore the fact that Ireland received more aid from England than Scotland, also suffering.

Queen Victoria proclaimed a day of fasting and prayer; subscription lists were opened, and British citizens from all over the world sent contributions for relief. The sum raised by Britain exclusively was over a million pounds, of which Ireland received five sixths and Scotland one sixth. Notwithstanding this generous contribution to Ireland from England, the Young Ireland party continued their abuse of England and kept on blaming her for the evils they had in a large measure brought upon themselves.

Since this famine members of the Celtic Irish race have been pouring into the United States until emigration laws have caused curtailment.

Many Celtic Irishmen fought in the Civil War, but comparatively few of this race were in America during the War of the Revolution, and some of these fought in the opposing army of England.

In a sketch of any people, their characteristics are always interesting and important. Thomas Babington Macaulay, an acknowledgeable writer and historian, comments on the characteristics of the Celtic Irish. He believes "they possess to an extraordinary degree, the power of assimilating those who dwell among them, to an extent unknown among other nations." He shows "they are imaginative, humorous, and susceptible. Passionate in everything, but without strength or solidity. The surface is seductive, but experience brings the knowledge of its instability." This deficiency, says Macaulay, "is conspicuous in their history, arts, and literature; their lyrical melodies are exquisite, and their epic poetry ridiculous bombast. As a nation they have done nothing they do not wish forgotten.

"They are attractive, brave to rashness, yet infirm of purpose, unless led by others. Their history they must trick with falsehood to render it tolerable even to themselves. They possess qualities, the moral worth of which is inestimable. In their weakness, boastings, and poor performances they are yet capable of loyal devotion to those who will lead and command them, but have not shown themselves specially devoted to persons of their own race."

Macaulay believes the Irish are distinguished by qualities which make men interesting rather than prosperous. He says they are an ardent and impetuous race, easily moved to tears or laughter, to fury or love, and that alone among the nations of northern Europe, they have the susceptibility, the vivacity, the natural turn for acting and rhetoric which are found on the shores of the Mediterranean.

Froude's opinion of Celtic Ireland is that had she "but fought as England fought, she would have been mistress of her own destinies and in a successful struggle for freedom, would have developed qualities which would have made her worthy of possessing it . . . yet Ireland would neither resist courageously, nor would she honorably submit, and there never was a time when there was not an abundance of Irish who would make common cause with the English when there was a chance of revenge upon a domestic enemy, or a chance merely of spoil to be distributed. . . . Their insurrections are disfigured by crimes, assassinations, and secret tribunals. . . . They irritated England into severities which gave their accusations a show of color."

Perhaps the opinion of a Catholic on his own countrymen might be of some interest. The Rt. Hon. Sir James O'Connor says, "He is a loyal son of the church [Catholic], intellectually convinced of its truth, yielding to it the most implicit obedience," etc. This historian, devoted to his people, speaks feelingly of the many virtues he has observed in the Irish people and mentions a lovely charity, fidelity to the home, good nature, good temper, courage, and loyalty to friends, which, he believes, makes them a very desirable people to live among. He then discusses some Irish failings which, he thinks, may be attributed to political life. "A lack of truthfulness," O'Connor thinks, is a predominant failing, and he continues, "The teaching of a love of truth has but little place in Ireland, and the standard of public opinion on the subject is exceedingly low."

Nassau Senior holds precisely the same opinion on the

lack of Irish veracity. We read in this author's Journal, "The Anglican and Presbyterian ministers enforce the virtues which produce prosperity in the world, thrift, diligence, and carefulness. The Roman Catholic priest—an ascetic by his faith, and still more by his profession—preaches contempt of worldly goods, and worldly pleasures, and dwells on the austerities, and the contributions which are to be rewarded with happiness hereafter."

O'Connor points out the intellectual roguery of his countrymen with its by-products of individual lying and dishonesty. Senator Douglas, a prominent Sinn Fein senator, remarked in the senate (Nov. 26, 1924) "that when he was in the United States recently, he found the reputation of Irish traders for keeping contracts was just as bad as it could possibly be," and Mr. Kevin O'Higgins, in an address before the Catholic Truth Society in October, 1923, said: "They were not Catholics in the measure to be expected—an unquestionable mixture and brigandage in one quarter, and a deplorable amount of grabber and gombeen morality on the other. If public men were churchgoers, excellent in private life, but had no political morality, how was the community to fare?"

An Irish statesman, Lord Clare, attorney-general, has accused the people of mendacity, dependent on concealment of evidence, and their own historian accuses them of dealing in "artfully altered news." The Irish attorney-general also said, "The Irish try to drown the voice of truth, by loud and confident assertion."

Would any one of us concede that a leaning towards mendacity could be caused by political contacts alone? Is not the truthful character the product of religious and secular training in childhood? If this ethical concept is not planted in early life, can it ever come to fruition? Is it not true that an absence of truth and honesty in any character is a very serious defect? That punctual attendance at church and the observance of rites and ceremonies fall far short of developing an exalted ethical sense and moral outlook on life, which makes the individual possessor of such qualities respected and honored for his integrity and value to the community, and places him on a higher level than the possessor of intellect or mere ability alone?

The Englishman, like the Scotch, prides himself on being able to say his "word is as good as his bond," surely a finer ideal than the motto of the Sinn Feiners, "For ourselves alone."

Sir James O'Connor points out another outstanding characteristic of the Celtic Irishman, which is vanity. The Irish Celt, ignorant of his own national history, will dilate on his nation of saints and scholars, and the culture of his people, when other nations were barbarians. He will dilate on his royal descent from one or several kings and so on. It is true that for a period of about two hundred and fifty years, Ireland really was a center of religious light and learning; but it was also true that in spite of clerical enlightenment, the masses remained rude and utterly ignorant. The Irish, we learn, are addicted to politics, politics that is distinct from statesmanship, and they believe themselves possessed of an intellectual superiority over others, who have furnished vastly better records. We learn, also from O'Connor, that the Irish are fluent speakers, and from the same source, that they present a "parasitic mind, quickly absorbing and emitting information but not necessarily possessing a power of discrimination, or of distinguishing between right and wrong; nor are they specially adept at drawing correct inferences from data at hand."

The above criticisms are those of an Irishman of his

own race; opinions of others on this subject must be formed from observation. Certain it is that a critic who alludes to any fault or failing of the Irish, must be prepared for the most violent abuse. Lord Clare, for instance, who dealt in facts, holding the mirror up to nature, was past forgiveness and even his dead body was abused and insulted. Daniel O'Connell, on the other hand, who gloried in extravagances of speech and attributed every virtue, grace, and glory that ever existed to the Irish, was worshiped, though the cabins on his estate were hovels without a pane of glass in the windows, and the swarms of people existing on his land were clad in rags and tatters.

O'Connor has also said: "The adulation which the Irish have been pouring on their country, and on one another, is almost incredible. A stream of sickening flattery has flowed without ceasing from pulpit, platform, and press." Kevin O'Higgins said: "We have been so stunned by the discovery that we are not better than any other races, that there has been a stampede from national vanity to national cynicism." The national vanity of Ireland has been a frequent topic of discussion by many nations, even those who were quite friendly toward the Irish. Another very serious defect of the race under discussion is an intolerance of the opinions and rights of others, coupled with an unforgiving spirit and a tendency toward vindictiveness. Perhaps these latter traits, with a somewhat unsteady veracity, may account for the violent and unceasing torrents of abuse which have been rained on England. In Ireland's campaign of vilification of England, the latter has been accused of lascivious practices, cowardice, treachery, inhumanity, etc. English literature was said to be a combination of filth and paganism and so on and on.

As a matter of fact England compares favorably with

other nations and is far ahead of most of them in ethics and altruism.   There is scarcely a civilized country that has not paid tributes of the most elevated character to English standards of justice, her sense of right, and other highly moral qualities.   Emerson, for instance, had a very high opinion of England.   Cavour said England is one of the greatest nations that has done honor to humanity; our Ambassador Page, Signor Nitti, and many others have given similar testimony.

It is undoubtedly true that many, perhaps most, of the evils from which Ireland suffered, she brought upon herself though she unhesitatingly and without examination blamed England for them all.

If the people were encouraged to breed like rabbits, and emigration was prevented, who was to blame?   And so when a wet season came destroying the harvests or the blight fell from heaven on the potato crops, Heaven could not be punished, but perhaps England might.   Again if greedy workmen placed such obstacles in the way of industrialists that factories could not be established, or if started could not carry on, and the people were poor and needy and miserable, of course it could only be the fault of England.   And if farms were reduced by the tenants' insistence on subletting, until farms were reduced to the size of a good-sized tablecloth, and the farmer was too ignorant and indolent to properly cultivate the ground and the yield was small, whose fault was it?

And now with regard to religious persecution.   In the reign of Elizabeth the war carried on in Ireland was not because of religion but because of the rebellions one after another against the authority of the Queen.   The pope had planted his banner in the dominions of Elizabeth, and absolved the people from their allegiance to her so Britain determined to conquer the rebels, and she did.   At the same time Roman Catholic chapels and churches were increasing in numbers and there was no persecution of the religion, although the Catholics complained as usual.

During the reigns of the Stuarts the Catholics were, as a rule, favored, especially during the reigns of Charles I, Charles II, and James II, while the lives of the Dissenting bodies were rendered almost intolerable by persecution of different kinds, so that at a very early period they began emigrating to America.

Then came the rebellion and massacres of 1641 when the Celtic Irish tried to exterminate the colonists root and branch, and brought upon themselves the punishment of Cromwell. The abuse of Cromwell must have reached high heaven, and what was it but a red herring drawn across the trail of their own savage atrocities towards the unarmed colonists, thus diverting notice from the one hundred fold greater cruelties they had perpetrated? Unlike the Irish Cromwell kept within the letter of the law, while the Celts were a law unto themselves.

Regarding the complaints of the destruction of woolen manufactures, these were not in the hands of Catholics at all, but carried on almost entirely by the Presbyterians.

Denunciations of England were heard again when destruction of life and property in Ireland and wild lawlessness was the order of the day, and Coercion Acts were placed upon the statute book to defend the more peaceful and law-abiding citizens. Great Britain was assailed as usual for her restrictive legislation, and howls of rage echoed round the world. And Britain received no gratitude when she did not retaliate in kind, and show the hateful cruelties practiced on helpless beasts as well as on human kind, which rendered her restrictive Criminal Acts necessary. Had the world been cognizant of the mutilations and tortures suffered by unoffending animals and helpless human beings, surely the world would have judged accordingly.[1]

The delay of Catholic Emancipation until 1829 was because of the falsehood and treachery which the Catholics had manifested towards the Protestants and which actually was the reason why it was thought a very risky thing to grant the long-delayed legislation.

Catholic Emancipation and the Attitude of Protestants Towards the Granting of This Power

The policy of Great Britain in Ireland affected similarly Catholic and Protestant. With regard to religion, the Presbyterian Dissenters suffered a great deal more than did the Roman Catholics. It is true, the penal laws remained upon the statute book, a humiliating fact, but actually the body affected suffered little from them, and viceroys from the castle while urging the observance of the penal laws, in private advised that the same laws should be ignored. Throughout the greater part of the Stuart reigns, the Catholics were favored while the Dissenters were plagued by irritating and restrictive tests, besides being persecuted by the prelates of the Established Church, who again and again pressed laws against the Presbyterians which should have applied also to the Catholics, but were not. During the reigns of George I, II, and III much was done for the Roman Catholics by Parliament, and still more was attempted. Practically from the be-

---

[1] It would be easy to see in the Irish character a blend of the Dr. Jekyll and Mr. Hyde fantasy, for among them are found those of charming personality, gracious, entertaining, generous, affectionate, obliging, sympathetic, and helpful to others, while some show a love of domination and a tendency towards cupidity and selfishness with little consideration for the opinions of others. Alas, we are all human.

ginning of the reign of George III, relaxation was being made in the penal laws, and the Catholics were admitted step by step not only to political power, but by the Emancipation Act of 1829 they were placed on a footing of equal civic equality with Protestants. As far back as 1791, the Belfast Presbyterians, through their denominational representatives, had asked for a complete removal of all Catholic disabilities, but the Irish House of Commons, less tolerant, and less enlightened than the petitioners, had refused. The Anglican prelates in Parliament were definitely opposed to Catholic Emancipation; nevertheless a Catholic Relief Bill was enacted in 1793, which annulled the disabilities affecting land ownership; Catholics were enfranchised, they were permitted to qualify for the magistracy, to carry arms, to act as grand jurors, hold commissions in the army and navy, qualify for civil appointments, and made eligible for entrance to Trinity College and the College of Physicians and Surgeons.

At a still earlier period the Presbyterian Volunteers had met in the Presbyterian church at Dungannon, that is, in 1783, when delegates from 272 companies composed almost entirely of Presbyterians, the chief speaker being the Rev. Robert Black, a Presbyterian clergyman, passed resolutions, prepared by Grattan, which were carried with only two dissenting voices. It was resolved, "That we hold the right of private judgment in matters of religion, to be equally sacred in others as in ourselves : that as men and as Irishmen, as Christians and as Protestants, we rejoice in the relaxation of the penal laws against our Roman Catholic brethren fellow subjects, and that we conceive the measure to be fraught with the happiest consequences to the Union and prosperity of the inhabitants of Ireland." Among the delegates were two Presbyterian clergymen and one Anglican clergyman, both of whom warmly supported the resolution. The attitude and action of such a large representative body in the very center of Protestant Ulster had a profound effect on public opinion, and was endorsed by leading gentry and by other Protestants in the province.

Undoubtedly Catholic Emancipation would have been granted long before 1829 but for the behavior of the Catholics themselves, for their conduct had been such that the public in general felt that power could not be safely trusted in their hands.

Pitt, who was a broad and liberal minded man, had hesitated for he was well aware of the deep and far-reaching belief against the trustworthiness of Roman Catholics in a Protestant government, because of their divided allegiance. To set doubts at rest, and to be able to answer the critics, Pitt wrote to the universities of Sorbonne, Douay, Louvain, Salamanca, and Alcala on the question at issue, and received reassurances from them. There was, however, a condition attached to the privileges to be granted though they were not such as a person of normal Christian ethics could object to. The conditions were abjuring the principle that a heretic could be murdered, declaring that wrong was not excused by being done for the good of the church; and it was provided that no injury should be done to the Established Church. These conditions indicate the prevailing opinion held of Catholic ethics and conduct.

An objection made by some critics was that the church in question had repeatedly set expediency above moral principle, besides glorifying its infallibility and intolerance, when the latter was possible. According to a Jesuit named Schrader, the pope in 1856 had condemned a Spanish law which tolerated other forms of worship, and in 1848, a papal concession to its own state made it a condition that non-Catholics should not have the franchise.[1] Up to 1796, a Roman Catholic bishop, on his consecration, took an oath, "Hereticos persequor et impugnabo."

The bill for emancipation of the Catholic abolished the Oath of Supremacy and the declaration against transubstantiation. The Test and Corporation Acts of Charles II which excluded Dissenters from offices of trust and prominence, unless they communicated according to the forms of the Established Church, were repealed in 1780.

The first important step towards the abolition of the penal code occurred in 1778, though we are told the entire Catholic system in Ireland had its existence in connivance, and this denomination, generally speaking, was unmolested in spite of the loudness and frequency of their complaints. However it is a fact that such positions as the magistracy and the legal profession were closed to them, nor were they eligible to administrative positions.

The demand of Ulster Presbyterians in 1778 for Catholic Emancipation was renewed in 1783 and again in 1792 when full emancipation was demanded.

The concessions granted to the Catholics were strongly opposed by almost all the bishops, by Lord Charlemont, and by Flood. Opposition came also from the king and the English cabinet, and from these men came secret instructions to organize resistance to the measure and to kindle an anti-Catholic feeling in Ireland. It will be remembered that in 1784 the Presbyterians or Ulster Volunteers had presented an address on the extension of political rights to Catholics to Lord Charlemont, but this statesman was opposed to Catholic suffrage.

---

[1] Even in the past century, between 1848 and 1853, the United States withdrew its minister accredited to the Holy See, because the Vatican refused to allow a Protestant church to be built in Rome.

VI

RELIGIOUS WARS

Misrule and inefficiency in government, with resulting discontent
and agitation—Parliamentary reform earnestly desired—Ireland left defenseless; her troops removed to fight on foreign
fields—Reforms demanded at Dungannon including emancipation of Catholics—Volunteer Association formed—Catholics remain unfriendly in spite of the fraternal gestures
made in Mid-Ulster—Catholics murder a whole family at
Forkhill, a priest removed by his bishop on account of the
crime—Protestants fraternize with Catholics in order to
have their help in working for reforms so badly needed—
Society of United Irishmen formed to include all citizens on
a basis of equality, but anarchy and terrorism spreads, and
Protestants fear for their lives; the effort to secure reform
develops into a religious war in the south led by priests, and
Protestants are murdered singly and in batches—Vinegar
Hill and Scullabogue barn attain a bad preëminence for the
murders there committed—Irish ideas in the ascendant in
Wexford; the assassins daily blessed by the priests before
setting out to plunder, burn, and slay.

TOWARDS the end of the eighteenth century
the misrule and inefficiency of the government
had increased the discontent and unrest of the
people. The Presbyterians were still shut out by law
from civil, military, and municipal offices. Practically all
positions of importance were in the hands of Englishmen,
notably administration of the executive and judicial
branches of the government, and the religion of the officeholders was that of the Established Church, although the
members of this denomination composed only one twelfth
of the population; and the wide-awake citizens of the

country saw their government absolutely in the hands of members of the Anglican faith who were large owners of land, and interested most in matters relating exclusively to their own affairs. At the time of the Union, about the beginning of the nineteenth century, more than sixty seats were in the hands of three families, and one half of the House of Commons was made up of a small group who used their offices for public plunder, and with rare exception the notorious fact was known that every man had his price, and the price, too, could be guessed quite accurately. Naturally, abuses of various kinds went uncorrected, and those who should have taken such matters under consideration were surfeited with bribes, preferments, pensions, and titles to leave the people's business alone in the interests of the purchaser.

It was members of this purchased fraternity who were advisers to the Lord Lieutenant, and it is not difficult to imagine the character of the aid a confiding executive would receive from such men, and yet it was these very persons who were practically the governors of the country. No wonder Ireland was considered the worst governed country in Europe, and it would have been still worse but for the fact that the Irish Parliament was subordinate to the English Privy council, and the tyranny of the chosen few in the Irish Parliament was subject to the check-rein held by England.

Grattan once said it had been the deliberate object of the English government by systematic corruption to give the monarch a power which the Constitution never intended; to make the king in Parliament everything and the people nothing, and thus to render absolutely abortive the Parliamentary rights that had been nominally conceded. And Grattan continued to say, "This attempt to regain by corruption what had been lost in prerogative was the true cause of the disaffection which had become so formidable. England had agreed to the independence of the Irish Parliament, and then had created a multitude of offices to make that independence an idle name."

The incorruptible Grattan also said that the Irish distraction towards the end of the eighteenth century was "due to the conduct of the servants of the government, endeavoring to establish by unlimited bribery, absolute power; and that the system of coercion was a necessary consequence of the system of corruption."

These are some of the reasons why Parliamentary Reform was so urgently desired by the Dissenters, and shows why, when England turned a deaf ear to the just requests of the northern settlers, a number of them decided to work for equal rights and privileges with their fellow countrymen. The mother country had again adopted the policy of playing one race and creed against the other, lest they should combine against herself, and in the north the feeling against the whole venal policy was very strong.

The country was without military protection, and in imminent danger of invasion by some enemy with whom England was at war. Under the circumstances it is not surprising that a volunteer association for the protection of the country sprang into existence, receiving its initiation in Belfast. The organization was entirely Protestant, and the movement quickly became popular. Two companies were enrolled on St. Patrick's Day, with the Rev. James Bryson, a Presbyterian minister, as chaplain. The movement grew rapidly, and in the closing years of the century was said to number 100,000 men.

Members of the organization came together to discuss political grievances, and in 1778 they met in Dungannon and again in 1783 at the same place. Here resolutions were passed demanding various reforms. One of these resolutions favored an independent Irish Parliament, which was conceded and tried for eighteen years, but unfortunately independence did not bring freedom from corruption. Other resolutions demanded concessions to Catholics including Catholic Emancipation.

In 1779 Ireland found herself without defense except what was given by these Volunteers. The men were loyal to the government and won undying praise for their bravery and prompt, intelligent, and efficient action. In 1796 the British navy again failed to afford protection to the northern colony, and a French fleet lay for a week in an Irish bay and only tempestuous weather prevented an attack.

The Volunteers for some time had existed in independent bodies and now efforts were made to form a union among the companies, which were found at this time to number 40,000 men. According to Hamilton the numbers in the companies grew rapidly and a later census showed 100,000 men; this large body of volunteers were practically all Presbyterians and though a loyal body, they decided to ask for the removal of trade and other restrictions under which they had so long labored. Demands were voiced for free trade, with free import and export in trade with foreign countries, which requests the mother country could not now refuse. Legislative independence for Ireland was secured, and a demand made for the full emancipation of Catholics. The latter demand when made in 1792 had caused great astonishment for the Catholics were the recognized foes of Protestants. "It is curious," writes Lord Sheffield, "to observe one fifth or one sixth of a nation, in possession of all the power and property in the country, eager to communicate that power to the remaining four fifths, which would, in effect, transfer it from themselves."

A second and treasonable body of Volunteers was formed in Dublin two years after the original northern body was established, but was refused recognition by the original body. The new Volunteers were arming themselves in spite of the law and had even sent an invitation to the French to enter Ireland. The Volunteers of Northern Ireland retained their original character, and their president was Lord Charlemont. In 1779 Ireland had no defense whatever except what her Ulster Volunteers afforded; and this body sent a request through their president, Lord Charlemont, asking that the right of voting be extended to the Catholics. Lord Charlemont, however, did not favor this measure. The Dissenters desired a real representative government.

The friendly and liberal attitude of the Protestants towards their Roman Catholic fellow countrymen met with no response, and the concessions granted to the latter seemed to stimulate the spirit of antagonism and hatred. Concessions to them were apparently regarded as weakness, and still more were desired. The Catholics now assumed a threatening attitude. Protestants were to be exterminated, and Ireland was to be their own again.

The Celtic Catholic attitude towards those of a different religious denomination is illustrated by an occurrence at Forkhill, near Dundalk. A philanthropist named Jackson had died in 1787 leaving property which he ordered to be used for the purpose of educating children of members of the Established Church in various trades, and settling them on the estate in small holdings. There was no eviction of former occupants, but some park and waste lands had been reclaimed and occupied by industrious families of the same religious denomination as the donor. The old residents remained in their former possessions, and were even given an abatement of rent, amounting to one hundred and seventeen pounds. The old residents, however, in the vicinity resolved to drive the Protestants out, and brought Defenders from other sections of the country, and so terrorized the Protestant families that only a few of them were left behind. The school, however, remained in a fairly flourishing condition in spite of a long series of outrages. The schoolmaster in charge was a worthy man named Berkeley, who, in the year 1791, was attacked by a gang of Celtic Catholic cutthroats, about forty or fifty in number, who forced their way into his home, stabbed him repeatedly, cut out his tongue, cut off his fingers, and then mangled his wife, and mutilated his son, a boy of thirteen years of age. No reason was given for the cowardly outrage, except that the schoolmaster was a respected leader in the new colony. On completion of their bloody work the gang marched triumphantly along the public highway, holding lighted torches in their hands, knowing the sentiment of the residents in the neighborhood was in sympathy with the dastardly work just performed.

For particulars of this crime, see a letter from the Rev. Mr. Hudson to Francis Dobbs, Jan. 29, 1791, in the Charlemont MSS.; also Musgrave's *Rebellion in Ireland,* pp. 59, 63. For account of schools, see Charlemont MSS. Irish Academy. Colonel Verner, one of the military leaders, said, "The declaration of Berkeley's torturers that this was what all his sort might expect, was the chief cause of the hostility manifested towards Catholics in the north, during the insurrection there."

A parish priest at Forkhill was removed by his bishop, because of his participation in the outrage on the schoolmaster and his family.

In spite of general unrest, agitation, and dissatisfaction the country was showing an advance in material prosperity. Lord Clare, the attorney general, said in 1798, referring to the preceding twenty years, "There is not a nation in the habitable globe, which has advanced in cultivation, commerce, agriculture, and manufactures with the same rapidity in the same period." Unhappily, material prosperity with political and religious concessions could not prevent complaint and a mounting discontent. Northern Ireland had warmly sympathized with America in her struggle for independence which her Peep of Day Boys, Steel-boys, and others of their kindred had done so much to win, and they now, in Belfast, celebrated the anniversary of the French Revolution, for the sentiment of Edmund Burke and the opinions of the people of Northern Ireland varied widely.

Lord Westmoreland observes, "The tendency of these Dissenters is to unite with the Catholics," and he continues, "the union would be very formidable."

In 1791 Wolfe Tone founded at Belfast the society of United Irishmen, and with him were associated Thomas Russell, Lord Edward Fitzgerald, Thomas Addis Emmet, Arthur O'Connor, Napper Tandy, Henry Joy Mac-Cracken, founder of the first Sabbath School in Belfast, and others. The leaders were almost all Protestants, and the agitation was said to run high among the Presbyterians, with the tendency on their side towards a Catholic alliance. Lecky thought that a republican form of government was favored by Ulster Presbyterians which was in accord with their form of worship, but the obvious fact remains that Ulster Presbyterians had suffered more, much more, political and religious disabilities than even the Catholics of the south. The woolen trade and the linen trade, ruined by England, had been in the hands of Presbyterian manufacturers and workers. Dissenters in Ulster had suffered greater hardships and persecution because of their religious beliefs than had the Celtic Catholics, whose religion had always received legal recognition and who were greatly favored during the Stuart reigns. The Test Act which had so long plagued Presbyterians was but recently abolished. Disabling acts had interfered with their representation in Parliament and their entrance into state and civil service, and tithes in support of a persecuting Anglican Church were exacted from them as well as from Catholics.

Notwithstanding, industry and self-denial had brought Ulster a measure of prosperity; she belonged to the Anglo-Saxon race, and set a value on the British bond of union. Ulster had been harshly treated, but self-relying and self-respecting as she was, her object was to achieve real political reform.

The avowed object of the society of United Irishmen in Belfast was, "the purpose of forwarding a brotherhood of affection, a communion of rights, and a union of power, among Irishmen of every religious persuasion, and thereby to obtain a complete reform in the legislature founded on the principles of civil, political, and religious liberty."

The men at the head of the United Irish movement were progressive enthusiastics, interested in much-needed political and other reforms. Catholics were made welcome as members, and the organization became diluted with men of the Defender and Whiteboy type until at the nether end of the body fanatics and blood-stained criminals found a place.

Londonderry was also a center of revolutionary spirit. The objective of the United Irish Society was perfectly legal in the early part of its history but gradually changed with the years and it was finally suppressed in 1794; and when reconstructed twelve months later, became actually treasonable.

The agitation beginning in the north, spread to other
parts of the country, especially the east and south, where
the populace was urged to join the United Irishmen, not
for parliamentary reform, a subject which was of no
interest to them, but in order to get rid of rent and tithes
and to acquire their neighbor's property, and at the same
time get rid of their Protestant neighbors.

It was reported that United Irishmen had instituted
a system of terrorism in the country. Magistrates and
others were intimidated, houses were robbed, and no one
dared to give evidence against the thieves. Assassination
Clubs were said to be formed, and witnesses to crimes were
murdered. "The Protestants in Antrim," writes a magistrate, "are in a most horrid panic about the United people
rising. They absolutely dare not go to bed at night, and
never without a watch. They tell me plainly every night
they expect to be murdered." Lord Castlereagh also mentions "the infernal system which prevailed of murdering
witnesses." There is evidence that the murder of Lord
Carhampton by his servant Dunn, who had long been a
member of the household, was discussed in a baronial
committee.

There is no doubt the assassinations and other criminal
acts were not approved by the leaders of the Association,
but men of the Defender and Whiteboy type are a law
unto themselves, and were beyond control.

Grattan said, "The irritation in Ulster would never have
reached its height, but for the flagrant corruption of the
Irish Parliament, and the obstinate resistance of the government to the most moderate reform." He showed the
policy of the government to be lawmaking in the spirit of
law breaking. Lecky says, "It is difficult to believe that
some compromise might not have been devised, so long as
the chief seat of disaffection was the province in which

an intelligent, industrious Protestant population predominated."

Anarchy was spreading in the north, and a system was instituted by the government of arresting men and carrying them off to the fleet without even a show of trial. Some Protestant districts were proclaimed by the Insurrection Act. Grattan indignantly protested this government action in the north, and asked, "Who are the people whom the ministers attaint of treason, and consign to military execution? They are the men who placed William III on the throne of this kingdom. The government have declared they will persist in proscribing Catholics, and they now consign the Protestants to military execution."

"The character of the people who inhabit the north of Ireland," said Fox, "has been severely stigmatized . . . it is said these men are of the old leaven. They are indeed of the old leaven, that rescued the country from the tyranny of Charles I, and James II, the leaven which kneaded the British Constitution."

In the south Protestants were being murdered. Forged Orange oaths were pasted on chapel doors in order to force the people into taking part in the revolt. The condition of a large part of the country would have been disgraceful even in a semi-civilized state.

Martial law was proclaimed in Ulster, where a state of terrorization was instituted and cruelties practiced, which, happily, have been surpassed but rarely in modern history. Property was destroyed, women outraged, and victims died under the lash, the common soldiers instituting their own punishments, under the command of General Lake.

Villages in Ulster were left desolate, the inhabitants fleeing for their lives from Lake's men. The drastic punitive measures exercised by General Lake in the north were incomparably more unjust and severe than those adopted by Cromwell in punishment of the murderers of 1641. Oliver kept within the letter of the law, frowned on the destruction of private property, and protected from violation the chastity of women, yet the name of Cromwell is held up to detestation, while the barbarous cruelties of General Lake have gone unnoticed; the latter also punished the innocent with the guilty, a wrong which Cromwell was careful to avoid.

The drastic punishment visited on Ulster, was because that province was the one most dreaded by the government. Britain knew her Ulster colony had been treated more harshly than the settlements in America which but recently had successfully resisted her authority.

Lake's action in the north increased the animosity of class and creed resulting in the transformation of lukewarm sympathizers to ardent supporters of the rebels. The Catholic and the Protestant viewpoint always differed radically, but were now temporarily united.

Marked disapproval of the action Britain had taken in the north was felt by the ruling classes in Ireland. The Duke of Leinster protested against the proclamation of martial law in Ulster by resigning his command of the Kildare militia, Lord Ballomore resigned his command of the Cavan militia, and Grattan resigned from the yeomanry because of it. It is interesting to notice some of the inconsistencies presented by the mother country in her treatment of Irish rebels. Her attitude towards the loyal and disloyal in Ulster has been the subject of comment. Now she presents political preferments to those who had stirred up strife in Parliament and urged on the revolution. A leading rebel, Lord Moira, was presented with the governorship of India, while the man whose work for England has rarely been equaled and never surpassed, the attorney-general, Lord Clare, she scarcely noticed, because he had deeply wounded the vanity of the people by showing them up in their true colors, and he was left like Cromwell to the vengeance of his enemies.

The Revolutionary Committee of the United Irishmen, working in dark and devious ways, continued its work of theft and murder without detection or punishment. The infirm government was aware of the machinations of the insurgents but was too feeble to interfere knowing its militia was corrupt and unreliable; even the army could not be depended on, and the Catholics held a wholesome fear for no one but the Orangemen. The Irish statesmen responsible for the condition of the country were well acquainted wtih the steps taken by the fomenters of rebellion, but hesitated to employ restrictive measures. They were profoundly affected by the behavior of Orangemen, but tried to avoid irritating Catholics by engaging the services of the loyal and efficient Orangemen. "The Orange combination," said Lord Camden, "was not aimed against the law but they irritated the Catholics and gave a pretence to the disaffected." Distrust of the militia was so great that permission was given to raise companies of yeomanry, upon whom dependence might be placed.

The conduct of the Irish statesmen of this period with their knowledge of the contemplated rebellion is far from edifying. They were filled with indignation at the disorderly conduct of Orangemen, while they feared to notice the violence and murders of the Catholics. In Irish debates of 1796, we learn that the conduct of Orangemen had been generally speaking justified. A disturbance between Orangemen and Catholics had occurred in Armagh in the county of an M.P. named Venner. Speaking of the occurrence in Parliament, Mr. Venner said, "If the Orangemen had come in contact with Catholics in

Armagh, the Catholics were themselves to blame." They had been robbing Protestants of their arms, in order to murder them. Under a pretense of making a peace they had attacked the Protestants. Of those who had fled from the country, many had been concerned in outrages, and were afraid of arrest. The Orangemen had been accused of many crimes. They had not threatened the lives of magistrates, or destroyed cattle or burnt the houses of those who had attempted to enforce the law. In some instances they had acted improperly, but not until they had been goaded beyond the endurance of human nature." The speaker said, "Orangemen had not interfered with Catholics, until the latter began to arm themselves in defiance of the law, and Protestants had learned from bitter experience what Catholic fanatics can do to unarmed Protestants." Because of turbulence and general insecurity, the Orange organizations offered their services to the government but these were not accepted, for the very name of Orangemen had been so vilified by their enemies, the viceroy, though convinced of Orange loyalty and efficiency, was afraid to employ Orange service.

The Orangemen, however, organized in self-defense. They had been forced to turn their homes into arsenals in order to protect their families from a treacherous and cruel enemy. Lord Camden held proofs of Irish rebel correspondence with France, and a list of the names of the men who constituted the Assassination Committee and the committee of the Revolution. He was greatly in need of loyal men, yet while convinced of the dependability of the Orangemen he dreaded irritating the Catholics by employing them as the latter were largely in the majority. A speech of the attorney-general, Lord Clare, a man of superlative ability, gives a vivid picture of the disturbed state of the country. Lord Clare accuses Lord Moira, a leading Catholic rebel, of falsehood, deceit, and of misleading the English Parliament with regard to the treatment Irish malcontents had received.

Lord Clare said: "It remains for me publicly and distinctly to refute the foul and injurious charges of tyranny and injustice which have been advanced against the government and Parliament of Ireland. *It has long been the fashion of this country to drown the voice of truth by loud and confident assertion."* The futility of conciliation was pointed out. "If conciliation be the pledges of tranquillity, there is not a nation in Europe in which it has had so fair a trial. Concession and conciliation has produced only a fresh stock of grievances, and the discontent of Ireland has kept pace with her prosperity." The speaker then showed how "the opening of trade in 1779 was followed in 1782 by demands for political change and how the Commons had promised the king that now no question could arise to disturb the national harmony." Pointing to the short-lived harmony, the attorney-general mentions a "succession of bills, one sent at the point of the sword, ending with appeals for the Volunteers to resume arms, and an outcry made for favor to Catholics, in which for the first time a great body of Protestant Dissenters joined, and Catholic emancipation and reform went forth as the watchwords of innovation and treason. . . . The noble lord who imputes Irish disaffection to a system of coercion, will please to recollect that the system of midnight robberies and avowed rebellion was completely established before any coercive statute was enacted here. In 1792 and 1793, the project of levying a revolutionary army had been formed. Soldiers were forthcoming in abundance. I will tell the noble lord the conspiracy has been disclosed by evidence the most clear and satisfactory by the testimony of gentlemen of rank and character, some of them at this moment high in military command in the king's service. If there be ground of censure of Parliament it is that the vigor was not proportionate to the magnitude and extent of the evil. Every man accused by the brotherhood of loyalty was stripped of his arms. If he presumed to defend himself he was murdered. In 1796, the Insurrection Act was passed. The United Irish combination was a complete revolutionary government organized against the law. Has the noble lord heard of the murders perpetrated by order of the Irish Union for the crime of putting the law into execution? Has he heard of the murder of Mr. Butler, a clergyman and a magistrate? Of Mr. Hamilton, a clergyman and magistrate? Of Mr. Cummings, whose crime was that he enrolled in the yeomanry corps? Of Col. St. George and his host Mr. Uniak? Of the two dragoons who discovered to their officers an attempt to seduce them and were murdered? In a word, has he heard of the numberless atrocious deeds of massacre and assassination which form part of the system of the Irish brotherhood, and are encouraged by the privileged order of innovators? I hold the dark and bloody catalogue, but I will not proclaim to the civilized world, the state of cannibal barbarism to which my unhappy country has been brought by these pestilent and cowardly traitors, these injured innocents who deal in robbery, conflagration, and murder, and scatter terror and desolation over the face of this devoted country. What alternative has been left to the Executive Government, but to surrender at discretion to a horde of traitorous barbarians, or to use the force entrusted to it for self-defense and self-preservation?"

Well history shows how poorly informed England has always been on the question of Ireland and her internal affairs. How she swallows the stories of her foes and permits the wool to be pulled over her eyes. She conciliates and bestows honors and emoluments on the disloyal and gives her friends the cold shoulder, and the Irish have always bitterly hated those who have told them the truth about themselves, while heaping honors and gratitude on those who paint them in colors not their own, provided those colors are of the required shade.

Lord Blayrey wrote, "The yeomanry of the north are your sheet anchor. Were it not for the confidence the United Irishmen have in the militia, matters would not have gone the length they have. . . . Among the observations I have made, the Roman Catholics alone have universally been guilty of robbery and murder." Lord Blayrey was one of the military commanders. Orangemen received permission to enroll in the district corps, and some of them entered the yeomanry.

At the time the attorney-general made his famous speech, Whiteboys were disarming Protestants, who were also being disarmed in Meath and King's County, and the plan adopted by the legislature for controlling lawlessness was more concilation, and more concessions, while there was great and well-grounded fear for the lives of Protestants scattered throughout the country, for with the United Irishmen leading the army of liberty there was no respect for law or order, nor any protection for life and property. In Parliament, the question was asked, "Of what benefit were the concessions granted to Catholics? for their turbulence seemed to increase with every concession."

Lord Camden, succeeding the recalled Fitzwilliam as viceroy, received a letter from the Duke of Portland who wrote, "The favorable disposition of the government to the Catholic pretensions must have tended to dispirit and enervate the Protestants in general," and he then goes on to enumerate a number of other concessions which could be made to the Catholic majority. England was again disposed to shower benefits on her enemies and left her friends to be rewarded by their conscience. It was said, "the magistrates had learned by centuries of experience that those who were loyal to Britain in her time of trouble, could expect no support when her attempts at coercion were followed by acts of conciliation."

The onset of the rebellion was fixed to take place May 23, 1798. Ulster, where the conspiracy was most dreaded, remained quiet for two weeks after the rebellion began. Skirmishes took place at various places throughout other provinces. The conspiracy had departed entirely from its original plan, that of fraternity and equality. It was now an insurrection and religious war. Every day brought an account of bloody savageries. Two magistrates were killed in open day in Kildare, with a group of workmen looking calmly on the murderers. The Orange lodges offered their services but the ears of England had been so poisoned against Orangemen, the viceroy was afraid to employ them. At the same time the insurgent chiefs pursued their plans without interference. The yeomanry could be trusted but as yet lacked military training. Portland, writing to the viceroy said, "I heard yesterday that the Orange Association in Ulster has been joined by all the principal gentry in that province, for the purpose of protecting themselves against the United Irishmen, and that they have bound themselves by an oath, to defend the king and constitution." Yet Camden still hesitated to employ the Orangemen for "he feared it would much increase the jealousy of the Catholics," although he continued, "the Orangemen are more to be trusted with arms in either kingdom."

According to Musgrave, Armagh, Fermanagh, Derry, and Tyrone furnished 14,000 yeomen for the protection of the country, and three quarters of these were Presbyterians, most of them Orangemen, and, he continues, "in spite of the recent disaffection of the Presbyterian body, he did not know of a single case of a Presbyterian yeoman having betrayed his oath of allegiance," and it is conceded if the yeomen lacked discipline, they showed patriotic energy, ceaseless vigilance, and were ever ready to encounter bodies five and ten times as strong as their own; and it was to them, indeed, the repression of the rebellion was mainly due.

During the succeeding struggle with the rebels, the yeoman officers discovered that many of their men had been seduced, so it became obligatory to impose tests, and Catholic yeomen were thus weeded out and disarmed, after which purge, the army of the yeomanry became almost exclusively Protestant.

The trend towards a religious frenzy was very noticeable at Prosperous, a town which had become a center of cotton manufacture, and owed its prosperity to an Englishman named Brewer, who was ruthlessly murdered by men under the command of a Dr. Esmond.

Dr. Esmond was a brother of Sir Thomas Esmond of Wexford, who made himself notorious for falsehood and treachery toward his Protestant associates and his government. Dr. Esmond was an officer in the army, and had seduced his men. In friendly and intimate fashion he had dined with Captain Swayne the previous evening, after which the two men proceeded to the chapel, where Esmond exhorted the men to deliver up their arms, and professed his own loyalty. The priest, Father Higgins, exhorted the congregation to submit to lawful authority. Dr. Esmond as a Catholic spoke to them in the same tone. The peasants in seeming obedience yielded up their pikes and professed regret for their compliance to conspirators.

Esmond in the presence of the priest spoke to Swayne on the real penitence of the peasants, who, said Esmond, would lay down their arms in the street but feared the sentinels. The unsuspecting Captain Swayne then issued orders to the sentinels not to arrest people who might be seen moving around, and Esmond, having thus averted suspicion, entered Prosperous with his seduced men at two o'clock in the morning. The sentinels giving no alarm were killed, the barracks forcibly entered, and Captain Swayne stabbed while springing from his bed. All in the barracks were killed or left at the point of death. The local men and women residents, forgetting their bene-factor, Brewer, who had brought them comfort and prosperity, fell weeping in each other's arms as they cried, "Down with the heretics," and "Ireland is ours." Esmond and his murderers returned from Prosperous, where the leader reached his room without apparent suspicion; dressed, and later appeared in the ranks in his usual manner. Meanwhile a messenger came with reports that Esmond had led the attack on Prosperous some hours earlier. He was arrested, court-martialed, and hanged.

In the early part of 1798, there was a sudden and very pronounced increase in attendance at the numerous chapels, and rumors were cunningly circulated that the Catholics were to be murdered, and at the same time persistent reports were made that Protestants were to be destroyed and their churches pulled down. Quite in harmony with the attitude of Dr. Esmond towards Protestants, Catholics were taking the oath of allegiance in chapels, and at the same time were actively engaged in the manufacture of pikes. This knowledge became so general that magistrates refused to accept the oath of allegiance, unless when accompanied by a surrender of arms. The priests, of course, could not have been ignorant of this double dealing of their parishioners. They doubtless gave the deception their encouragement and blessing.

Scenes similar to those enacted at Prosperous were occurring all over the country where Protestants were found. Smoke arose from burning homesteads, and inmates who had not escaped were piked. Camden writes, "The rebels have been guilty of the most barbarous and dreadful cruelties, . . . the feelings of the country are so exasperated as scarcely to be satisfied with anything short of extirpation."

Protestants and especially clergymen were exposed to the fanaticism and atrocities of 1641. Another message from Campbell runs, "The loyal parts of the country are so indignant, that I almost tremble that their zeal will drive them to acts of retaliation." Lord Castlereagh wrote, "It is difficult to bring the rebels to action. They commit horrid cruelties, and disperse when troops appear." Dundas, who was now commanding in the army, was believed to be a traitor himself.

It was in Wexford more than anywhere else that the rebellion bore all the earmarks of a religious war. Father John Murphy placed himself at the head of a band of rebels, including women skilled in the use of firearms which they had used in duck-shooting. The followers were not concerned with political problems, but they had been taught to support their religion above everything, and to hunt down and destroy the hated heretic. That part of the Christian religion which inculcates the manifestation of love and forgiveness towards the erring was apparently unheard of, and Christ's admonition to his follower who cut off the high priest's ear went equally unnoticed. It was noticed that the houses plundered and burnt belonged to Protestants, and those who were murdered also belonged to that denomination.

The country had been placed under martial law, and the yeomen and militia armed for the protection of their homes and families. The number of men who could be relied on to defend the country was totally inadequate, and although England had been notified of the desperate condition of the minority in Ireland she showed little concern, sending a regiment of cavalry which was practically useless. The men upon whom dependence was placed for protection were so few that in a general uprising before the completion of the disarming process, the yeomen and militia would themselves be the first victims. Peremptory measures were therefore necessarily adopted with insistence on the observance of the order. The measures used did not compare with the violence suffered in Ulster during the disarming process there, though the less voluble and more reticent northerners have said much less about their disarming experiences.

Wexford had a fertile soil and was a prosperous civilized town. No Whiteboys and no Orangemen had yet invaded Wexford nor had it been in touch with the revolutionary spirit. Arthur Young believed the peasantry in Wexford superior to the natives in the south and west. A large Protestant congregation was found in the town and the different denominations had lived peaceably together, and their harbors were crowded with shipping.

At Gorey some parishes were placed under the Insurrection Act and the priest loudly complained of the insult to his harmless loyal people. The parishioners swore in the presence of Lord Mountmorris they were not United Irishmen and that they never would be, and those who took the oath included John and Michael Murphy who were filled with rebellious ideas and bigotry and in view of the Protestation the enforcement of the act mentioned was suspended for the time being. A sketch of Father

John and his activities will furnish a picture of the rising in the east. In spite of ready oaths and denials, the inhabitants were well provided with arms. Father John Murphy, a peasant's son, and a large coarse man of forty years, had recently sworn allegiance, and solemnly protested his loyalty. It was he who lighted the signal fire on Corrigua Hill to call Catholics to action. The priest and his army of pikemen soon appeared at the door of the Protestant Parson Burrows. The parson's house was fired, and he with his son and seven parishioners were piked on the lawn. The party next arrived at the palace of a heretic bishop, having fired all the Protestant homes on the way. The house was plundered and then burnt. The bishop and his family had escaped. The holy Father was now joined by brother Michael, also a priest. They marched on plundering, burning, and killing every heretic identified. They met on the way a small number of soldiers and the rebels swarming around in incredible numbers dispatched every man. Twenty priests were included in Father John's forces. At feeding time cattle were knocked senseless, and the bleeding beasts were cut up and slices from their warm bodies basted on the point of pikes. If after gorging themselves they went to sleep, they were careful to lie with their face downwards, and with their hats and shoes on, lest they should awake to find these coverings had been appropriated by a needy comrade. Humanity might be left in the background, but religion, so called, was remembered. A score of priests said mass every day, a tub of water was made holy, and with this water the rebels were sprinkled, and then sent forth to plunder, burn, and slay.

The incendiaries would sometimes stop and pray, and after battle, priests were found dead, clad in their sacerdotal vestments.

The country around Vinegar Hill was plundered, and Protestants were brought to a barn at the foot of a hill and there murdered. A few were dismissed in safety who had written protection from a priest. Gordon, a reliable authority, states that unquestionably four hundred Protestant victims perished here. The activities at Vinegar Hill were mainly directed by priests. Mass was celebrated every day, and fanaticism sustained by fiery denunciations of heretics. Piety and murder went hand in hand, and it was noticed that those most scrupulously observant of ceremonies were the most cruel and murderous. The enlightened and the unenlightened seemed to suffer from the same bloodlust, and the same passionate hate of their fellow man. The education received in early youth had borne fruit not, alas, in the region of higher ethics but in the baser qualities which some day, perhaps, will be regarded as sub-human, very close to the beast.

Scullabogue barn served as another house of detention for prisoners brought there to be murdered at leisure. The number of prisoners here has been placed at 234, who were guarded by 300 rebels. A messenger came from New Ross with orders from a priest who was fighting there, to slaughter the Protestant captives as the battle was going against the Catholics. In obedience to the priest's command fifty-seven were shot or piked, and the remainder kept inside the barn, where they had been confined through a hot summer's day, so closely packed together that they were all obliged to stand. Twenty of the number were women and children. The windmill on Vinegar Hill was kept full by gangs who scoured the country for Protestant victims. At Ringwood victims were piked on the spot. Prisoners brought in batches to the Hill were passed out to instant execution. As the windmill prison was emptied by death, it was refilled from the barn. As long as the camp existed, the bloody work continued. A large tub of water was blessed every day, and it has been expressly recorded that those most ready to serve in these executions were not the peasantry but those who had received an education. A picture is given of the gentle priest with pistols in his holster, a sword at his side, and a huge crucifix in his arms. With thousands of followers swarming around him he met two companies on the way to Wexford. The soldiers were surprised by wild yells as if from a pack of hyenas. The small number of half-trained soldiers was surrounded, the priest refused quarter, and every soldier was slain.

Some ships in the harbor were filled with men and women flying for safety to England. These were captured and returned to prison or put into an old hulk in the harbor as captives, and were afterwards drowned, although they had paid for their passage to safety.

England though notified of the desperate need for assistance in Ireland did not show any concern though she was the immediate cause of the rising, aided by the foolish Irish Parliament.

When the rebels began action in Wexford they forced Protestants into their ranks who might in some measure act as commanders but these were in a sense prisoners themselves, and dare not follow their own direction. Protestants, too, were forced at the point of the pike into chapels to become Catholic converts; no doubt some went without compulsion to prevent their own slaughter. Some liberally-minded gentlemen were offered the alternative of entering the rebel army or yielding up life.

In Ulster where a lively discontent had prevailed from 1791 to 1797, alarm and consternation prevailed at the tales of plunder, incendiarism, and murders daily taking place in the south. The Scotch-Irish had dreams of a fraternity of liberty and equality. They had asked for Catholic concessions and for equal privileges for all. Down and Antrim had sent emigrants who fought at Bunker Hill and Lexington, and in spite of the dread memory of 1641, Ulster was stunned, and Ulster remained quiet, but not before the insurrection had started. In Ulster the rebellion was confined to the centers of theoretical republicanism where the long-lived persecution of Presbyterianism was allied to the dissatisfaction engendered by the legal robbery of landlords and by commercial injustices. In the eyes of the despotic and intolerant Established Church, Dissenters were the enemy of Ireland, and this attitude influenced the opinions of the castle, for the Episcopalians, though but a fraction of the whole number of Protestants in Ireland, "could point with pride" to the large number of Englishmen among them who practically held all the important and well-paid positions, and consequently were very powerful. The Ulster insurgents had some success at first, but the massacres of Vinegar Hill and Scullabogue barn opened the eyes of northern discontents, and thousands who had hesitated rallied to the Orange standard, and northern Catholics too found the companionship of "heretics" undesirable. No party in Ireland had suffered as severely from every point of view as the Dissenters. Their ethical standards were high and their self-reliance undimmed but they realized now the unwise decision which had been made when they chose to cast their lot with their Celtic Catholic countrymen, and they returned to the allegiance that befitted the descendants of the supporters of William III and the defenders of the Maiden City. The insurrection in Ulster was confined mainly to Antrim, Down, and Derry. The "frightfulness" campaign of Lake had borne fruit, and the rebels were poorly armed and not well disciplined and so were quickly conquered. Henry Joy MacCracken and William Orr were executed; and other Protestants, remembering how they had agitated for an equality of privilege with Catholics and for Catholic Emancipation, decided they could have no partnership with disorderly Catholic mobs who plundered their victims and then murdered them. Yeomen were placed on permanent duty, and acted as patrols throughout the night, a very necessary precaution. At Omagh, 6,000 Presbyterians offered their services to the government, and the example was followed in other localities. The ranks of the Orangemen filled rapidly; large numbers of them offered to march anywhere to aid in the suppression of the rebellion. Lord Camden had been intimidated by the outcry of the Catholics and had been afraid to accept the proffered services of the Orangemen; they were now accepted without question, and it was this body with the large number of neutral Presbyterians and the yeomanry which was able to stem the first part of the insurrection in 1798 until England found it convenient to extend her assistance.

A government report states, "The Catholic atrocities caused the Presbyterians to dread Catholic ascendancy" (see Bishop Percy to his wife, May 28, 29, 1798. British Museum).

A report published in May, by the government, stated that "Catholic atrocities were hindering the Presbyterians from giving their support to the rebellion, and causing them to dread a Catholic ascendancy." Another communication said, "The north is perfectly safe, the Protestants being here in some places murdered by the Irish papists has turned all Dissenters against them. The murders of the Protestants in the south will prevent them ever joining again with them, much less in the present rebellion." (May 28, 29, 1798, British Museum.) James Dicky, one of the northern rebels who was executed, said before his death, "The eyes of the Presbyterians were opened too late; the massacres in Leinster showed that if they had overturned the Constitution they would have to contend with the papists."

Lecky states, "The rebellion in the north while comparatively short was untarnished by the cruelties and murders of the south, but was repressed with an equal ferocity and barbarity."

In a communication of Castlereagh to Pelham, June 18, 1798, the yeomen of the north are described as "being equal to the best troops."

Gordon, an historian of acknowledged ability, and for a long period a resident in the locality in which he resided, says, "The war from the beginning in Wexford, in direct violation of the oath of the United Irishmen, had taken a religious turn; as every civil war in the south and west of Ireland must be expected to take, because of the prejudices of the inhabitants"; and he continues, "So inveterately rooted are the prejudices of religious antipathy in the minds of the Irish Romanists, that in any civil war, however originating from causes unconnected with religion, not all the effects of the gentry or even the priests to the contrary could, if I am not exceedingly mistaken, restrain them from converting it into a religious war."

England was unable to understand how a Jacobin conspiracy could be transformed into a Papist insurrection, and credited every charge brought against the yeomanry, no matter how unfounded, and yet it was the same yeomanry to whom Britain was indebted, in the main, for quashing the rebellion.

The Catholic religious war against "heretics" outside of Ulster continued for some weeks, manifesting always the same savage cruelty.

A Protestant family named Dale living in Kildare was sentenced to death, by Pat Dowling, an insurgent leader, unless Dale joined the rebels, which to escape death he did, and marched away with the band. Mary Dowling, Pat's wife, with her two daughters, James Byrne, a boy of sixteen, and a few other lads entered Dale's house and found Mrs. Dale reading her Prayer Book. Mrs. Dale was knocked down with the handle of a churn, dragged out to the road, and there stoned to death. The guilty were tried and convicted at the spring assizes in Naas and convicted of the crime in 1801. One of the boys on being questioned why he had joined in the murder, answered, "Because she was a Protestant."

The burning of homes accompanied with plunder and massacre continued in the southern counties. It was characteristic of the rebels to refuse quarter and to disfigure their victims. The savagery and atrocities practiced so infuriated their opponents that they too refused quarter to the rebels when the tables were turned. When the insurgents found their match, they broke up into companies of banditti and spread over the country robbing and murdering wherever possible (see Cornwallis Correspondence). It was said the perpetrators were slaughtered in revenge, but Cornwallis admits the atrocities committed by the rebels were greater than the retaliation visited upon them. Father John ended his days on the gallows like a number of his fellows. Emmet, O'Connor, and MacNevin were protected because those having a knowledge of their conspiracies refused to appear against them. Wolfe Tone died in prison of a self-inflicted wound. Rufus King, the American Minister to Britain, protested in the name of the United States against Emmet being sent to the States, denouncing him as "a pernicious miscreant" (King to Portland, Sept. 3, 1798). O'Connor went to France.

Irish ideas had been in the ascendant on Vinegar Hill. One of the executioners, who himself was executed a year later, said that what he had done had been in obedience to the orders of his superiors. This man said before the rebellion, Catholics and Protestants had lived peaceably together, that Protestants were considered better and more indulgent masters than Catholics, but after the insurrection began, every one was called an Orangeman, and every one must be killed (Confession of James Quigley, Aug. 24, 1799). Quigley also said his people had hoped to kill all the Protestants including those who had campaigned with them. All Protestants who had under compulsion joined the rebels were executed. Quigley must have believed he had a passport to glory, for it was the current belief among the rebels that killing a Protestant ensured them entrance to heaven. The rebel flag, appropriately enough, flying in Wexford, was a red cross on a black ground.

Camden resigned. Criticism had been made of his management, though Pitt knew he was obliged to do many things not generally explainable. The cabinet was fully acquainted with the current conspiracies and held the names of the conspirators, but dare not make public their convincing evidence. Portland had said that the conspirators could not be brought to trial, without exposing secrets of the last importance to the state, the revealing of which might involve the safety of two kingdoms. In all probability France was meant, then suffering from the machinations of Bonaparte. When the French did arrive with assistance for the Irish rebels, she had waited too long, and achieved nothing.

The result of the war was to undo the work of half a century. Relgious antagonisms and distrust were renewed. It has been computed that 30,000 men were lost in the warfare, and again Ireland by her own action was left prostrate and dishonored.

The war, though of very much shorter duration than the Irish St. Bartholomew of 1641, resembled it in many respects. The same spirit of religious fanaticism, intolerance, and savagery was manifested and similar attempts were made later to palliate and minimize the shocking occurrences.

VII

THE UNION AND HOME RULE

Union of the two countries—Material prospects—Taxation—
Education outside of Northern Ireland clerically controlled
—Enormous number of Roman Catholic clericals—The Land
League—Agricultural systems—Murder of Sir Frederick
Cavendish in daylight near his home—"Martyrs' meeting"
to raise fund for murderers, held in New York—Opinions
of Henry George on the Irish land question—Coercion Acts
were Crimes Acts—The Land League assisted by Celtic-
Irish in America—The Irish Agricultural Organization Society, its beneficent effects—Censorship laws—The Ne
Temere and Motu Propriu decrees—Irish Trades-Unionism
—The Irish Republican excesses—The Black and Tans
—Protestants murdered in south and their property appropriated—The Irish-Irish Free State outrages—Irish Communism sanctioned by De Valera—The Celtic-Irish and their
Sinn Fein friends in the United States—American men in
uniform assaulted on the streets of Cork—Ireland suffered
nothing, and gained much by the World War—Fought conscription aided by the priests—Ulster signs Solemn League
and Covenant—The Ulster Divisions in the World War
and their amazing feats—Memorial tower to Ulster dead at
Thiepval in France.

THE rebellion of 1798 had aggravated the antagonisms of race and creed and it was thought
that a union with England would act in many
ways to the advantage of Ireland. The latter country
had indeed petitioned in 1703 and again in 1707 for such
union but no serious attention was given to the request.
Now it was felt that some new arrangement was necessary, and the British cabinet, headed by Pitt, took steps
to effect a union between the two countries. As the Irish

Parliament was notorious for its corruptibility Pitt found it desirable in putting the measure before the House to deal with the corrupt oligarchy on its own terms, a proceeding which earned for him very severe criticism.

Ireland had experienced a prosperity in the closing years of the eighteenth century, varied with periods of depression and distress, but all classes had not participated in the well-being which existed. The fortunate ones were those who were able to furnish England with the necessaries required for her troops during the wars in which she was engaged.

The Union became effective in 1800 and had the hearty support of the Catholic hierarchy but was bitterly opposed by the leading men of the old ascendancy, who dreaded the loss of their predominance and power.

The Union had the effect of removing all restrictions on Irish trade, giving Ireland, at the same time, access to English markets, and for twenty years, a protection to the struggling Irish industries. The representation of Ireland in the British Parliament could cause no complaint, for to England and Wales was allotted a representation of 513 members, Scotland 45, and Ireland 100. In 1920, when the population of Britain had reached forty millions, her representation in the Commons was 565, while Ireland with a population of five million had 105. As standards changed, Ireland was over-represented. Before the World War Irish representation was 103 when it should have been 86 and if based on Irish revenues Ireland should have had only 55 representatives. The Union was unequivocally of great advantage to the lesser partner. The French writer Cavour, one of the best informed writers on the subject, wrote in 1844, "As regards the civil and economic relations of the two kingdoms, the Act of Union is irreproachable. England and Ireland are placed by it on a footing of the most absolute equality. If there were sacrifices or concessions on either side, it is by England they were made, since it consented to open its colonies to Ireland, and to share the benefits of a monopoly of which it alone had the privilege."

Ireland's material prospects advanced amazingly under the Union. In 1800, according to D. A. Chart, the annual value of exports was four million pounds. In 1826 this amount had reached eight million pounds, with a corresponding increase in imports. In 1895, Sir Robert Giffen estimates Irish imports at twenty-five million pounds, and exports at twenty millions. In 1910, imports had reached the sum of sixty-five millions, and the exports 65,800,000 pounds. Ulster, like Scotland, flourished remarkably under the new tie, not because she had received any special favor, as envious critics have asserted. Belfast with true Yankee energy and initiative adapted herself to the new circumstances, and when the time arrived, seized the opportunities presented, and went on to success, while in other parts of the country, manufactures similar to hers dwindled away and disappeared.

Investigators who have examined the taxation problem in Ireland have testified that it was fair and just. It was arranged for Ireland to pay two fifteenths of the imperial burden, but this share was never paid. The country went into debt for it, and in 1817 when the exchequers of the two countries were amalgamated the Imperial Government became responsible for Ireland's debt. It was also shown that the taxation rate in Ireland would fall far short of paying the cost of running a country, meeting the national debt, and the expenses of a military and naval establishment, not to mention other expenses of a socio-economic character. Indeed, Redmond himself estimates that Ireland, from 1886 onwards, was run at a loss to the Imperial Government.

Ireland, too, was a backward country, afraid to come in contact with modern progression; and it is interesting to note that while Ireland was sobbing over her financial relations with the Imperial Government, she was actually the least taxed country in Europe, relatively to the services she enjoyed at her partner's expense.

The matter of contributions is too lengthy and complicated to discuss fully here; suffice it to say that during the period when Ireland was said to have contributed 330,000,000 pounds, Great Britain can be shown by exactly the same method of calculation to have contributed the sum of 5,800,000,000 pounds to the imperial expenditure for the use of the islands.

With regard to exemptions and abatements, the share of Scotland in these favors was less than Ireland enjoyed. Many taxes payable in Britain, were not levied in Ireland. For almost a century, there was a lighter tax on legacies, deeds, probate, and letters of administration. The income tax was not levied in Ireland until 1853. In 1912 the following imposts were not applied in Ireland, on Inhabited Houses, Railway Passenger Duty, and duties on Patent Medicines. Some critics have stated that the cost of Irish administration to the Imperial Government was excessive. The estimated cost for this purpose in 1913 was about five million pounds, which compared with the Civil Cost of the Irish Free State government in 1924 for running only twenty-six counties is less than moderate, for the cost of the latter was twenty million pounds excluding the cost of the military establishment.

The most reliable authorities believe and state that Ireland was not over-taxed during the Union, and there is absolutely no evidence of indebtedness to Ireland on the part of England. The contention of Ireland and her visionary claims of debts to her from the other side of St. George's Channel are but a ruse to avoid paying debts —just debts—to English taxpayers. It has been said by a Celtic Irishman that Ireland detests creditors. Ireland has contributed less to the British exchequer, and taken out proportionately more than the other partners in the concern, and while enjoying under-taxation has been greatly over-represented at Westminster.

From 1815, down to 1848, England gave preference to home-grown British products, a preference which was of enormous value to Ireland although she never refers to this advantage. The Corn Laws were then repealed. Ireland, however, has not evinced any appreciation of the many beneficent activities provided for her.

Further facts point to prosperity under the Union. There was the increase in tonnage entering Irish ports, which was, in 1800, 642,477, and in 1841, 1,994,285, showing a gradual increase and a stable progress. The excise revenue increased from 475,000 pounds in 1800 to two million pounds in 1843. In this year (1843) the yield of Irish taxation according to Martin was 4,392,101 pounds, which amounted to ten shillings per head, and that was lower than any of the other nine European countries with which comparison had been made.

With regard to education in Ireland, the Irish peasant, especially of the south and west, is almost always represented as being very poor, and very ignorant, though why he should be so, with the multitudes of priests caring for his interests, it is difficult to understand. However under the influence of the Imperial Government a system of National Education was established in Ireland, said to be superior to that used in England. The system became effective in 1831. The teachers were carefully trained for their work and the utmost care was taken that no proselytism should be possible. Gradually, however, what were known as the Christian Brothers' schools began to attract Catholic pupils. These schools multiplied, until now, outside of Northern Ireland, Irish education is controlled by the priests. Most earnest efforts were made to bring these sectarian schools into the system of the National Board of Education, but without result. Now the Christian Brothers' Schools are found everywhere in Ireland, and in many places have taken the place of the schools of the National Board. The Dissenting minorities in Ireland have to contend with this peril to their religious beliefs, this sectarianizing of primary schools by Roman Catholics. Protestant families living in certain districts find no school available for their boys but those of the Christian Brothers, and none available for girls but the convent schools. It has long been the aim of the Irish Roman Catholic hierarchy to denominationalize, in the interests of their church, all branches of Irish education. In contrast with this narrow outlook of those who control these schools may we compare the generous conduct of England toward the minority of differing faith in her island. England, with a population of about forty millions, is a refuge for between two and three millions of Irish within her borders, almost as many as in Ireland, and England generously furnishes funds to provide the education which they desire. A prominent Irish Celtic Catholic says: "In no non-Catholic country in the world, and in few Catholic countries, is the Catholic Church treated with such consideration as in England today." Where the local Catholic community maintains a school for its own members, the local educational authority defrays the cost of the education given in the schools. Grants are even made to train teachers for these foreign schools, and the teacher is amenable, not to those providing the funds for the maintenance of the school, but to the authority of those providing the school.

Speaking of education, O'Connor says that "Irish education controlled or imparted by priests has hitherto failed to turn out the proportion of able, progressive, earnest citizens that should be expected."

With regard to education by Catholic priests, a prominent writer says: "Separated from most of the ties and affections of earth, viewing life chiefly through the distorted medium of the casuist or the confessional, and deprived of those relationships which more than any other soften and expand the character, the Catholic priests, too often, have been conspicuous for their fierce and sanguinary fanaticism, and for their indifference to all interests except those of their church; while the narrow range of their sympathies, and the intellectual servitude they have accepted, render them peculiarly unfitted for the office of educating the young, which they so persistently claim, and which to the great misfortune of the world, they were long permitted to monopolize."

Another instance of the effort on the part of the Catholic clericals to denominationalize educational institutions in their favor, and their contracted views on this subject, is the National University of Ireland, which was created by the Birrell Act of 1908. This National University was represented to the English Non-Conformists as being absolutely free from religious tests, and yet it is now, as boasted by Cardinal Logue, completely Roman Catholic, in spite of the boasted paper safeguards.

The clerical population of Ireland is enormous, says Frank Hugh O'Donnell, a faithful son of the Catholic Church. He says, "The German Empire with its 21,000,-

ooo Roman Catholics has fewer mitered prelates than Ireland with a population of 3,000,000 Catholics, and that this huge number of churchmen, far beyond even the luxuries of service and worship, would be a very heavy tax on even a large and wealthy country. That the priests are the despotic managers of all primary schools, and can exact what homage they please from the teachers, whom they dominate and keep completely under their thumb. They own and control secondary schools, with their private profits and government grants. In the University, what they do not dominate they mutilate. Every appointment from dispensary doctors to members of Parliament must pay toll to their despotism. The County Councils must contribute patronage according to their indications, and the parish committees of the congested districts supplement their pocket-money. The priests have annexed the revenues of the industrial schools, and take not less than five million pounds from the Irish people every year by their numerous agencies of clerical suction." Mr. O'Donnell lost a position in public life for his plain speaking. No one must object to clerical absolutism. According to Sir James O'Connor, with a Catholic population of 3,243,000 in 1911, Ireland boasted 15,397 priests, monks, and nuns. Somewhat later it was estimated that the members of religious orders in Ireland had increased 150 per cent during the past fifty years while the population has decreased 30 per cent. The Roman Catholic Church, says Dr. Horton, "dominates Ireland as completely as Islam dominates Morocco."

The closing years of the nineteenth century, and especially its last quarter, saw many outrages, including murders, necessitating Coercion Acts for public protection. The ostensible object of these activities was a lowering of rents, preferably no rents at all, and other privileges. The real object of the agitators was the separation of Ireland from the mother country. The poor crops of 1878 and 1879 gave impetus to the mounting discontent, which was gladly seized by the Nationalist Party as an excuse to make demands on the legislature, as well as to play on the emotions and excite the cupidity of the populace.

Under Gladstone, a Land Act had been enacted which gave to the Irish tenant better protection than his English brother enjoyed in 1860, while the Land Bill of 1870 bestowed on the tenant a property right in his holding, secured to him the benefit of his improvements, and the right to a dual ownership in the land. It was in 1881, however, that a Land Act became law which was regarded as almost revolutionary in character. Freedom of contract because of this legislation was practically abolished, and the hold of the Irish aristocracy on their estates was greatly enfeebled, so that this event really marked the beginning of the end of their domination.

The great trouble with the small landholder was the love of subletting. The tendency was inveterate. The little farm would be sublet perhaps nine or ten times, at a constantly increasing rent, until the owner would be in receipt of several times as much rent as he paid to his landlord. If the progressive landholder tried to increase the size of his farms, his livestock would be maimed or otherwise injured, perhaps his home would be burned down, and if he still refused to listen to reason, his own life would pay the penalty.

Yet though too poor to pay his rent, he spent almost the same amount in alcoholic beverages, and his rent was actually lower in 1881 than in 1843. The peasant proprietor was a backward farmer, and could scarcely make ends meet. The rents, it was believed, amounted to about one quarter of the whole agricultural yield, but there is overwhelming evidence which proves that a reasonably efficient cultivation of the land would have produced a great deal more.

The Ulster tenant was in better circumstances, which Irish writers have ascribed to various causes. One of these was the "Ulster Custom," which was merely an understanding between landlord and tenant that the latter would be treated fairly. The Custom did not have the force of law, did not prevent the landlord from increasing the rent because of improvements the tenant had made at his own expense, did not prevent the landlord, when a lease expired, selling the ground to the highest bidder, and finally did not prevent the farmers from emigrating in swarms to America, to escape legal robbery. As a matter of fact, the Custom seemed to have little force except with the friendly and kindly disposed landlord.

With regard to the character of the soil, Ulster was the least fertile and least desirable from the land cultivation point of view of the four provinces. Gladstone himself furnished proof of this statement. After the massacre and rebellion of 1641, parcels of land in 1,000 acre lots were offered for sale in each of the four provinces, which were valued as follows: In Ulster, the price of 1,000 acres was two hundred pounds, in Connaught three hundred pounds, in Munster, three hundred and fifty pounds, and in Leinster the price asked was four hundred pounds. These statements were made by Gladstone, when introducing his Land Bill of 1870.

In addition to the poor soil found in Ulster, the climate is bleak, very different from the genial atmosphere of the salubrious south.

A Tenant-right League was formed as far back as 1850, to secure fixity of tenure, fair rent, and free sale. The Presbyterian Synod of Ulster presented a petition asking that the Ulster Custom should be given the force of law. At a meeting held to secure the measure, there were present as many as sixteen Presbyterian ministers, as well as one Catholic priest. However nothing came of the efforts made, for the agitation, so promising for a time, disappeared soon after the great famine.

All writers are agreed that the Land League was never able to secure a footing in the north, and the agricultural community of Protestants was practically free from agrarian disturbance which caused such havoc and distress in other provinces. The north, though without the advantages of soil and climate enjoyed elsewhere in the country, declined to introduce a criminal despotism in its province; though redress of agrarian grievances was just as earnestly desired and as badly needed in the north as anywhere in the island. The law-abiding, industrious Ulsterman felt no inducement to join an agitation made up of priests, and others whose intelligence and business capacity he could see no reason to respect. Ulster formed her own opinions and acted accordingly, which, of course, she had a perfect right to do.

When the beneficent Land Acts became law, and could be taken advantage of in a legal, orderly manner, the Ulster farmer was among the first to go to the courts, have his affairs reviewed, and a fair rent agreed on. The great Land Act of 1881 was supplemented by other acts in 1887, 1891, and 1896. Within three years after the first act was passed, fair rents were fixed in 70,000 cases, the average reduction being 20 per cent. The Act stopped arbitrary increases of rent, as well as evictions for non-payment of rent.

The Protestants of Ulster paid rents as high, perhaps relatively higher than was paid in other provinces. In 1870, Gladstone showed the rental of counties in Ulster where the Custom prevailed. In the north in 1779, the rent paid amounted to 900,000 pounds. In 1870 it was over three times as much, or 2,830,000 pounds, while in the rest of the country the rent in 1779 was 5,000,000 pounds, and in 1870 the increase was only 9,200,000 pounds, showing that the less fertile soil of Ulster had paid a much higher rent than the richer land in other provinces.

According to Kohl, the Protestant agricultural community in Ireland has been on the whole free from agricultural disturbances. "They appear superior in thrift, industry, and skill, to the rest of the island." Then again the northern farmer had a better comprehension of methods used in agriculture. McLennan says: "The northerner was better lodged, clothed, and fed than the others; wages of labor higher. . . . A frugal, industrious, and intelligent race, inhabiting a district for the most part inferior in natural fertility to the southern portion of the island, but cultivating it better, and paying higher rents in proportion to the quality of land, notwithstanding the higher rate of wages."

"The system of agriculture which prevails in the counties of Derry, Antrim, Down, and other Northern Counties is so superior to that which prevails in the west as to amount to full 50 per cent difference value in the land." (Evidence of Griffith before Valuation Commission, p. 59.)

Baker Greene, scientific agriculturist and journalist, said, "Ireland is always on the verge of famine, because Irish agriculturists do not practice agriculture."

In 1906, the Catholic archbishop of Tuam said, "In no other part of the world is agriculture in such a deplorable condition."

A German publicist, sent to Ireland by German and

Australian journals to see conditions in 1880, reports:
"Much misery, more ignorance, no intelligent demand for
reforms. The peasants headed by townspeople mostly.
Good soil, agriculture not merely bad, but worthless. German Bauern could treble all crops yearly. Priests in everything. . . . Mr. Parnell does not know how to manage
his own estate. Vast sums coming from America with the
object of political revolution more than economic reform.
No visible way out."

A report of the Irish Agricultural Commission in 1880
states, "Small farmers of south and west are poor, lands
undrained and neglected. Thousands and thousands could
easily double income."

Such was the land situation in Ireland when three successive poor seasons not only in Ireland but in England
also had made a bad condition worse. England was suffering too much herself to employ as usual extra agricultural help, so Irish privation and dissatisfaction was
increased, and the perennial Irish agitator saw a ready and
waiting harvest. The result was the Land League of
malodorous reputation established in 1881 with Charles
Stuart Parnell one of the leading directors. Parnell was
a small squire, with a heavily mortgaged estate, and on
the paternal side was descended from one of Cromwell's
soldiers. His mother was of Scotch-Irish-American
ancestry.

The League endeavored to coerce the public into accept-
ing its arbitrary rulings in lieu of the law of the land.
From its origin, its progress was marked with coercion,
intimidation, and murder. Regular meetings were held,
and murders of persons discussed, with the price to be
paid the murderer and his assistants. The Land Leaguers
were members of the Home Rule party. It was their

policy to attack and obstruct all beneficial legislation, lest the tenant should become satisfied with his condition, and refuse assistance to the agitators. From the origin of the Land League in 1881 to 1882, the official Parliamentary returns furnish the following record of its crimes: murders 49, attempted murders 124, killing and maiming cattle 299, incendiary fires 637; threatening letters sent to probable victims 4,906. In the south and west the chairman of the local Land League was the priest (Labouchere). Monthly assistance was obtained from America, without which the plans of the bloody League could not be carried out.

John Bright said, "Rents are refused to be paid, even by those tenants who could pay them." Although the crops of 1880 were good, men were shot here and there in broad daylight. Lord Mountmorris was shot to death at Clonbur close to County Galway, although he had a good reputation. The government decided to prosecute the League for the murder, and priests in every county rallied to the support of the League. The country was in a state bordering on anarchy and civil war, due to the work of the League.

The Land League was suppressed, but the National League took its place. Morley describes the country in 1882: "The Invincibles roved with knives through the streets of Dublin. . . . Over half the country, there was demoralization of every class; the terror, the fierce hatred, the universal distrust had grown to an incredible pitch. . . . The clergy hardly stirred a finger to restrain the wildness of the storm; some did their best to raise it."

In 1882, Earl Spencer became Lord-Lieutenant, and his new secretary was Lord Frederick Cavendish, a man well liked for his many noble qualities. He came from England with messages of hope and conciliation for the Irish people, and he was determined to do all in his power to aid them and their country.

On Saturday, May 6th, in the late afternoon, but in daylight, as he was on his way to the viceregal lodge in Phoenix Park, he and his secretary Burke were attacked by five men, and brutally murdered with knives, quite close to his residence. A reward of 10,000 pounds was offered for information leading to the detection of the assassins. A murderous attack made on a Mr. Fuld, because he had sat on a jury that had convicted another murderer, led to the detection of the criminals.

On May 10th, five days after the murders, Patrick Egan, treasurer of the Land League funds, declared that if a penny of these funds were used to offer a reward for detection of the Cavendish murderers, he would resign from his office.

It became known, eventually, that the perpetrators of the double murder were the "Invincibles," all Fenians. A man named Carey was the leader, and their object was to murder all the prominent "tyrants in the country." The membership included Father Murphy, also McCaffrey, Brody, Curley, all of Dublin. Carey held the position of town councilor, and swore he had been a Fenian. Councilor Carey turned informer, and was subsequently shot by one of his own countrymen; the others were convicted.

In March, another gang of murderers, named the "Patriotic Brotherhood," were tried at the Antrim assizes. It was organized by Parnell's chief organizer, and its business was murder; it was in fact a Murder Club, and its victims were chosen by the Land League. The Murder Club was run on strictly business principles and books were kept with details to be acted on in the regular way. On May 24, 1882, the following entry was made: "At the request of the Land League, conveyed through Thomas Murphy, men have been sworn in to kill Mr. Brook." So much evidence was obtained with regard to the sanguinary activities of the Murder Club, that its stalwart members decided that discretion was the better part of valor, and the "patriots" fled for safety to America, finding refuge under the sheltering wings of Patrick Ford, owner of the *Irish World,* and the advocate of dynamite, in whose office, and under whose auspices, a "Martyrs' Fund" was opened for the benefit of the patriotic murderers and their assistants, provided the beneficiaries should neither plead guilty to the crimes they had committed, nor confess those crimes.

A "Martyrs' meeting" was held on July 2d in support of the Fund. The murder gang "gloried in the deeds of these few brave men who struck dead the chief of the Irish banditti" (from Parnellism and Crime, *The Times,* 1887). What a brave deed for five armed men to slay two unsuspecting and unarmed men who had only friendship and good-will in their hearts.

Although the Irish tenants very willingly obeyed the order not to pay rent, these same tenants raised 39,000 pounds, and presented the money as a free gift to the leader Parnell.

The Land League, in spite of repeated efforts, never succeeded in securing a foothold in Ulster, where the shocking tales of murder and rapine were received with amazement and disgust. The north, however, did send a company of Protestant men down to County Mayo, to the assistance of Captain Boycott, when he became the first victim of the inhuman measures afterwards known as boycotting, and was in sore need of assistance.

After the beneficent Land Acts had been enacted into law, Henry George, of single tax fame, made a visit to Ireland. In "The Irish Land Question" George quotes the charge of Mr. Justice Fitzgerald to a Dublin jury in a Land League case, who said that "the Land Laws in Ireland were more favorable to the tenant than those of Great Britain, Belgium, or the United States"; and George continues, "As a matter of fact Justice Fitzgerald is right." "It is not true that there is—in an economic sense at least —any peculiar oppression of Ireland by England now. To whatever cause Irish distress is due, it is certainly not to any English laws which press on industry more heavily in Ireland than in any other part of the United Kingdom. And this atrocious land system is essentially the same land system which prevails in civilized countries which we of the United States have accepted unquestioningly, and have extended over the whole temperate zone of a new continent, the same system which men all over the civilized world are accustomed to consider natural and just. As to England it is well known the English landlord exercises freely all the power complained of in the Irish landlord without even the slightest restrictions."

In Belgium, quotes the distinguished Belgian publicist M. Émile de Lavelogue, of the University of Liége, "the Belgian tenant-farmers are rack-rented with a mercilessness unknown in England, or even in Ireland, and are compelled to vote as the landlords dictate."

An authority has stated that the incendiarism, dynamite outrages, and other crimes were suffered to a greater extent by the people than by the landlords. Of course there were fewer landlords and they were better able to defend themselves.

Chamberlain stated, "We have had fifty Coercion Acts since 1830, and the Earl of Derby said in the House of Commons, 'The record of crime in Ireland almost passes belief.'" Chamberlain continued, "There are two nations in Ireland, two communities separated by religion, by race,

by politics, by social conditions. . . . I can quite understand that a Dublin Parliament without the power to tax
Ulster, might find itself in financial difficulties." The
speaker continued, speaking of Ulster, "They have reared
up great industries, with which they have held their own
against the competition of the world. They have created
a vast foreign trade, and a prosperous shipping trade."

Mr. Gladstone in further discussion of the Ulster problem said, "Ireland has more justice than England, or
Wales, or Scotland. . . . Ireland is better off than the
sister country. In Ireland, every tenant has security in
his holding, he has fixity of tenure, and the right of free
sale. Thousands and tens of thousands in Wales would
give their eyes to have the same laws for Wales, which
we have freely conceded to Ireland.

"We have made laws against murder, against outrage,
and against theft, and these things embarrass the National
League." Gladstone thus furnishes the reason why Coercion Acts were necessary. They did not muzzle the press,
or interfere in any way with the law-abiding citizen.
These Coercion laws were Crimes Acts, passed to, as far
as humanly possible, restrain the criminal. The Rev.
R. W. Oliver, D.D., said, "Under the name of boycotting
deeds have been reported that would disgrace a community
of savages." Apparently the national character had not
changed since 1847 when Lord Palmerston wrote to Lord
Minto as follows, "I really believe there never has been,
out of the central regions of Africa, such a state of crime
as now exists in Ireland."

"Ireland," says Sir George Campbell, "in the west,
southwest and northwest is inhabited by a people, so far
as their material condition is concerned, as savage as any
savages in the world."

It was stated in the House, that wherever the League

has power, the land is going out of cultivation, and there was no doubt of the demoralization, the degradation in ethics and morals of a people subjected to the intimidation and coercion of the League, with the savage brutalities and murders inflicted on the people by the National League they were obliged to support.

This League of blackest criminal fame could not long have existed without aid from America, whose citizens of Celtic Irish extraction were thus largely responsible for the dire condition prevailing in Ireland. John Redmond, and John Dillon readily admitted this fact. Dillon said publicly, "The National cause would not survive six months if deprived of the aid of the Irish across the Atlantic." And as a matter of fact the Irish members of Parliament were really representing their American employers. Redmond once reminded the people that the Nationalist party would not be able to carry on without help from America, and also said "he did not think that fact was creditable to the people of Ireland."

The dynamite outrages in Great Britain in 1883 and 1884 followed the publication in the *Irish World* of Ford's dynamite policy. Ford raised enormous sums of money for this kind of destruction and death. Fifty of his emissaries were convicted in England of their crimes. Ford was the paymaster of Redmond.

Mr. John Dillon and his paper fought tooth and nail against the beneficent Land Purchase Bill, accepted so gladly all over Ireland, becoming popular almost immediately. He was afraid the people might become contented, and satisfied with their condition, and his trade of agitator would be destroyed.

The Land Acts of 1870 and 1881 were designed to convert the Irish farmer into the sole owner of his holding, but the machinery for this purpose was not adequate until the Ashbourne Land Purchase Acts of 1885 and 1889 provided the methods. By means of these acts in a period of six years 27,000 tenants taking advantage of the ten million pounds advanced them by the Imperial Government became proprietors of their farms. The good work did not stop here and the tenants received further assistance through the Arthur Balfour Act of 1891, amended in 1896, by means of which in a period of twelve years an additional 44,000 tenants became independent owners of their holdings. Following the ripe experience of nearly twenty years the Irish Land Act of 1903 was enacted with the support of the government behind it. Under this act the direct sales to tenants in six years amounted to 217,299, that is from 1903 to 1909 when its beneficent efforts were strangled by the Birrell Act of 1909 supported by Mr. Dillon and his fellow nationalists, who were aghast at the success of the previous acts in creating a people bereft of a grievance.

England taxed her people one hundred and fifty million pounds to lend aid to Ireland in buying out the Irish landlords. This sum, however, was not a gift, and Ireland pledged herself to pay a certain amount annually to England for the benefit thus received, and did so, until the president of the Free State, De Valera, figuratively speaking, tore up the agreement, appropriated the amounts paid in by the liberated farmers, and started a tariff war with England causing the country financial loss, misery, and discontent, besides defrauding English taxpayers of their just dues.

Another institution of vast benefit to the country was introduced by Sir Horace Plunkett, and known as the Irish Agricultural Organization Society. From its birth the I.A.O.S. was the object of intense hostility from the Nationalist party. Eventually the soundness of its doctrines and its businesslike application of its beliefs brought astonishing success, and its progress was rapid. It established creameries, Agricultural Societies, Village Banks, Societies for Poultry-keepers, Flax Societies, and other progressive institutions to further industries and other activities. The I.A.O.S. was regarded as the most hopeful of its kind in the country and it obtained a generous grant from the Unionist government but was consistently maligned by Dillon, McCarthy, and their fellow Nationalists. The aim of the Nationalist party, said Goldwyn Smith, "has always been to create Nationalist feeling which would end in political separation, not the redress of particular wrongs and grievances or the introduction of practical improvements, . . . and I think I am justified in saying that there is not one of the great measures passed by the Unionist governments since 1886 which has not been either opposed by the accredited leaders of the party, or, at best, received with carping and futile, rather than helpful, criticism."

That the Roman Catholic church claims political as well as religious power no one can question. It has claimed the right to depose kings, and absolve subjects from allegiance to the sovereign. When it gains a foothold in a country it becomes more and more aggressive and its demands keep increasing until they become wellnigh intolerable. Such demands became too much for Italy and Spain. The Vatican would like to rule church and state in Malta, and is wellnigh omnipotent in Quebec.

Lord Clare, when attorney-general in Ireland said, "There is now and always has been, a constant correspondence and communication kept up between this country [Ireland] and the court of Rome, and the spiritual power of the pope is at this day acknowledged in Ireland as implicitly as it ever was at any period of Irish history."

The Vatican frowns on liberty of the press, is hostile to free speech, and disapproves of the modern spirit of scientific research and philosophy. It demands strict and unquestioning obedience to its edicts; it extirpates when it can heresy and heretics so-called; it sets itself above civil law, and claims the right to enforce canon law when it can. The Vatican claims supremacy in everything, and boasts of the claim; always insists on compliance with its demands unless other forces are too strong for it. Pope Benedict XIV laid down the principle that when it becomes impossible to resist the encroachment of adverse customs the popes shut their eyes to unwelcome incidents, and tolerate what they have no power to prevent. The Vatican bows to the storm when it is not expedient to resist. In a Roman Catholic country, members of Parliament are the servants of the Vatican, and promises made by them are but scraps of worthless paper for it is always the Vatican that must be reckoned with.

Everything considered, it is not surprising that the Irish Free State has established censorship laws of the press, and literature in general, appointing the Minister of Public Justice as the censoring authority. Many books and papers have been banned, and some of these are: *Count and Counterpoint,* by Aldous Huxley, *The Well of Loneliness,* by Radcliffe Hall, *Conjugal Happiness,* by Dr. Lowenfeld, books on Birth Control by Margaret Sanger, *Home to Harlem,* by Claude McKay, *Intimate Journals,* by Paul Gauguin, an enormous German book named *Schlump,* and many others. It was noticed that the first list of banned books followed a few weeks after the death of the last of Ireland's intellectual weeklies *The Irish Statesman,* which had vigorously protested against censorship in Ireland. Six other newspapers were barred soon after censorship was established. Newspaper proprietors have no right of defense, although editors, publishers, and authors may appeal to authorities. Other papers banned were Lord Riddel's *News of the World,* Thompson's *Weekly News, The World's Pictorial News, Weekly Record* of Glasgow, Reynold's *Illustrated News,* and others. The business appears in a flourishing condition.

Two very important papal decrees introduced in Ireland are the Ne Temere and the Motu Propriu decrees. The first command decrees the marriage of a Protestant and a Catholic null and void unless performed in a Roman Catholic edifice by a Roman priest. It might be well to say here that the Home Rule Bill of 1893, designed to safeguard the marriage of persons of differing faiths, was rejected by a vote of the Irish Nationalists party, which refused to exempt marriage and other religious ceremonies from the legislative powers of the Dublin Parliament. That such a law was desirable and very necessary, became evident from the widely known McCann case. Mrs. McCann was a Protestant, her husband a Catholic. The incident occurred in Belfast; the marriage though in conformity with the law of the land was declared void by the Roman authority. McCann deserted his wife and kidnaped their two children. McCann said his marriage was not binding because not performed in a Roman Catholic church.

The second Vatican or Motu Propriu Decree automatically places any Catholic under the bann of the church who violates the decree. It is designed to set the Roman clergy above the law of the land, and rules that whoever, without permission from an ecclesiastical authority, summons any ecclesiastical person to a lay tribunal, and compels him to attend publicly such a court, incurs instant excommunication, and absolution for such a crime is reserved for the Roman pontiff. This decree, so terrifying to the superstitious, is abrogated in such countries as refuse recognition to the papal power. These decrees have been introduced in a country possessing free representative institutions, and is a testimony to the wellnigh omnipotent power wielded by the Vatican in a Catholic country.

It is quite in accordance with Irish traditions to approve and support a pro-Celtic organization called the Ancient Order of Hibernians, also known as the Molly Maguires. Though a secret society, the pope was said to be one of its powerful friends. It has branches in many lands and is making efforts to draw to its ranks all Catholic people of Irish descent. The object of the organization "is to give preference to its own members first and afterwards to Catholics as against Protestants on all occasions." Whether it is a question of custom, office, public contracts, or positions on public boards, Molly Maguires are pledged to support a Catholic as against a Protestant. A serious feature of this system, according to John E. Healy, editor of the *Irish Times,* was the system of boycotting by the guardians, of all candidates who had not graduated from the Roman Catholic University; so that the most highly gifted and best trained men from Dublin University (Trinity College) had practically abandoned competition for Dispensary offices, outside the province of Ulster. The Dispensary Districts in Ireland number 740, and constitute a factor in Poor Law Reform.

A spirit of impatience of criticism expressed by the interested minority and an intolerance of independent opinion have been very noticeable in the east and south. These minorities though furnishing the major part of the contributions and taxes are, we are told, "virtually excluded from local councils and from paid places in their gift."

Trades-unionism took root in Ireland when industries were born, but its history is far from gratifying. A spirit of anarchy, cupidity, and a disposition to use brute force has been noticed among the Irish trades-unions to an extent rarely equaled. The attempts to obtain what is desired have not been overscrupulous. Campbell Foster, writing in 1840, says, "It is a remarkable fact, that there is scarcely a trade that has prospered in Ireland, save that of brewers and distillers." This trade does not necessarily require a large staff of workers, and so has managed to survive. Almost every other trade was ruined by the combinations of skilled workmen making demands impossible to meet. It has been said, "Irish skilled labor in the south is the most costly commodity of its kind in the world. The Labor Unions in the south will stop at nothing to achieve their purpose. Some of those who do not wish to commit murder themselves, are willing to pay three shillings a week out of their wages to hire assassins." (See Nassau Senior, p. 40.)

Strangely enough, there is none of this anarchy with tendency toward destruction of life and property among the laboring classes in Belfast. In 1923, it was shown that building a certain type of laborer's cottage cost in England $1,500, in Belfast $2,000 and in the Free State $3,500.

The acquisitive spirit of trades-unions reacted by driving industry and manufacturers to more friendly localities thus depriving the laborers of needed work, but who did not seem able to learn the lesson and continued on their course. Fontaine, we learn, tried to establish a fishing industry in the south, at Berehaven, but found it impossible because of this grasping, hostile attitude on the part of the workmen. The Berehaven occurrence was but one of a number of similar incidents, and may account for much of the poverty complained of in the southern province.

In the House of Commons the hazard and difficulty experienced by the prospective employers of labor in Ireland was discussed by Daniel O'Connell who stated in 1838 that "wages amounting to 500,000 pounds were lost in Dublin through the workmen's combinations." O'Connell said "shipbuilding firms had been driven out of Dublin from the same cause, and that in a period of between two and three years, thirty-seven persons had lost their sight through vitriol burns by the strikers, and there was not a day when such crimes were not committed." Nassau Senior, discussing the same subject, said, "The introduction of capital was prevented, and capital (already established) was driven away by the workmen" who prevented the use of machinery, and forced the importation of materials in the least finished state; that force was used to equalize the wages of skilled and ignorant, and that the manufacturer, the mechanic, and the chemist was coerced by the workmen to act under the dictation of the myopic and rapacious employees. The means employed by the workers in this warfare were torture, mutilation, and murder. These combinations are today as active as they ever were. Senior thought the Irish "were naturally an indolent people"; and it was the opinion of Kohl, that, "The main root of Irish misery is to be sought in the indolence, levity, extravagance, and want of energy in the national character." Griffith testified before a Committee on Values that "under a good system of farming, the farmers in Ireland might not only pay much higher rents, but live much better than they did." Evidence before the Poor Law Commission showed that it took ten laborers in Ireland to do the same amount of work which two laborers produced in England in the same length of time, and even then the Irish product was generally of an inferior quality.

In addition to the handicap of labor, was the encouragement tending to overpopulation. O'Connor quotes the testimony of a parish priest before the committee mentioned. The priest said: "I have married girls of twelve to thirteen years, and at this moment there is a married woman in Templemore who has just had a child before the age of fourteen." W. E. Foster quoted by the same author says, "The families are something fearful." And for this teeming population, the relief of emigration was not allowed, but violently opposed by priests and politicians. Emigration was anathema until the arrival of the famine of 1845-6, after which it was compulsory. Shipload followed shipload from 1846-7 onwards until in less than a decade between two and three million Celtic Irish immigrants reached the hospitable shores of America. The great west was then opening up and the new immigrants were able to furnish just the kind of labor required at a wage above what they were accustomed to receive. Relatives quickly followed, glad of the opportunities offered, and these were sedulously instructed to regard themselves as "exiles," yet they were glad and willing to make their homes in the new land.

The Anglo-Irish war so-called was a mode of savage warfare carried on by an army of gunmen who instituted a reign of terror in Ireland, during which neither life nor property was safe, and while the Roman Catholic clergy denounced the shootings and looting, no condemnation came from the Bench of Bishops as a whole; and yet it was a common practice for these thieves and assassins to say their rosaries at night, and to receive the "Sacraments" before going to battle. It was reported that the perpetrators of "Bloody Sunday" did so.

Innocent policemen, while in the performance of duty, were ambushed and killed, jurors who would not vote to clear the assassins, disappeared. Any paper brave enough to give an honest opinion of the daily outrages committed had its offices wrecked, and the publisher was lucky to escape with his life. Buildings were destroyed, the gunmen acting as if they were in an enemy country. No one dared to write the word murder or even to whisper it to a friend. In this land of liberty, no one dared to call his soul his own.

It was to curb these outrages that the notorious Black and Tans were sent to Dublin and vicinity. The people were terrorized, guardians of the law killed without provocation or compunction, and it was doubtless no easy matter to obtain men willing to engage in such warfare. The Black and Tans instituted reprisals for the murder of their companions and the destruction of property. General Macready says there were four occasions when the regular troops engaged in unauthorized reprisals—at Fermoy, after the kidnaping of the brigade commander, at Queenstown as the result of an attack on unarmed soldiers at Mallow when the barracks were seized, and at Ennis as a reprisal for the murder and mutilation of policemen on the streets of the village.

While the Irish gunmen were making themselves notorious in real Hibernian style, the sob sisters and brothers in the United States organized an "American Commission on Conditions in Ireland" which made touching appeal to the American citizen for funds for "starving Ireland," "for sickness, pestilence, and death in humble homes, and to avert the struggle against hunger, cold, and death." It is perhaps needless to say the condition had no existence whatever except in imagination, though in all probability, the sympathetic, overcredulous American contributed to the Irish hoax. Where the funds went no one knows.

When Terence McSwiney died in consequence of his hunger strike, in his possession was found an order to construct a bomb factory, also a key to the police cipher code, which would certainly have meant the death of many innocent men. It was shown he had approved the death of two innocent men of the R.I.C. who were executed by the lawless gunmen.

Seeking a new field for the exercise of their martial prowess, the Republican gunmen, in 1920, invaded the hitherto peaceful province of Ulster, and immediately began their work of destruction and death. They set fire to the Grand Central Hotel, and the income tax offices. Important documents were destroyed in the Custom House. A district officer was murdered on the street in Lisburn, and there were a number of other disturbances including one hundred and seventy fires in Belfast. The city was in a state of siege and the military in occupation, the streets wired and sandbagged. A county inspector from Ulster named Smith was murdered in Cork. In Belfast a number of murders occurred.

The Black and Tans became members of the police force in June, 1920. Recruiting for the police force had stopped because of the unusual and terrible risks and exposure to unusual perils.

On November 21st, fourteen officers of the British army were shot in their beds, there were ambushes, and murders. The rebels captured a Mrs. Lindsay, who had foiled one of the Republican ambushes by giving information she had obtained from a priest, and they shot her dead. Men were dragged from their homes and shot. Attempts were made to derail trains, policemen were ambushed and killed. Roads were torn up and bridges destroyed.

The Republican brotherhood continued its destructive work in the north. Protestant workmen were irritated by the fact that Catholics had taken the posts of Protestants who had volunteered and gone to the war, and accused the former of not having done their bit. The destruction of property continued, and the interests of a busy manufacturing city were at the mercy of a lawless gang, while other intruders continued to enter the northern province. Finally the Home Rule Act became law on Dec. 23, 1820. Ulster received her own Parliament and administration, and six of the Ulster counties, while the other twenty-six counties became the Free State. A boycott was immediately declared against Northern Ireland but proved of trifling consequence; indeed it was a failure. Ulster, taking advantage of the Home Rule Bill, opened her new Parliament on June 22, 1922. King George was there in person, and made an appealing plea for peace in Ireland.

The Sinn Fein element took the responsibility of placing De Valera in charge of their government, a man of mediocre ability and one who does not seem to possess much respect for treaties or official agreements, which he seems to regard as of no consequence if he happens to change his opinion. This official is credited for the continuance of these Irish disorders and outrages which have attracted so much attention.

In the south, violence did not abate. Protestants as such were murdered and their property destroyed or appropriated, the so-called Irregulars carrying on the war.

When the provisional government of the Free State began to function it was found that in spite of the capital which had been made of England's harshness and cruelty, the new government treated those resisting its authority much more severely than had the Imperial Government.

Many of the rebels were executed. The hunger strikes formerly capitalized by them were now regarded with crushing indifference, and the Irregulars were ruthlessly punished without a trace of the gentle hesitating mercy to which England had accustomed them. The provisional government again proved absolutely merciless to the destroyers of country mansions, railway stations, roads, and bridges.

It was really thought that the actual object in view in the destruction of country houses was to secure demesne lands for men who had none. Protestants were attacked and their property appropriated when possible. Protestant churches were destroyed and the ministers' houses looted, although the destruction was not confined to the houses of Protestants. The amount of damage caused by these lawless acts has been estimated at $100,000,000. The fine old buildings in Dublin destroyed by the Irish themselves in this Irish-Irish war was generously made good by the Imperial Government.

A number of Irregulars, who thought they might be a law unto themselves, were captured in Kerry; they numbered twelve. Again the provisional government, discarding the gentler measures of England, gave the prisoners a taste of their own medication. The captives were tied together, and a mine exploded under them which blew them to pieces, and that was the end of their mischief.

The Black and Tan outrages were completely overshadowed by the Irish-Irish Free State outrages. It was evident England could never hope to compete with Ireland in this, her own field. According to the Republican press, a boy of sixteen was tortured by putting a spiked metal cap on his head, and sending electric shocks through him, in order to force him to give names of wanted persons. These measures were quite in keeping with those employed by the Irregulars. On March 24, 1924, the Irregular forces used a machine gun on a party of unarmed British soldiers at Queenstown, Cork. One man was shot dead and twenty-one wounded. The assassins escaped.

The atrocities of this Irish-Irish war, which had received some ecclesiastical sanction, produced a wave of crime unequaled even in Ireland for at least two hundred years. Irish lawlessness became a boomerang. The conditions were appalling. It was quite the usual thing to decide quarrels by means of the gun and the knife.

Private business houses, post offices, and banks were held up, and the money carried off. Cardinal Logue said the plague of bloodshed, destruction, pillage, rapine, robbery, even sordid theft, had invaded at least a part of his archdiocese, with a virulence which left in the shade even the most outrageous excesses of the Black and Tans (Lent Pastoral, 1923). Dr. Doherty "deplores the fact that the houses of unoffending Protestants have been bombed, and one family in the diocese, at least, was forced to fly from home under the threat of death."

Dr. Hoare, Bishop of Longford, said, "Could you ever have thought it possible that Irishmen could be so cruel, so lost to all the finer feelings of religion and civilization, as to organize a system of assassination, and robbery, and destruction, such as we have seen before our eyes? Call to mind the destruction of roads, the land mines, the diabolical sending adrift the locomotive engine at full speed with its human and commercial freight to meet the blown-up bridge, and to be precipitated into the valley or the torrent; the firing of houses where were old people and helpless and innocent children; the dragging of men out of their homes and shooting them without priest or trial." (Lenten Pastoral.)

Mr. O'Hegarty said, "Every devilish thing we did

against the British went its full circle, and then boomeranged, and smote us tenfold" (*Victory of Sinn Fein,* p. 73).

The northern government, functioning since 1921, by resolution voted itself out of the Free State, Dec. 7, 1922, as authorized by the treaty.

In the south, the Protestant minority coöperated readily with the Free State government and when the state called for a loan of $50,000 it was the Protestants who supplied the most of it.

The communistic spirit in Ireland is voiced in the cry of "the land for the people." In the Irish struggle for a republic, a messenger was sent to soviet Russia, but Moscow declined any affiliation. Still the communistic principle was not to go begging. Factories and creameries were seized, and soviets established on the Moscow model. De Valera himself displayed communistic leanings. In a document which he issued in November, 1922, he makes the following statement: "Under the Republic all industry will be controlled for the workers' and farmers' benefit. All transports, railways, canals, etc., will be operated by the state—Republican state. . . . All banks will be operated by the state, and lands of the aristocracy will be seized and divided amongst those who can and will operate them for the national benefit."

Irish self-determination also cropped out among the laborers of Waterford and Wexford. "We are the people," they shouted, and they burnt the farmers' houses, and destroyed other property, shooting down the owners without a vestige of compunction, as similar farmers had shot down the honest farmer who tried to pay his rent in the old Land League days. Now the tables were turned, but when the laborers had their own houses destroyed and some of them were killed, this little war was halted. Notwithstanding the punishment, the gun and the torch were helping "the poor man" to become a rich one overnight. Raids on banks and tin boxes were supplying the wherewithals to set bandits up as gentlemen, who later on will become leaders of the people, and pillars of the law.

The Celtic Irish, and their Sinn Fein friends in the United States, were opponents of the Allies throughout the World War and were opposed to the League of Nations. Meetings were held in America where Woodrow Wilson, President of the United States, was hissed, as well as other leading American statesmen, like ex-President Taft. These hyphenated Americans sought aid from the Kaiser, and they aided him in return. In southern Ireland the American flag was publicly insulted and burnt in Irish towns when the United States joined the Allies in 1917. At anti-recruiting meetings the echoes waked to the shouts of "Up the Kaiser," "Up the Germans," and in the Irish National Assembly, grave insinuations were made against the President until the speaker appealed to members not to make too many open attacks upon him, as it might do harm to the cause. The *Gaelic American* of April 29, 1916, stated "the administration in Washington would go down in history coupled with the name of Woodrow Wilson, and make his memory infamous."

There was a meeting in Philadelphia at which Judge Rooney and Judge Cohalen were the principal speakers; the band played "Die Wacht am Rhein" followed by the "Wearing of the Green." When hyphenated Irish fervor had reached the proper pitch, a party of Irish volunteers in uniform entered the stage on one side, and a party of uniformed Germans came in from the other, and according to the *Gaelic American* "the two captains of the com-

mands, August Hueges for the Germans, and John Caven-
agh for the Irish, clasped hands in the center" (*Gaelic
American,* May 13, 1916).

Besides other abuse from the hyphenated patriots, Mr.
Wilson was accused of betraying his trust, and selling the
United States to the British autocracy.

At a meeting in Chicago Mr. De Valera found it necessary to warn his audience against hooting President
Wilson, and also made an attempt to minimize the demon-
stration which the hyphenates had made in Madison
Square Garden, which, he said, had been due to "agents"
sent hither by enemies of the Irish cause.

Passing over the disloyalty of the Celtic Irish in America, the Irish on the native soil were equally antagonistic.
Marked and open hostility was shown to American soldiers at Queenstown, Cork, on several occasions. In the
spring of 1918, several American sailors were stoned on
the streets of Cork. An eyewitness states that passing
Americans in uniform were often hissed and otherwise
insulted by Sinn Feiners. Riots followed these demonstrations of dislike. "I saw Sinn Feiners walk down the
streets behind two American naval officers, and when their
offensive personal remarks were ignored, spit on the
officers' uniform, who then turned and fought in blind
rage, orders to the contrary entirely forgotten."

Sinn Fein attempts to defend support of Germany, and
its opposition to the Allies, on the ground of an intolerable
tyranny on the part of England towards Ireland, but this
contention falls to the ground on examination. Ireland's
material condition had been improving ever since the
eighties or since the beneficent land legislation became law.
Other beneficent measures, mostly at the expense of England, had placed the Irish farmer in a position superior
to persons of his class in Continental countries. Then,

the relation between the countries, while advantageous to both in more recent years, was unquestionably in favor of Ireland. No country in the world had received such benefits from recent legislation as Ireland, which had received more favors than Scotland or Wales. Imports and exports showed a remarkable increase. Savings bank deposits testified to an unusual prosperity. Food was good and plentiful, wages high, and plenty of work was waiting for workers.

During the war, Ireland lost nothing, and gained more proportionately than any government in the world. The country was far removed from the European battlefields; no rent was to be paid to landlords; the industries of the country had been benefited by the war; munition works engaged many at high wages; trade was booming. In 1920 Irish exports and imports were, in proportion to the population, both in amount and in value, more than any country in the world. Ireland was actually a wealthy country and few countries had received the benefits of a more liberal legislation which had been bestowed on Ireland by Britain, among which may be mentioned the Old Age Pensions' Act, the National Insurance Act, the Workmen's Compensation Act, the Housing of the Working Classes Acts, Factory Acts, the Children's Act and other Acts of beneficial character. Much of this legislation, by the way, had been made at the expense of England, perhaps in the vain hope that some day Ireland might be contented.

Recruiting in Ireland for the World War and also conscription was fought obstinately by the Celtic Irish. The people, led by the priests, refused participation in the struggle. England had decided to render assistance to stricken France and Belgium, while Sinn Fein in a spirit of crass selfishness, saw, or thought it saw, an opportunity of winning something more for itself, by rendering aid to the fomenter of war, the enemy of peace, and was bending all its efforts to that end, thus hampering England in the aid she hoped to render to the Allies.

Prior to the war, Nationalist Ireland was pressing the passage of the Home Rule Bill, and the progressive north was determined that it would not come under the rule of a Parliament for which it had neither respect nor confidence. Celtic Ireland amused itself caricaturing and deriding the north, and leading Nationalists busied themselves in threatening and denouncing the province which preferred to avoid any close relationship with the Free State; Ulster "was to have the lead" if it did not at the crack of the whip immediately come into line.

Meanwhile, demonstrations in Ulster testified to the dogged resolution of a determined race to protect themselves from coercion and intimidation and to preserve the free institutions for themselves and their children they had always held so dear. Five hundred special services were held in various Protestant churches in Ulster, and a Solemn League and Covenant was signed on September 28, 1922, which pledged the signers to stand by each other in resisting the conspiracy to introduce Home Rule in Ireland; and in the event of a Home Rule Parliament being thrust upon the people to refuse it all recognition. Sir Edward Carson was the first to affix his signature to the Covenant at a large gathering in the Belfast Cathedral, and he was followed by Lord Londonderry, then moderator of the Presbyterian General Assembly. The Episcopalian Bishop of Down and Connor was next to sign. More than 200,000 men then added their signatures. It was an impressive and historic occasion; the Orange banner of King William III floated over the assembly, reminding those present of the successful resistance made by Ulster at Londonderry against the Catholic armies of James II assisted by the French, then the most military nation in the world.

The number of women who signed a similar covenant reached 200,000. Men were being drilled all over the north, and it was reported that 85,000 men were equipped with arms. General Sir George Richardson was appointed commander in chief of the Ulster force, and when the Ulster provisional government was formed in September, a fund was set in motion which was expected to reach one million pounds. Sir Edward Carson immediately subscribed $50,000 and was quickly followed by others.

The first step taken by the parent government savored of poor judgment, for in the month of March, 1914, British troops were ordered to the north, and warships appeared in Belfast Lough. Was England really going to discard her friends when they were no longer of assistance to her, and force them to fight for their lives against superior numbers as they had been obliged to do on more than one occasion? There were rumors of forces "marching on Ulster," and of a blockade to be erected against it by land and sea; the leaders were to be disarmed and then imprisoned. The government declared these rumors to be without foundation, and that the naval movements were a part of a general precautionary movement. It is not impossible that the knowledge of the army being in sympathy with Ulster had been noised abroad, and that discretion might prove the better part of valor. However, several officers in the English army resigned, among whom were General Gough, General French, commander in chief of the forces of Great Britain, Colonel Seely, the Minister of War, and General Ewart. Subsequently these gentlemen withdrew their resignations but not before the public became aware that the north had many influential sympathizers.

On May 25th, the Home Rule Bill passed its second reading, and the following March an amending bill was offered, which received still further alteration in the House of Lords. By these changes Ulster was excluded from the effects of the bill. The amending bill, however, was suspended by the war.

In April, the north had obtained 35,000 rifles from a small steamer, which had landed at Larne near Belfast with her consignment of arms for the Unionists, and Mr. Asquith was much perturbed by the occurrence. An information against the leaders was prepared, and ready to be served when events proved even a prime minister may change his mind, for a telegram was sent withdrawing the orders, which, doubtlesss, was the best way out of what might have proved a very serious occurrence.

The World War now intervened, and many national affairs were necessarily held in abeyance.

England had decided to aid with men and arms France and stricken Belgium; her money too was poured out in the effort to stem the tide of barbarism and cruelty which was threatening to engulf the European continent; but Celtic Ireland refused to help stem the tide of militarism surging over frightened peoples who did not know where to turn for safety. The motto of Ireland was Sinn Fein, and that shield she hugged to her bosom. The Roman Catholic Church, the Nationalist party, and the Clan-na-Gael were stubbornly opposed to recruiting in Ireland, even when men were urgently demanded for the holocaust on the battlefields of France. The woes of Belgium, the misery and near-despair of France, and the example of England sacrificing men and money in a cause which was not hers, left Celtic Ireland unmoved, and even when the news came that America, too, had heard the call of a common humanity and was pouring out her wealth of men and her treasure into the maelstrom swirling on the fields where poppies were to grow, the Irish people remained untouched by woes which were not their own.

Celtic Ireland was pro-German during the World War as well as the American Sinn Fein, and in spite of the fact that American youth were sacrificing their young lives by thousands in France, Sinn Fein was contributing funds to help the German cause. An Irish Roman Catholic, Rt. Hon. Sir James O'Connor, says, "Money for the cause came from the Clan-na-Gael of America," and the Hon. Francis Patrick Egan says, "I do not know how much German money has been collected by the Clan-na-Gael or how it has been expended, but I do know they sent $80,000 to Ireland to foment the final rioting, and I also know that no such sum as this was at hand at the beginning of the war, and that no such sum has been collected in the meantime from the members in America."

"Some of the young secular priests openly, and some of the regular order secretly were pushing the Sinn Fein policy" (O'Connor). Meanwhile Haig was saying (April 13, 1918), "With our backs to the wall, and believing in the justice of our cause, each of us must fight on to the end." Men were so badly needed for the army, that the age for compulsory service in Britain was placed up to 50 and 55 years of age.

As much as two hundred thousand pounds were collected in Roman Catholic churches and chapels to resist conscription; the act, however, was not enforced in Ireland, and no one ever knew where the large sum of money collected for the purpose went. It just disappeared.

The pro-German activities of Catholic Ireland interfered with and impeded Britain in her efforts during the war, as troops necessarily were kept in Ireland that could have been used on the continent. Meanwhile the male population of Ireland remained comfortably at home protected by the soldiers and navy of Britain.

Although Ireland suffered no hardship or other drawback because of the war, she made immense profits from it. There was no restriction of food here, no butter or meat was exported; there was plenty of fine white flour and other provisions now regarded as luxuries in other places. Sinn Fein was now working for a German victory in Ireland, and, as has been stated, defending its opposition to the Allies with its usual self-deception on the ground of the intolerable treatment Ireland was receiving from England. The Sinn Fein section of the Irish volunteers were said to number 65,000. The Nationalist press was very active and disloyal and dealt largely in its perquisite "of artfully altered news." Drilling went on and parades of armed and disloyal men were held.

On December 9th there was an attempt to shoot Lord French which failed, when the Catholic archbishop with keen diplomacy sent a telegram of congratulation on his escape to Lord French, and then squared himself by sending $500 to the Irish rebels. It was just a year earlier that the American Archbishop Hayes sent $1,000 to Mr. De Valera who had been imprisoned in a Lincoln jail for assisting in a German plot.

So conscription was not enforced in Ireland, but in Ulster conscription was not necessary. An official statement made in the House of Commons showed that Ireland contributed 123,585 men to the English army, more recruits being added later on. Of these volunteers, Ulster with perhaps one third of the population contributed 45 per cent of the men who joined the British army from Ireland, and 40 per cent of this total belonged to the Presbyterian and Protestant churches.

Of the total, Ulster contributed 58,438, and the rest of Ireland 65,147 men. Catholic workmen took the places in industry left vacant by the northern volunteers, and those of the latter who were able to return home had some difficulty in regaining their positions.

The 36th Division from Ireland was known as the Ulster Division, and the 107th Brigade was raised from the city of Belfast, and known as the 8th, 9th, 10th, and 15th Battalions of the Royal Irish Rifles. The 108th Brigade was recruited from the counties of Antrim, Down, Armagh, Monaghan, and Cavan and were the 11th, 12th, and 13th Royal Irish Rifles, and the 9th Royal Irish Fusiliers. The 109th Brigade drew its units from the counties of Tyrone, Londonderry, Donegal, and Fermanagh, with one battalion from the city of Belfast, which were the 9th, 10th, and 11th Royal Inniskilling Fusiliers, and the 14th Royal Irish Rifles.

Among the divisional troops, the pioneer battalion, the 16th R.I.R., came from County Down; the service squadron of cavalry, the 6th Inniskilling dragoons, from the town of Inniskilling; the 121st, 122nd and 150th, Field Companies, R. E. Signal Company, the 108th, 109th and 110th Field Ambulances Section, were raised chiefly from Belfast. The Divisional Cyclist Company Section was recruited from the whole of Ulster.

The 36th Division had a method of recruiting peculiarly its own which was most effective. Officers and men of the original force were sent back to their homes in cities, towns, and villages, and returned bringing with them their relatives and friends. In many cases, entire companies and platoons were formed by men from certain streets, or from villages. Brigadier General Ricardo, D.S.O., has mentioned the case of one section, composed entirely of cousins bearing the same family name.

The first big engagement in which Ulster took part was afterwards commemorated at Thiepval, a little village on the Somme, where Ulster's memorial to her heroic sons was unveiled five years after. It was here the great Franco-British offensive on both sides of the Somme began on the morning of July 1, 1916. It was here the 36th (Ulster Division) began to make history. It came into prominence again on June 7, 1917, when side by side with another Irish Division (16th), it fought its way into Wytschaete, and on many another day during the long struggle; but Thiepval was Ulster's day of days, and its story will be told while the English tongue survives.

An English eyewitness described the Division's feat as follows: "I am not an Ulsterman, but yesterday as I followed their amazing attack I felt that I would rather be an Ulsterman than anything in the world. My position enabled me to watch the beginning of their attack from the wood in which they had formed up, but which long prior to the hour of assault was being overwhelmed with shell-fire, so that the trees were stripped, and the top half of the wood ceased to be anything but a slope of bare stumps with innumerable shell-holes peppered in the chalk. It looked as if nothing could live in the wood; indeed the losses were heavy before they started. Two companies of one battalion were sadly reduced in the Assembly trenches. When I saw the men emerge through the smoke, and form up as if as on parade, I could hardly believe my eyes.

"Then I saw them attack, beginning at a slow walk over no man's land and suddenly let loose as they charged over the two front lines of enemy's trenches, shouting the famous challenge renowned since their famous victory at Londonderry 'No surrender, boys.' The enemy's guns raked them from the left, and machine guns enfiladed them on the right. But battalion after battalion came out of the awful wood steadily, bayoneting and chivying their enemies until the trench was free. Then on to the next line, where support was received from other regiments in the Division. And that was the story of Thiepval. The advance cost Ulster some 7000 casualties, and there was scarce a village in Ulster that did not lose a gallant son that night. Later days saw deeds just as brave, and the sons of Ireland won undying fame in many a hard-won fight, but that day of July 1st belonged to Ulster, although it was said the Somme ran red with blood from every province in Ireland."

The actual memorial to the sons of Ulster takes the form of a tower, which is an exact copy of Helen's tower at Clandeboyne, County Down. The original tower was built by the first Marquis of Dufferin as a memorial to his mother, the author of *The Irish Emigrant*. The height of the Memorial Tower is seventy feet, and it is surmounted by a flagstaff thirty-five feet high. It stands near the village of Thiepval on the site of the old German front line, overlooking the river Ancre, and commands from its turret a view of the surrounding country for thirty miles. It contains a memorial chamber sixteen feet square, and here there is an inscription tablet in memorial marble with an inscription on the four walls. A little cemetery stands at the gate of the Ulster Tower, fenced in and studded with white crosses. A signboard stands at the entrance of the plot, the words on the signboard reading "The Connaughts," and here all sleep peacefully together.

A caretaker has been engaged to care for the tower, where he will live, and the maintenance of this post will be a permanent charge on the people of Ulster.

Lord Carson, who was unable to be present when the

tablet was unveiled sent the following message: "On July 1st at Thiepval Ulstermen won undying fame for themselves, the Empire, and their province. Ulster mourns and will continue to mourn the thousands of her sons, but will appreciate with pride the monument which is dedicated today to their memory, which will ever record in the annals of the world's history, the contribution that Ulster made to the civilization of the world, etc. Major General Nugent, commander of the Ulster Division, was present at the unveiling of the tablet, as well as General Weygand of the French army. The Marquis and Marchioness of Londonderry were there, and the Marquis and Marchioness of Dufferin and Ava. The Prefect of the Somme was present, also Captain C. Craig and several members of Parliament from Ulster with a number of others from both Ulster and England." (This account was taken from *The Irish Times* of Nov. 19, 1921.)

VIII

THE SCOTCH-IRISH IN AMERICA AND THE REVOLUTIONARY WAR

Large numbers of Protestant emigrants to the American colonies had fled from their homes because of persecution on account of their religion—The Established Church in the colonies demanded special privileges—The Maryland colony and the Baltimores—William Penn and Secretary Logan—The Quakers—The Scotch-Irish in education—William Tennant and his "Log College"—Scotch-Irish quick to respond to call for men in revolt against England—Ferocity of English commanders and their men in Revolutionary War—Saratoga and King's Mountain—Campaign of Colonel George Rogers Clark.

IT has been said that "Tyranny and injustice brought to America persons nurtured in suffering and adversity" and that "a history of our civilization is a history of the crimes of Europe."

America proved a refuge and a blessing for persecuted European Protestants, a fact recognized by a number of Old World men of affairs. The early colonial period in America was coincident with the threat of a reviving power and will to persecute proceeding from the Vatican. In the Middle Ages, France, Spain, Austria, and the German Empire were united as a great league of Catholic powers, upheld and blessed by the Roman pontiff; and the sovereign power of these Catholic kingdoms was commended, strengthened, and exalted by connection with a powerful church. Consequently this outlet provided for a Protestant world in chains, was thoroughly appreciated and its advantages eagerly seized.

Gustavus Adolphus, alive to the possibilities in view by means of emigration advised German colonization in America, believing it was a boon to the Protestant world; and Chancellor Oxenstiern in April, 1683, voiced his belief in the wisdom of German people emigrating to America.

Not so long after this proclamation a Germany colony was settled on the Delaware, and within the century, German Protestants had appropriated a large portion of the excellent land stretching from the Mohawk region to the valley of Virginia.

When John Huss was burnt to death for holding Protestant opinions, a number of his disciples, abandoning their native land, fled to Holland and from thence embarked for America. There was no room on the European continent for those who believed in worshiping God in their own way, and persecution had taken its toll for many weeping decades. Pope Pius V urged Philip of Spain to deal with heresy in the Netherlands by means of the sword, and Alva's butcheries in the Low Countries were the answer to that bloody counsel. The Waldensian people, secluded in their mountain retreats between France and Italy, had long anticipated the reforms of Luther and Calvin and were ordering their worship accordingly, and for these independent religious convictions they were stricken to death by a tornado of intolerant persecution, designed by its authors to sweep Protestantism out of existence. Waldensian mothers, clasping their infants in their arms, were hurled down rocks and precipices, and the bones of a righteous God-fearing people whitened the Alpine mountains, until but few were left to tell the tale. The city of Amsterdam, which had suffered the same brand of cruel, relentless persecution, gave aid to Waldensian fugitives yet alive to forge their way to America.

French Protestants, too, had drained the bitter cup of religious intolerance. On August 24, 1572, one hundred thousand French Protestants were ruthlessly slain, including Admiral Coligni and other leaders, after which the furious zeal of the assassins spread from town to town, as they waded deep in the blood of their countrymen. This massacre of the Huguenots was pompously celebrated at Rome by the order of Pope Gregory XIII and a Te Deum was sung in the churches in celebration of the violent death at the hands of Catholics, of the followers of the founder of the Christian religion.

The policy of the papal court is "too infallible to err and too immutable to change." Blessings were sent from the Vatican to the Spanish Armada designed to crush English Protestantism, and even "Bloody Mary" herself was commended and blessed by the Roman pontiff.

The revocation of the Edict of Nantes in October, 1685, drove out of France a million of her best subjects, the very cream of the French nation in ethics and morals, many of whom came to America; indeed the Huguenots arrived in such numbers that public documents in the colonies were issued in French as well as in Dutch and English. The distressed people from Salzburg also found a refuge in America. The Roman Catholic Archbishop of this city, who was also its ruler, in his merciless bigotry, with cruel and relentless fury drove out of his dominions those who had adopted Lutheran opinions, and he subjected the helpless people to brutal tortures to compel them to renounce their faith and become perverts. Fugitives from Salzburg began their quest for a land where liberty of conscience could be enjoyed, and while on their way, history records the names of towns closed against them by Roman Catholic magistrates and other civil officers in the year 1733. The exiles made their way to England

and there embarked for the colonies where they found the long-sought homes near the Savannah River. The king of Spain at this time was perpetrating his autos-da-fé and enjoying the sight of Spanish heretics burning at the stake on the order of blood-stained ecclesiastical assassins. In February, 1568, Philip of Spain sentenced to death as heretics 3,000,000 people of the Netherlands.

Thus it transpired that the population of the American colonies was almost entirely Protestant, although the people belonged to different sects. In Maryland, where Catholics were most numerous, Montgomery estimates the number at one fifth of the population. Doubtless because of their previous history of intolerance Catholics in America were regarded with question and in most of the settlements were not allowed equal political privileges.

The ministers of the Anglican Church although in the minority were not satisfied to enjoy equal rights with their fellow citizens, but demanded special privileges for themselves, the vested rights they had enjoyed in England. There the Established Church, created by the arbitrary will of Henry, was a dependant of the state and a creature of Parliament. The articles of its creed were prescribed by statute, as was its book of Common Prayer, and high officers of the Anglican Church were not selected for the discharge of their ecclesiastical duties because of their piety, learning, or love of humanity, but rather for their ability to please the powerful patron, or for political or family reasons, or for some other more or less trivial cause.

In England positions of honor, trust, and power were, in the main, monopolized by certain families who possessed a powerful patronage, which was used as fancy or interest dictated, so that British governors in American colonies were not chosen because of their ability but were sent to America to retrieve their fortunes or to be out of the way. These men were often obstinate, irascible, unjust, and ill-tempered, without a sense of justice or square dealing. The Duke of Newcastle, it is said, conferred American office on some Englishmen too vile to be employed at home.

The British governor in America usually favored the Anglican minister. Lord Cornbury, an acknowledged good-for-nothing but related to Queen Anne, was an ardent supporter of Episcopalianism, and showed his partiality in a practical way by ousting a Presbyterian pastor from his manse and bestowing it on an Anglican. This peer prosecuted the Rev. Francis Makemie for preaching in a private house without a license, and for failure to use the Book of Common Prayer.

Lord Fletcher maintained that only Anglican clergy had a right to support at public expense, and in 1704, Lord Granville, supporting Fletcher, refused to Dissenters the right to sit in the Assembly, but mortified his Episcopalian friends by a law compelling reverend culprits to answer for their misdeeds before a lay tribunal. The royal assent, however, was not obtained for either law.

Industrial restraints were similar to those imposed in Ireland. Although native furs were good and plentiful in the colonies, Great Britain looked disapprovingly and with jealous eyes on American-made hats. She banned the forge, and wished to prohibit the making even of bar iron. American looms, even the making of stockings, or manufactures of any sort were denied to the colonists, and a system of inquisition of American industry was established, creating not only discontent but apprehension as well. The colonists might struggle with the Indians, brave scalping and death in the protection of their homes, and wring a living from the land. Such actualities they might monopolize, but the rewards of their toil, the emoluments, were to go to England. Commercial relations with other countries, too, were not allowed.

The slave trade, however, was placed in a different category, for it was enormously profitable to England, and was fostered by English legislation and by royal power; the laws regarding it being enforced for more than a century by successive ministries. The traffic brought to English traders and merchants an income of one hundred thousand dollars a year. Between the years of 1680 and 1700 England obtained from Africa by purchase or kidnaping, 1500 persons annually, who were obtained from far distant regions, speaking different dialects, and even differing in color. Ships were prepared in English ports, with the special approval of the royal family, the ministry and Parliament, and under the ægis of British authority one and a half million negroes were purchased in the first half of the 18th century. The slave ships were insanitary and overcrowded. The miserable captives huddled together under a tropical sun sickened, and about an eighth of them were thrown into the Atlantic. The American colonists objected to the slave traffic, but England was inexorable, and the former were obliged to submit to her despotic commands.

According to Bancroft, "There is not in all the colonial legislation of America, one law which recognizes the rightfulness of slavery. Every province favored freedom in the abstract, and laws designed to restrict the importation of slaves are scattered through the records of colonial legislation." The first American Congress gave expression to the opinions of the colonists when it resolved "that no slaves be imported into any of the thirteen colonies." A Virginia statesman testified that the British government consistently checked the efforts of the state to stop the slave traffic.

The New England colonies were homogeneous in race and spirit; those of different descent were but an insignificant minority. In New England schools were set up except in the Plymouth colony. Massachusetts required a school in every town having fifty householders, and in addition a grammar school for twice that number of families. Marriages were for a long time celebrated exclusively by civil magistrates. Greek and Latin studies were fostered. Roman Catholics were disfranchised.

In New York there were no schools except in Manhattan. Here the Dutch had established schools but when the English were in authority, these were neglected. Here Governor Sloughter was instructed to give religious liberty to all but Roman Catholics. In 1700, the Assembly of New York enacted "Every priest removing in or coming into the province after November 1, 1700, shall be deemed an incendiary and disturber of the peace and safety, and an enemy to the true Christian religion, and shall be adjudged to suffer perpetual imprisonment."

Governor Andros writes in 1678 of the religious sects found in New York. He said there were religions of all sorts, one Church of England, several Presbyterians, Independents and Quakers, anabaptists and some Jews, but Presbyterians and Independents most numerous and most substantial. When the Duke of York, afterwards the notorious James II, wielded authority in New York, he appointed in 1683 as Governor a soldier named Dongan, an Irish Catholic, who was a nephew of the Irish Lord Tyrconnel, also known as "lying Dick Talbot." The Celtic Irish Catholic was at that time in New York, conspicuous by his absence.

In 1700 when laws were passed expelling Roman Catholic priests the "Papist recusants" were included. In the time of Governor Cornbury a law remained on the statute books ordaining that a Papist priest if he came into New York voluntarily, should be hanged; and here J. P. Zenger struck a blow for public liberty and free speech by defending himself with the aid of Andrew Hamilton against the attack on the New York *Weekly Journal* of which he was editor, and won his case.

Governor Clinton of New York was the second son of the Earl of Lincoln. In his day the population of the colony was said to be mainly Dutch, English, and some Huguenots.

In New Jersey religious liberty was conceded to all except "Papists." The germ of Princeton University was a "Log College" established by the senior Dr. Tennant, and the colony was indebted to the Presbyterians and Congregationalists for what was done to promote the education of the people.

The statutes of Rhode Island showed a law, thought to date from the time of Bellomont, excluding Roman Catholics from voting or holding office.

In New York, toleration was generally practiced except towards Quakers and Roman Catholics. The danger of invasion by France from Canada and the influence of the Jesuits also created a feeling of hostility toward the Catholic body.

In New England in 1708, a synod met at Saybrook, and a system of church government was adopted midway between Congregationalism and Presbyterianism which was approved by the legislature.

A number of the early colonists in Virginia possessed excellent libraries, and we learn that every man according to his ability taught his own children. In 1693, however, largely through the efforts of a Scotchman, the Rev. James Blair, who had been ordained in England in the Episcopal Church, a charter was obtained for William and Mary College, and their majesties also bestowed an endowment on the institution which held its first Commencement in 1700, the same year in which Yale College was founded. Orders were received compelling the benefits of the English Toleration Act granted to Dissenters in England to be enjoyed in Virginia. Even at this early period Scotch-Irish were planted in the valley of the Potomac. The same race erected a Presbyterian church in the locality afterwards known as Winchester. In 1732 they went over the mountains and settled in the Shenandoah valley. In 1737 arrived more Scotch-Irish, from whom have descended the Alexanders, the McDowells, and other distinguished families.

After the death of the Rev. James Blair, the clergy of the Established Church were accused of looseness of behavior.

The father of Presbyterianism in Virginia was the Rev. Francis Makemie, later to be prosecuted by Governor Cornbury for preaching without a license in New York, and who was there acquitted after making an able and telling defense. The real founder of Presbyterianism, however, was the Rev. Samuel Davies, who made it an effective and organized body. Towns were few and schools not yet established, but the higher education was obtainable at William and Mary College.

The Episcopalians boasted forty-eight parishes and their ministers received stipends. Lawrence Washington points out that usurpation by churchmen and the absence of religious freedom, prevented a normal growth of population. Lawrence Washington married a daughter of Lord Fairfax and his brother George Washington, then

sixteen years of age, was employed to survey the estate
of Lord Fairfax beyond the Blue Ridge Mountains.
Hanna states there were 75,000 Scotch in Virginia at the
time of the Revolution of the Protestant faith.   In the
time of Charles II dissent from the Church of England
was frowned upon, and the people taxed for its support.
Dissenters were forbidden to teach, marriage was celebrated according to the Prayer Book formula, and Quakers
were fined for not attending the Established Church.   In
the Carolinas, Scotch-Irish founded homes at Williamsburg and others from Virginia, Pennsylvania, and the
coast settled in the "up country."   In 1697, religious liberty was adopted by laws applicable to all "except Papists."
Huguenots were treated liberally.   In 1704 efforts were
made to establish Episcopacy, and the churchmen were
disturbed by a law which brought their culprits before a
lay jury.

In 1653 a company of Dissenters from Virginia began
the Albemarle settlement which included Quakers, and
English colonists came to Clarendon.   Another company
of Scotch-Irish came in 1683 who were joined by Huguenots in 1685, after the revocation of the Edict of Nantes.

Great Britain made grants of large tracts of land in
the colonies, sometimes as a special favor, or perhaps to
liquidate a debt, or for some other reason.   The persons
receiving such grants were known as proprietaries, and
the prerogatives of these favored individuals were almost
regal in character.   Maryland was such a colony, and the
grant was made to George Calvert, the first Lord Baltimore.   Calvert was descended from a decent Yorkshire
family, and in 1617 was created a knight by James I.
Later Sir George received a grant of land in Longford,
and then became enrolled in the Irish peerage as Lord
Baltimore.   In 1625 he forsook the Protestant faith, and

became a Roman Catholic after he had received the grant of land in Maryland. He died, however, before his Maryland charter had received the royal seal, when the grant was handed on to his son Cecilius in 1632. The Maryland charter was made out to George Calvert when he was a member of the Church of England, and while that church was recognized in the charter, no bounds limited the full toleration of other Christian bodies. Indeed it was understood by grantor and grantee that such toleration was to be practiced, and Roman Catholics were not to be molested in the practice of their religion. The Baltimores were not propagandists and were more concerned with building up the colony than interfering with the creeds of the colonists; at the same time any attempt to proscribe Protestantism would have destroyed the infant colony. A formal document states that certain privileges usually granted to Roman Catholic ecclesiastics in their own country could not be granted in Maryland without grave offense to the king and the colony of Maryland, etc. The population of the young colony showed a majority of Protestant settlers, and these were increasing. Two Jesuit priests who came to the colony in 1633 were charged while on the voyage to abstain from religious manifestations likely to give offense to Protestants. Lord Baltimore became dissatisfied with the Jesuits, characterizing their demands as most extravagant, and instituted measures to prevent other priests from entering the colony; and the Jesuits themselves were somewhat later carried back to England. In 1648, under the Protestant Governor Stone, an act of religious freedom was passed, by which liberty of conscience was granted to all Christians in Maryland.

After the Revolution of 1688, the ecclesiastical designs, affiliations and actions of James II had their repercussions in America, and Maryland was made a royal province.

The possibility of a Jacobite revolt caused the institution of severe measures against Roman Catholics and Quakers. Puritan intolerance, however, lasted but a few years. The Anglican ministers, though in the minority, were antagonistic to the proprietary, and Episcopalian intolerance was of long duration, though many of these men, history relates, led profligate lives.

The son of the third Lord Baltimore renounced Roman Catholicism, and returned to the faith of his ancestors. The sixth and last Lord Baltimore was of little account in the colony.

As in Virginia, the majority of the Maryland population were of British extraction, and the unworthy character of the Anglican clergy, when they happened to be in power, increased the power of the Dissenting sects, besides contributing to a religious indifference.

William Penn, the famous founder of Pennsylvania, was a Quaker and a believer in religious tolerance. The colony grew rapidly. In 1683, Mennonites settled Germantown and in 1730 townships called Derry, Donegal, Tyrone, and Coleraine named after the towns in Northern Ireland existed in Pennsylvania. In 1723, Benjamin Franklin came to Philadelphia and was instrumental in founding the University of Pennsylvania, one of the first educational institutions in America, which had for its first provost Dr. Allison, a Presbyterian minister from Ulster.

The earlier sects were said to be Quakers, Lutherans, and Presbyterians, but as early as 1685 the people were English, Dutch, French, Scotch-Irish, Finns, and Swedes, and the Scotch-Irish in the middle regions were said to differ from the frontier population because of their higher grade of intelligence. The Scotch-Irish we learn "cherished the Bible and established schools." The secretary of William Penn was James Logan, an Ulster Presbyterian born in Northern Ireland in 1674, and one of the most literary and scientific men of his time. He made famous translations of the classics, and corresponded with the leading men in Europe interested in the same fields. Besides being a staunch Protestant this outstanding man was remarkable for his tolerant spirit. He founded the Loganian Library in Philadelphia and presented it to the city. He was related to the famous founder of the first "Log College," William Tennant, the senior. Religious freedom prevailed in Pennsylvania.

The sect of the Quakers, founded in England by George Fox, was not as a rule popular. The Quakers departed from the common pattern of Christianity and were not understood. The Quaker ideals were high and their lives admirable, but being steadfast in their opinions, their obstinacy and the strangeness of their ways counted against them. Quakers demanded freedom of conscience, emancipation from superstition, and they refused to recognize the delusion of witchcraft. They protested against priestcraft, demanded a pure life rather than vows of celibacy, disapproved of nunneries and monasteries, and tried to have their marriages founded on permanent affection. Militarism was denounced and the taking of oaths. They insisted on absolute liberty of worship. The blessings of what was called "the inner light" knew no distinction of sex. They claimed for woman, because of the dignity of her moral nature, the culture and free exercise of all her endowments. The Quaker did not believe in kings, and thought himself the equal of any human being. The pleasures of the senses were mentioned to be condemned, and superstitions derided and denounced. Surely a sect pursuing such ideals should be the cream of the earth, and it might have been that their opponents were unable to reach their altitude.

The Scotch-Irish have been styled builders of common-wealths. Strong and brave, staunch and valiant, self-reliant, self-respecting, industrious, and orderly, hating sham and pretense, truthful and law-abiding, they have shone in all walks of life, and achieved success, not only with the ax which made clearings in the forest but with the plow and the loom. Their desire for education coupled with their intellect and intelligence has placed them in the most important and honorable positions in the country of their adoption. Their love of civil and religious liberty is a racial characteristic, and in the words of an historian and orator they have shone "in every walk of private usefulness and public honor, in every avenue of enterprise and popular progress, and in every department of literature and every branch of science; in every theater of honorable ambition; in the pulpit and at the bar; on the field and in the cabinet; on the bench and in the halls of legislation; in the chambers of our highest courts, and in the Presidential chair, they and their sons have written their names in imperishable characters upon the brightest page of our country's history."

The Scotch, whether in their native country, or as sojourners in Northern Ireland, or as American colonists, were always energetic and steadfast promoters of education. Religion and education they ever placed on a lofty plane. How often has the local school found a place close to the Presbyterian church, the teacher frequently no other than the pastor himself, or maybe, a theological student, getting his hand in, or perhaps an elder or pillar of the church with special teaching talent. Wherever the Scotch-Irish settled in the new country, there educational facilities for young members received energetic attention.

Persistence and zeal in a good cause is not always appreciated, and early in the eighteenth century an attempt was made to exclude Non-Conformists from the teaching field where they were pioneers. A ruling was made in New York that no one was to teach a school unless provided with a certificate from the Bishop of London.

The name of William Tennant stands prominently on the page of pioneer education in America. He was a native of Armagh, Northern Ireland, and married Catherine, the daughter of an Irish Presbyterian minister. Dr. Tennant came to America in 1716, and in 1726 was ordained pastor of the Presbyterian church as Neshaminy in Bucks County, Pennsylvania. Here he started a school to prepare young men for the ministry, and his financial equipment leaving much to be desired, the building was poor, so the school was derisively styled the "Log College." The founder of the college planned to give a thorough classical, philosophical, and theological training, and time proved the graduates of the school to be zealous and successful men. The New York colleges were hostile to the pioneer "Log College" and their ministers wholly opposed to evangelical religion. David Brainerd was expelled from Yale because he had attended a prayer meeting; and these conservatives complained because he received ordination from a Presbytery. In the same spirit, Harvard was antagonistic to the evangelical Wesley because he addressed his audiences without the aid of manuscript. Plans were made and the Dissenters were informed no charter would be granted to their body, and it was only when the "Log College" proved its value that its charter was granted.

The Tennant couple had four sons; one of these, Gilbert by name, becamse a leader in spiritual development in America. Among the notable graduates of the "Log College" were Samuel Finlay, Samuel and John Blair, John Robinson, John Rowland, and Charles Beatty.

Schools planned on the Log model appeared in Pennsylvania and Delaware as well as in the south, which brought education to the very door of the people, and that without assistance from the government. Scotch-Irish instructors not infrequently gave their services without pay. Samuel Blair established a school at Fagg's Manor, Chester County, Pennsylvania, in 1790, which subsequently came under the care of Francis Allison who later was a professor in the Philadelphia College. Nottingham Academy in Maryland was established by Dr. Samuel Finlay in 1744, who was descended from John Finlay, an early martyr burned at the stake in Scotland. With the academy at Nottingham were associated some of our leading men such as Governor Martin of South Carolina, Doctor Benjamin Rush, Colonel Bayard, and such preachers as Waddell, McWhorter, etc. Pequa School in Lancaster County, Pennsylvania, was established by Robert Smith, a disciple of Dr. Tennant, and also an Irishman. His wife was a sister of Robert Blair, and their son, Samuel Stanhope Smith, became president of Hamden, Sydney, and Schenectady colleges successively. A school was opened at Neuville in Cumberland Valley, Pennsylvania, by John Blair, brother of Robert, and another at West Canococheague by John King.

The Rev. David Caldwell of North Carolina with a superabundant energy was at the same time in charge of an academy, a theological college, and a seminary, while he overflowed with a glowing patriotism. John McMillan established a church and a Log College in western Pennsylvania, and Thaddeus Dodd did likewise in Red Stone in the southwest of the same province. John Smith also opened a school.

The western institutions developed into Washington and

Jefferson Colleges, and the academies were supported until the colleges had multiplied and prepared the way for chartered institutions.

In 1748, the roll of trustees at Princeton included with others Gilbert Tennant, William Tennant the junior, Richard Treat, and Samuel Blair, all graduates of the first "Log College."

The reputation of the Princeton institution for learning and piety was such that Lady Hamilton and others collected funds to further the Princeton ideals.

Other schools modeled on the early pattern were established, which evolved into our American type of college in the middle and western states which were homes of leadership, high ideals, and religion, and which were besides independent of state control. Education was thus brought close to the homes of the people, and youth trained in patriotism and citizenship, rich and poor alike being placed on the same educational plane.

When special disabilities were placed on the Scotch-Irish race because of their non-conformity, they forced their way to the same results as the New England colleges, manifesting a zest for religion and for learning that was not surpassed.

James Bryce has made allusion to our admirable and accessible American colleges, pointing out how they train, not only business men, but those who have achieved eminence in special fields, and he mentions United States presidents who have taught school in the earlier days of their career.

The Scotch-Irish with extending vision established schools and colleges not only in America, but even in far away Calcutta and other lands beyond the sea, as Robert's College in Constantinople and Beyrout College in western

Asia, bringing light to dark places. In Pekin, Canton, and Tokio, also, the torch has been lighted. The University of Tokio was placed under the control of Dr. Martin, an American missionary, and Ward, of an international faculty of education.

South Carolina is indebted, not only for much of her general literature, but for most of her physicians, clergymen, lawyers, and school teachers to the Scotch-Irish, for they provided most of the schools and churches. In North Carolina the same race was present in such numbers that they gave color to its history, and it was due to their efforts that educational advantages were readily obtainable. The colony possessed not only classical schools but academies and colleges. David Caldwell established a classical school at Greensborough in 1767, which was styled the "Eton of the South." Another institution, Queen's College, in South Carolina was chartered in 1770; its charter, however, was repealed by George III. In 1777 it was incorporated as Liberty Hall but was closed when the Revolutionary War was started. Lord Cornwallis burned the building, but Davidson College, in the north of Mecklenburg County, was established by Presbyterians after the war.

Lord Cornwallis honored Mecklenburg County by designating it "the hornet's nest of the Revolution," and it was the Scotch-Irish people of North Carolina who formed the first colony to vote for independence. In the words of Bancroft, "The first public voice in America for dissolving connection with Great Britain, came not from the Puritans of New England, the Dutch of New York, nor the planters of Virginia, but from the Scotch-Irish Presbyterians." The people of this colony were the first to secede from the mother country.

"Manhattan and Plymouth and Jamestown,
   Can boast of their heritage true,
But Mecklenburg's fame is immortal
   When we number the stars in the blue.
The Scotch-Irish Puritan fathers
   First drafted the words of the free,
And the speech of Virginia's Henry
   Is the crown of our liberty's plea."

In Virginia there was a church establishment, and toleration, not religious equality, in spite of Scotch-Irish services in protecting the west from Indian raids. It was however due to the influence of the Presbytery that the right to worship as each thought best was incorporated in the Virginia Bill of Rights. It was the same Presbytery which sent a memorial, written by one of them, Caleb Wallace, showing a guarantee of religious liberty which influenced Jefferson to write his Act for the establishment of religious liberty. Thus was effected the divorce of church and state throughout the Union. Virginia also owes her earliest educational institutions of repute to the Scotch-Irish race, except the William and Mary College, founded by a Scotchman.

Dr. David Ramsay, historian of South Carolina, mentions Huguenots and foreign-born in the State, but points out that no country had contributed so many inhabitants as Ireland, and he continues to say that the Scotch and the Dutch were the most useful emigrants.

Dr. Archibald Alexander was president of Union College in Virginia in 1796, and in 1810 was elected president of Union College, Georgia. One of his sons was the first president of the Equitable Life Insurance Company of New York, which he helped to establish.

When the American war of independence began the

population in general held a warm affection for the people of their motherland; a number remained loyalists in spite of the provocation received, and the grasping spirit displayed by the imperial power. In New York, men of wealth with very few exceptions were loyalists, but as the war proceeded this cherished affection of the people was changed to dislike and distrust.

George III obstinately refused the desired rights the colonists claimed. The monarch was half insane and utterly unreasonable, and as it happened the British ministry of that time were notoriously inferior and unequal to the average thinking English public who were on the whole in sympathy with the demands of the colonists, as were also the best men in the kingdom. The same spirit existed among the leaders in the navy who refused to serve in America against a people who only sought the rights and liberties which England herself demanded, and for which British blood had been shed. The sordid truckling ministry must carry the blame for the barbarous methods of warfare practiced by British commanders and soldiers on the colonial battlefields, which stimulated the unswerving spirit of resistance to the end. At this time England was without a friend in all Europe, was at war with France and Spain, and had antagonized the other powers by her imperious actions; and in defense of their maritime rights Russia, Sweden, Denmark, and Portugal had united in defense of these rights of sea-going vessels. Therefore Britain's military and other exploits demanded men, and these she expected to purchase in the continental market. Frederick of Prussia refused to sell the blood of his soldiers to be shed in England's wars, and Switzerland scorned the idea of making merchandise of her free-born citizens; but other states in central Europe were not so scrupulous. Some of the petty German states could barter a few hundred men for a price, and the notorious Hessians were there for sale, and certainly lived up to their reputation when they reached America. The English conduct of the American war appalls by its ferocity—its cold-blooded brutality. America was just a struggling young people, her soldiers untrained, her resources undeveloped, and England was bringing her trained soldiery backed by mercenaries to strangle the ideas of liberty she had long nourished on her own shores. The measures adopted by the older country proved poor policy and her violation of her own tactics was widely condemned.

Lord Rockingham, voicing his opinions in the British Parliament with regard to the American war, said, "Since the coming of Christ, war had not been conducted on such inhuman ideas," and from the Bishop of Peterborough came the statement that "Great Britain defeats any hope in the justice of her cause by means like these for its support."

Washington appears to have been profoundly moved by the savageries and brutalities visited on combatants and non-combatants alike, and said, "The injuries we have received from the British nation were so unprovoked and have been so great and so many, that they can never be forgotten. Our fidelity as a people, our character as men, are opposed to a coalition with them as subjects."

Not content with plundering and burning the homes of the people, even tombs were broken open in the hunt for treasure. Jewelry, money, and plate were purloined. Precious objects of art, not readily transportable, were broken up, and porcelains, mirrors, and windows smashed. Carefully kept gardens were laid waste and rare plants destroyed. The uncontrolled rage of low-grade minds extended even to domestic animals, killed not for food but from petty spite; sometimes not even a chicken would be

left behind. Negro servants too were appropriated and
shipped for sale to the West Indies. The very name of
the British, once mentioned with affection, was now detested and hated.

For families known to be specially patriotic were reserved special atrocities, including outlawry, incendiarism,
and assassination. Women and children fled to the forest
to escape their bloodthirsty enemies; districts were deso-
lated, and thickly populated stretches of country laid
waste. British and German officers worked overtime to
get rich quick on plunder while opportunity remained.

If proofs were not incontestable, it would be difficult to
believe Englishmen, supposedly gentlemen, and natives of
a civilized country, could be so dead to every feeling of
honor, honesty, and humanity. Tarleton, who served
under Cornwallis, massacred the American soldiers who
sued for quarter, and received praise for the butcheries.
Cold-blooded assassinations were perpetrated in the homes
of the victims, and in the presence of wives and children,
and the commissioned British officers guilty of these murders were commended and rewarded for their zeal.

American prisoners died on British ships in large numbers, others were impressed into the British service and
sent to Jamaica, their families left to shift for themselves.
Thousands confined on prison hulks met an untimely end.
The story grows monotonous. It is recorded that Tarleton, after he had destroyed houses and food, beat a widow
lady who was unable to supply him with the information
he wanted; he then burned the roof over her head and left
her with scarcely a rag of clothing to cover her. The
same commander's line of march was marked by groups
of wretched starving women and children.

James Caldwell, a Presbyterian minister in New Jersey,
had achieved a reputation for his glowing red-hot patriot-

ism, so to reward such a natural feeling, a British soldier deliberately went to the minister's house, put a gun through the window, aimed at and shot Mrs. Caldwell as she sat with her infant on her knee, and surrounded by her children. The man then set fire to the house and outbuildings and all were destroyed.

After the battle of Bunker Hill, eight regiments of Celtic Irish were given to Lord North for service in the colonies, while Ireland was left unprotected.

All the British commanders in America seemed possessed of ferocious tempers. Lord Rawdon, in command of the Celtic Irish army, offered ten guineas for a dead Irish deserter soldier but only five if he were alive.

Whatever the reason, the brand of humanity prevailing among the men of the American army was incomparably superior to that generally practiced among the British forces. The American soldier-patriots Greene, Sumter, Williams, Pickens, Marion, and others were noted for the merciful treatment of their enemies, and that, too, in the face of unusual provocation. Certainly only men of a very superior type could control their feelings and judgment under such circumstances, though perhaps if a few of the British commanders had been forced to take a dose of the medicine they so willingly dealt out to others, the effect might have been salutary.

Colonel Greene accused Lord Cornwallis himself and others high in the British command of inhuman practices and sent a list of fifty men hanged by Lord Cornwallis and others associated with him, and called on mankind to sit in judgment on the order given to Balfour following the action at Camden, as well as to pass judgment on the atrocities of Tarleton.

At Charleston after the capitulation of the American soldiers and when the capitulation was formally signed and interchanged, the American officers in charge of the men were hanged, and the prisoners slain by Colonel William Cunningham with his own hands. This person then asked his men to follow his example. Such dastardly conduct would be thought scarcely possible by the soldiers of a civilized state, if the facts were not so well attested and established.

Towards the end of the war the British commanders in America were selected because of their brutal characters and the men under such command might burn, plunder, destroy, and murder at will, as they did in the south and elsewhere. One such commander, a Colonel Fanning, a man empowered to grant commissions to subordinate officers, was pensioned after the war, apparently for his misdeeds.

Another of these sub-human English commanders was a Major General Grey, who bayoneted his opponents after they had sued for quarter. Another white savage was Patrick Ferguson, who killed his prisoners, burnt their homes, and left their lands desolate.

Women and unarmed men met violent deaths at Fairfield where the Hessians and their associates were given free rein. They and the British soldiers gorged themselves with plunder, then burned down the houses, and wound up by attacking the women and children.

The Indians, more savage, if that were possible, than their British employers, were freely employed in the British work of destruction and death. Under Macdonnel, the Indians laid waste the land on the west bank of the Susquehanna until, as the commander stated, "the savages were glutted with plunder, prisoners, and scalps," and thirty miles of closely settled country were laid waste.

To their great credit, the American officers, pushing

aside the debasing example of the British, set a uniform example of humanity and mercy, and refused to degrade themselves by theft or cruelty. Any nation permitting her employees to act the part which Britain encouraged in the American war of independence undergoes a humiliation among civilized peoples which is not easily forgotten. When Lord Shelbourne was placed at the head of the English ministry the savage tactics of the previous administration became but a memory; and when Sir Guy Carleton, an Ulsterman, superseded Clinton in New York State, the former disgraceful orgies of brutality immediately ceased and clemency became the order of the day.

The Mecklenburg Declaration of Independence is dated May 20, 1775, and was prepared by men of Scotch-Irish extraction, and according to Bancroft the blood that was first shed in the cause of liberty came from the same race, which did so much throughout the war to win independence for America.

From the beginning to the end of the war, the steady zeal, unflinching courage, and brilliant exploits of the Scotch-Irish were commended and appreciated, even by Washington himself, who on more than one occasion showed his trust and confidence in them, and he paid them perhaps the highest compliment paid to any of those taking part in the conflict when he said, "If all others failed him, he would plant his standard on the Blue Ridge Mountains of Virginia, and rally around him the people of the valley, and then make his last stand for the liberties of America."

The battle of Saratoga, one of the fifteen famous battles which have changed the history of the world, was won under the command of the Scotch-Irish Daniel Morgan. America had already shown her mettle when this battle was won, but it had the immediate effect of inducing France to acknowledge American independence and to enter into a treaty of alliance with the colonies.

The battle of King's Mountain also had a far-reaching effect. The British occupied a very advantageous position, besides being superior in numbers. Here Patrick Ferguson, British commander, was killed with eleven hundred and four men either killed or taken prisoner. On the American side twenty-eight were killed and sixty-four wounded. Almost the whole number of men in this engagement on the American side belonged to the Scotch-Irish race. According to Washington and Jefferson this battle was the turning point of the war, giving fresh life to the discouraged colonial army. The Carolinas were overjoyed and stimulated to fresh effort, and Virginia was also lifted out of the slough of despond. The battle of King's Mountain occurred in 1780 and subsequent events led to the surrender of the British army. In the succeeding battles of Cowpens and Guilford the same Scotch-Irish element also did telling work.

In 1778 Colonel George Rogers Clark with Scotch-Irish men from west of the Blue Ridge Mountains and from Kentucky, conducted a campaign unequaled in valor and daring. Colonel Clark captured Hamilton, the British governor, and secured to Virginia the northwest. The campaign was conducted with less than two hundred Virginia militia. The entire conquest was conceded to the United States, and when later on England and Spain tried to appropriate the domain during peace negotiations, the American commissioner relied on the conquest of Colonel Clark as support of the American claims. Clark's campaign was compared to that of Hannibal in Italy, and its results were decisive.

The advance guard of Scotch-Irish coming to the colonies in the beginning of the seventeenth century had been so quickly followed by others that before the beginning of the Revolutionary War they were found in very imposing numbers not only in Pennsylvania and Virginia, but in Maryland, North and South Carolina, also in Georgia. It was because of their bravery that Tennessee was called the "Volunteer State," and it was first settled by "Regulators." These were Scotch-Irish Presbyterians who in 1771 came to Governor Tryon of North Carolina, asking for redress of their grievances, but Tryon redressed their grievances by shooting them down on the spot. As a result of this unexpected savage attack, others of this race abandoned their homes and laid the foundations of a new town at Wautauga in Tennessee, and it has been said that this State may be called the center of the Scotch-Irish blood of the United States.

Before and during the war the same race was very active in subduing the Indians of the west and southwest, whose unexpected and merciless attacks were profoundly dreaded. In North Carolina the Scotch-Irish were so numerous that they have peopled its history. It was due to their efforts that educational advantages were so readily obtainable.

The stream of pioneers continued to flow westward and was followed by other bold and adventurous spirits. Their discontent with local conditions rested on no slight foundation. In North Carolina the courts of law offered no redress for extortion; the justices themselves were implicated in the pilfering of public money, and these men named the juries who were to give opinion on the cases brought to them. Sheriffs and receivers of taxes extorted money from the people, much of which was embezzled. Art was employed to increase the expenses of the law, and the oppressors goading the people to resist injustice had them punished for their acts of anger, and themselves received the protection which the injured citizens demanded. Thus arose the Regulators, anxious to obtain or compel justice, and who for asking it were shot to death by foreign officeholders, such as Tryon.

The State of Georgia owes something to its McKays, McIntoshes, and others of their kin. Kentucky has been called a Scotch-Irish State. A roll of the Presbytery here in 1802 showed forty-three names almost all Scotch-Irish, as Clark, Brown, Breckinridge, Campbell, Bullitt, Wallace, Robertson, Preston, Todd, McKee, and others. Many of the race rose to eminence in the State.

Texas entered the Union through the efforts of Samuel Houston who was victorious over Santa Anna in 1836. He was the first president of the State and the first to make efforts to effect its annexation to the United States.

No racial element in the United States has had a more profound or more beneficent influence on the destinies of the country than that race which was first to secede from the parent country, and the first to shed its blood in the cause of liberty and independence.

IX

THE SCOTCH-IRISH IN AMERICA (*Continued*)
MANY EMINENT NAMES

Population of country when Revolutionary War began—Most of
early successes due to Scotch-Irish—Friendly Sons of St.
Patrick, organized by Scotch-Irish with only three Catholics
—Organizing for war; the patriots found Bank of Pennsylvania to supply army for two months; their contributions
—The Hibernian Society, founded by the same race—The
Scotch-Irish in Virginia, North Carolina, New York, Pennsylvania, and other colonies are quick to respond to call for
men; voice their unqualified support of independence of
England—Names of presidents of the United States of
Scotch-Irish descent—Names of famous men of colonial and
revolutionary times who have shed luster on the country of
their adoption, both in war and peace.

WHEN the Revolutionary War broke out, the
population of the country was almost entirely
Protestant. We learn from Bancroft (Vol.
IV, p. 416), "Yet the thirteen colonies were all Protestant
except in Maryland, where Catholics were one twelfth to
one eighth of the people, their presence except in Pennsylvania hardly perceptible." In Vol. II, p. 568, we read,
"The colonists were almost entirely Protestant though of
different religious creeds." In Vol. VI, p. 171, it is stated
that "Carroll gave hearty support to the cause of independence, but the mass of the Romish church, who were
about one in seventy-five of the whole population of the
United States and who were chiefly newcomers in the middle states, followed the influence of the Jesuits in whose
hands many of them still remained. In Philadelphia, the

British commander Howe formed a regiment of Roman Catholics."

The Frenchman Vergennes wrote, "I would count upon the Catholics . . . the principle of their religion attaches them specially to the monarchical system . . . the fanaticism of the Presbyterians make them enemies of all civil or religious authority concentrated in a chief." *Ibid.*, Vol. VI, we learn, "The sentiments of nationality and the influence of the Jesuits swayed the Catholic Irish of the United States to the side of Great Britain."

During America's Revolutionary War, Sir John de Blaquire presented from the Roman Catholics of Ireland an address to the king of England "justly abhorring the unnatural rebellion which has lately broken out among some of his American subjects."

"Catholic Ireland was against America in the war of independence" (O'Connor).

When the tidings of Lexington and Bunker Hill reached the Irish Parliament it voted that "it heard of the rebellion with abhorrence, and was ready to show its attachment to the sacred person of the king. Lord North asked for 4,000 men and received eight regiments which were shipped to America to fight the colonists." (O'Connor, Vol. II, p. 378.)

According to O'Connor, "After the first shedding of American blood in 1775 over one hundred Irishmen speaking for their Roman Catholic fellow subjects in Ireland addressed the English secretary in Ireland and made a tender of two million faithful and affectionate hearts and hands in defense of his person and governments in any part of the world."

The Ulster colonists on the other hand were in warm sympathy with their blood brothers fighting for liberty on the other side of the Atlantic. The Oakboys and the Hearts of Steel with their other relatives were being well and favorably heard from in Washington's army, and Ulster's sympathy and best wishes were with them and the cause they were fighting so hard to win.

Indeed we can learn from a number of historians just what part the sons of Ulster bore in the American war of independence. Plowden, for instance, states in his *Historical Review*, p. 458: "Most of the early successes in America were immediately owing to the vigorous exertions and prowess of the Irish emigrants chiefly from the North who bore arms in that cause." Further evidence is given by Bancroft, Vol. IV, p. 349: "The Presbyterians of Pennsylvania, Maryland, and throughout the colonies arose as one man for the rights and liberties of America." According to Froude, "Throughout the revolted colonies all evidence shows that the foremost, the most irreconcilable, the most determined in pushing the quarrel to the last extremity were the Scotch-Irish whom the bishops, Lord Donegal and others of their kind, had driven out of Ulster." William Grace says, "Probably one third of the officers and a large proportion of the army were of Irish birth and parentage." According to Lecky, "The famous Penn line was mostly Ulster Irish." Ramsay says, "The Irish in America were almost to a man on the side of independence." Lecky also said the Ulster Irish furnished some of Washington's best generals. General Lee said, "Fully half of the Continental army was derived from Ireland." The adopted son of Washington, Mr. Custis, said, "Of the operations of the war, I mean the soldiers up to the coming of the French, Ireland had furnished in the ratio of a hundred to one, of any foreign nation whatever." "You lost America by the Irish," declared Lord Mountjoy in the British Parliament. Dr. Killen said we can name a dozen Scotch-Irish around Washington for every one of another race.

So retributive justice balanced her scales and the sufferers from religious intolerance, landlord cupidity, and commercial tyranny had their day in court at last, and compelled the justice they demanded and deserved.

As was natural the Scotch-Irish emigrants in America, having so much in common, associated themselves together in various ways. One of their organizations was known as the Friendly Sons of St. Patrick and in the election of a president of this organization they again showed that absence of bigotry and the same broad spirit of toleration they had shown in 1732 when they passed what is known as the Dungannon Resolution which approved what had been done for Catholics and asked for them still further concessions of religious and other liberties in spite of the many unfriendly acts practiced on themselves by the same fellow countrymen. Stephen Moylan, a Roman Catholic, was chosen president of the new organization.

The Association of the Friendly Sons of St. Patrick was organized on St. Patrick's Day, March 17, 1771. Appended is a list of the members: Stephen Moylan, President, John McNesbit, Treasurer and Secretary, Thomas Barclay, John Boyle, Andrew Caldwell, Samuel Caldwell, George Campbell, George Davies, Thomas Fitzsimmons, Francis Tench, Col. Francis Turbutt, Benjamin Fuller, George Fullerton, Ulysses Lynch, George Meade, James Mease, John Mitchell, Randle Mitchell, John Nixon, John Shee, William West.

Honorary members were: John Dickinson, William Hamilton, William Hicks, Henry Hill, Robert Morris, James Searle.

Campbell tells us that on November 17, 1774, the Light

Horse Cavalry of the city of Philadelphia, which became known as the First Troop Cavalry of Philadelphia, was organized by the "Sons," and of the twenty-eight men who formed this troop upon the date of organization the names of nine of them were: James Mease, John Mease, Henry Hill, John Boyle, John Mitchell, George Campbell, Samuel Caldwell, Andrew Caldwell, and William West, Jr. These were all members of the Friendly Sons of St. Patrick and two more, John Dunlap and Blair McClenachan, afterwards became members. Among the eighty-eight members on the roll of the troop during the Revolutionary War were thirty members of the Friendly Sons.

When news came of the battle of Lexington, enrollment of citizens began at once. John Dickinson became colonel of the First Battalion; John Cadwalader, also a colonel; John Nixon, lieutenant colonel; Samuel Meredith, colonel of the First Battalion. Enrolled were: Richard Peters, Francis Tench, Lambert Cadwalader, John Shee, as captains.

Before the battle of Lexington two companies had formed the Quaker Blue, the Greens, and the Silk Stockings Company. These were seventy in number and drilled twice daily in the yard of Captain John Cadwalader's house.

A Committee of Safety was formed with the following members: John Dickinson, Anthony Wayne, John Cadwalader, Robert Morris, Francis Johnson.

A navy was also created with John Maxwell Nesbitt as paymaster.

The Friendly Sons of St. Patrick had a fine record of patriotic service on land and sea, and in giving freely of time, goods, and money to the Revolutionary cause.

Andrew Caldwell was appointed commander of the Pennsylvania navy and was in command of the fleet which repelled the British ships *Roebuck* and *Liverpool,* in 1776.

Of the four battalions organized for Continental service Colonel John Shee and Colonel Anthony Wayne commanded two of them; Lambert Cadwalader and Francis Johnston were lieutenant colonels.

John Dickinson, Thomas McKean, and Robert Morris were members of the Continental Congress, and the two latter signed the Declaration of Independence. Charles Thompson, Secretary of Congress, prepared the Declaration, and John Nixon read it. Thomas Dunlap printed it.

Colonel Anthony Wayne commanded a regiment in the Canadian campaign. Colonel Edward Hand commanded the oldest Continental regiment in the army at New York. Colonel John Shee commanded another regiment. Captain Thomas Procter, afterwards a member of the Friendly Sons, commanded the First Company of Pennsylvania artillery; and of associate battalions of State troops who saw actual service outside of the State, three out of six were commanded by Col. John Dickinson, John Cadwalader, and Thomas McKeon.

The Light Horse, numbering many of the "Sons," were directly under Washington himself, and in the retreat from Princeton, they were the last to cross the Delaware River.

On December 25, 1776, the troops recrossed the Delaware at McConkey's Ferry, eight miles above Trenton. This famous passage has been reproduced in paintings and prints because of the risk, danger, and difficulty encountered in the passage.

The Light Horse with its number of the Friendly Sons continued in active service until January 23, 1777. These numbered twenty-five, ten of them Friendly Sons. Washington called them "his aides."

In the Navy Board of the city, eleven in number, were

Andrew Caldwell, Thomas Fitzsimmons, Thomas Bailey, and Paul Cox, later a member.

Funds necessary for the successful prosecution of the war were urgently needed; the army was poorly clothed and badly fed, clothes were in shreds, shoes almost dropping off the feet, while the British army was well fed and well clothed. Patriotic women had torn up their house linens and were using them for army purposes; still the men were on the brink of starvation in spite of the burning appeals of Washington, and the strenuous expostulation and recommendations of Congress.

In this distressing situation the Bank of Pennsylvania was established by the patriots, June 7, 1780, for the express purpose of supplying the army of the United States for two months. Twenty-seven members subscribed $577,500 and the names of the subscribers were: Robert Morris, $50; Blair McClenahan, $50; William Bingham, $25; J. M. Nesbitt & Co., $25; Richard Peters, $25; Samuel Meredith, $25; James Mease, $25; Thomas Barclay, $25; Hugh Shiell, $25; John Dunlap, $20; John Nixon, $20; George Campbell, $10; John Mease, $20; Bunner, Murray & Co., $30; John Patton, $10; Benjamin Fuller, $10; George Meade & Co., $10; John Donaldson, $10; Henry Hill, $10; Kean & Nicholls, $20; James Caldwell, $10; Samuel Caldwell, $10; John Shee, $5; Sharp Delaney, $5.

This bank was opened July 17, 1780, and continued in operation until the establishment of the Bank of North America, January 7, 1782. Additional subscribers to the Bank of Pennsylvania were John Mitchell, $1,000; Joseph Carson, $20,000; Thomas McKean, $12,500. Ninety-three merchants of Philadelphia came with offers of assistance whose aggregate subscriptions were $2,500,000.

In gratitude to the organization of the Friendly Sons

of St. Patrick, General Washington accepted membership in the organization.

In 1781 other members added to the Navy Board were: Colonel Charles Stewart, Captain Isaac All, Director of Hospitals in Continental Army, DeJohn Cochrane, Edward Hand, Colonel Henry Knox, Captain Thomas Reid, Colonel Thomas Robinson, Captain Thomas Green.

A new society was organized for the relief of emigrants in 1790 which was in effect an offspring of the older organization of the Friendly Sons, and like the parent organization was composed almost entirely of men of Scotch-Irish extraction.   It was named the Hibernian Society.   Most of the members of the parent organization became members in the new one and the following names were added: John Barclay, John Dunlap, Sharp Delaney, John Barry, Hugh Boyle, John Bleakley, George Campbell, James Collins, James Campbell, John Donaldson, Thomas Fitzsimmons, Robert Gray, Charles Healey, Edward Hand, James Hawthorn, John Leacey, George Labmer, George Meade, Jasper Moylan, Blair M'Clenachen, John Mitchell, Alexander Nesbitt, Francis Nicholls, Michael O'Brien, John Patton, Robert Stewart, Robert Rainey, Charles Stewart, Walter Stewart.

Ramsay says, "The Irish were almost to a man on the side of Independence"; this statement refers, of course, to the Scotch-Irish rather than to the Celtic Irish, who were largely counted on the opposite side.

Most of the wealthy residents of America at the time of the Revolution were loyalists in their sympathies but Livingston of Rhinebeck, a very wealthy man of Scotch extraction, was an unqualified supporter of the rebels against Britain's authority.

Another charitable society organized by the Scotch-Irish was known by the name of the Boston Irish Charitable Society. It, too, was organized on St. Patrick's Day, in the year 1737. The members were nearly all Protestants and they again showed the tolerant spirit manifested by those members of their race who organized the Friendly Sons of St. Patrick. The Sons admitted three Roman Catholics to membership, and the Boston Society also admitted a few Catholics. The names of the twenty-six original members are as follows: Robert Duncan, Andrew Knox, Nathaniel Walsh, Joseph St. Lawrence, Daniel McFall, Edward Allen, William Drummond, William Freeland, Daniel Gibbs, John Noble, Adam Boyd, William Stewart, Daniel Niel, James Mayes, Samuel Moir, Philip Mortimer, James Egart, George Glass, Peter Pelham, John Little, Archibald Thomas, Edward Wilderchurch, James Clark, Thomas Bennett, Patrick Walker.

The second name on this last—Andrew Knox—was that of the father of Henry Knox, who rose to the rank of Major General in the Revolutionary army, became Secretary of War and Navy in the cabinet of the new nation, and whose entire career in peace and war rendered his name second only to that of Washington himself.

Campbell speaking of the Friendly Sons of St. Patrick says: "Most of them were what would now be considered Scotch-Irish; yet they organized an Irish Society not a Scotch one; they met on St. Patrick's Day not on St. Andrew's Day, and though composed originally of Presbyterians and Episcopalians with but three Catholics among their number, yet so far were their thoughts from any idea of illiberality that they chose one of those Catholics, General Stephen Moylan, who was not Scotch-Irish, to be their first president."

The Presbyterians of North America, most of whom were of Scotch-Irish descent, were according to Briggs not only the earliest but the staunchest friends of American colonial independence. The Scotch-Irish on the frontiers of Virginia, in North Carolina, in the Presbyteries of Hanover and Orange, were the first to issue a declaration of their independence of Great Britain. These people met in council at Abingdon, January 20, 1775, and there wrote an address to the Delegates of Virginia. This statement was in the following words: "We are willing to contribute all in our power if applied to constitutionally, but cannot think of submitting our liberty and property to a venal British Parliament or a corrupt ministry. We are deliberately and resolutely determined never to surrender our inestimable privileges to any power on earth but at the expense of our lives. These are our real and unpolished sentiments of liberty and loyalty, and in them we are resolved to live or die."

Bancroft states (IV, p. 100): "The Scotch-Irish of Mecklenburg County in western North Carolina took a still more determined stand. They assembled in convention May 20, 1775, where the following resolutions were unanimously adopted:

" '1. Resolved, That whomsoever directly or indirectly, abetted, or in any way, form or manner countenances the unchartered and dangerous invasion of our rights, as claimed by Great Britain, is an enemy to this country, to America and to the inherent and inalienable rights of men.

" '2. Resolved, That we the citizens of Mecklenburg County, do hereby dissolve the political bonds which have connected us to the mother country, and hereby absolve ourselves from all allegiance to the British crown, and abjure all political connection, contact, or association with that nation, who have wantonly trampled on our rights and liberties, and inhumanly shed the blood of American patriots at Lexington.

" '3. Resolved, That we do hereby declare ourselves a free and independent people; are, and by right ought to be, a sovereign and self-governing association, under the control of no power, other than that of our God and the general government of Congress; to the maintenance of which we solemnly pledge to each other our mutual cooperation and our lives, our fortunes and our most sacred honor.' "

The Presbyterians of New York, New Jersey, and Pennsylvania, while perhaps not quite so prompt in action were just as decided in their views, and deliberately and decisively reached the same conclusions. The colonists including the mechanics of New York and those from New England voiced their enthusiasm for resistance to royal authority. The landed aristocracy were hesitating and divided but we learn the Dutch and the Scotch Presbyterians and especially Schuyler of Albany and Livingston of Rhinebeck were willing to risk their all, which means a great deal for wealthy men, in the great cause of American independence and freedom.

Bancroft states: "The Presbyterians of Pennsylvania, Maryland and throughout the revolted colonies rose as one man for the rights and liberties of America."

The Rev. John Witherspoon, the only clergyman in the Continental Congress in 1776, voiced the Presbyterian decision for the Declaration of Independence. He said: "To hesitate is to consent to our own slavery. That noble instrument upon your table which ensures immortality to its author, should be subscribed this very morning by every pen in this house. He that will not respond to its accents and strain every nerve to carry into effect its provisions is unworthy the name of freeman . . . although these gray hairs must soon descend into the sepulcher, I would infinitely rather that they descend hither by the hand of the executioner, than desert at this crisis, the sacred cause of my country."

The Rev. Mr. Inglis, rector of Trinity Church, New York, writing October 31, 1776, said: "I have it from good authority that the Presbyterian ministers, at a synod where most of them in the middle colonies were collected, passed a resolution to support the Continental Congress in all their measures. This, and this only, can account for the uniformity of their conduct; for I do not know one of them nor have I been able, after strict enquiry, to hear of any, who did not by preaching, and every effort in their power, promote all the measures of the Congress, however extravagant." (*Documentary History of New York*, III, pp. 1050-51.)

From Hawkins, *Historical Notices*, pp. 328-9, we see that "The Presbyterian Church suffered severely by the War of Independence; its ministers and elders went into the struggle for constitutional liberty with all their strength. Churches were destroyed, ministers and elders slain, congregations were scattered. . . . The leading ministers took an active part in the struggle. Dr. Witherspoon was an influential member of the Continental Congress. Dr. George Duffield was one of the chaplains, Dr. John Rodgers of New York was chaplain of Heath's Brigade; James Caldwell of Elizabethtown, of the New Jersey Brigade; Alexander McWhorter, of Knox's Brigade; Adam Boyd, of the North Carolina Brigade; Daniel McCall of the expedition to Canada.

"Jacob Green was member of Congress for New Jersey; Henry Patill for North Carolina; John Murray for Massachusetts. David Caldwell was a member of the convention of North Carolina in 1776 which drew up its Constitution.

"Abraham Kettelas of the convention of New York.

James Hall, of Iredell, North Carolina, was captain of a cavalry company as well as chaplain of a regiment."

Dr. Thomas Smyth gives us a careful statement of the activities of the Presbyterian elders in the war of independence in the province of South Carolina: "The battles of the Cowpens, of King's Mountain, and also the severe skirmish known as Huck's Defeat are amongst the most celebrated as giving a turning point to the contests of the Revolution. General Morgan, who commanded at the Cowpens, was a Presbyterian elder and lived and died in the communion of that church. General Pickens, who made all the arrangements for the battle, was also a Presbyterian elder and nearly all under their command were Presbyterians.

"In the battle of King's Mountain Col. Campbell, Col. James Williams (who fell in action), Col. Cleaveland, Col. Shelby, and Col. Sevier (the latter probably of Huguenot extraction), were all Presbyterian elders; and the body of their troops were collected from the Presbyterian settlements.

"At Huck's Defeat, Col. Bratton and Major Dickson were both elders in the Presbyterian Church. Major Samuel Morrow, who was with Col. Sumter in four engagements and at King's Mountain, Blackstock and in other battles, and whose home was in the army till the termination of hostilities, was for about fifty years a ruling elder in the Presbyterian Church." (Thomas Smyth, *Presbyterianism and the Revolution,* etc.)

"The ecclesiastical polity of the Presbyterian Church influenced the government of the state (*Ibid.,* p. 355). The doctrine of the separation of church and state was inscribed upon the banners of American Presbyterianism (*Ibid.,* p. 356). There is no reason to doubt that Presbyterianism influenced the framers of the Constitution in their efforts to erect a national organism—a constitutional republic."

Smyth points out that the Presbyterian form of government was familiar to the great mass of the inhabitants of the middle and southern states.

Scotch-Irish influence and support had much to do with securing the establishment of religious tolerance in Virginia and elsewhere throughout the country. It was Patrick Henry of Scotch descent who was leader of the movement which secured the insertion of the famous Bill of Rights of Virginia with its declaration that one of the inalienable rights of man is his right to worship God according to the dictates of his conscience, and it was because of the insistence of Scotch-Irish Presbyterians that Jefferson in the next session of the Assembly was influenced to write, and by their votes that he secured, the passage of the act for the establishment of religious freedom, which has done so much to cause the divorce of church and state in Virginia and throughout the Union.

W. W. Henry states: "Thus there was completed by the Scotch-Irish in Virginia in 1776, the Reformation commenced by Luther two hundred and fifty years before."

A number of counties in Virginia populated mostly by Scotch-Irish, when the Revolutionary War was impending, effected control of their representatives in the House of Burgesses, and it was by their votes and under the leadership of a Scotchman, Patrick Henry (see W. W. Henry in *Appleton's Cyclopedia of America*), that was passed in opposition to the combined efforts of the old leaders of the province, those resolutions denying the validity of the Stamp Act which roused the continent. The Scotch and their blood brothers the Scotch-Irish held similar sentiments throughout the colonies.

It was four months before the Mecklenburg County resolutions were passed, that the freeholders of Fencastle County, Virginia, presented an address to the Continental Congress, in which they voiced their willingness to shed their last drop of blood, etc. Almost three weeks before the Declaration of Independence eighty-five men from the Scotch-Irish town of Peterborough, N. H., signed the following resolution: "We, the subscribers, do hereby solemnly engage and promise that we will to the utmost of our power, at the risk of our lives and fortunes, with arms oppose the hostile proceedings of the British fleets and armies against the united colonies" (Parker, p. 186). Even after the Declaration of Independence had been adopted by Congress it has been stated and believed that it would not have been signed but for the influence of John Witherspoon, a delegate from New Jersey, a Scotch-Irish clergyman as well as President of Princeton College.

Professor Macloski of Princeton College says that the Declaration of Independence as we have it today is in the handwriting of a Scotch-Irishman, Charles Thompson, Secretary of Congress. The Declaration was printed by Captain Thomas Dunlop, another Scotch-Irishman. Captain John Nixon of Philadelphia first read it to the public.

The Scotch-Irish served in great numbers in the Continental army and in the militia of several states all through the Revolution, and their martial achievements were of the most brilliant order. When the British army entered Charlestown there were two Londonderry colonels among those sent to oppose them and it was here they joined the forces of General Putnam and the regiment of Colonel Prescott at the rail fence, which was really the focal point of the British attack.

John Stark, too, displayed his capacity by getting together about 1,400 trained militia from Vermont and New Hampshire, and winning a victory over Burgoyne.

During the attack at Crown Point, three companies were chosen from New Hampshire to act in the capacity of rangers. Many of these were from Londonderry, three captains coming from that town; their names were Robert Rogers, John Stark, and William Stark. Captain Rogers was created a major.

Parker says (p. 239) that Archibald Stark was a native of Scotland and emigrated in his early youth to Londonderry, Ireland.

The New Hampshire Convention held at Exeter, April 25, 1775, had the troops of that State formed into two regiments which were placed under the command of Colonels Reid and Stark, both natives of Londonderry.

When Congress called for troops to defend Boston, Daniel Morgan, a Scotch-Irishman (see W. W. Henry in *Scotch-Irish in America*, First Congress, p. 118), raised a company of riflemen among his people in the lower valley of Virginia and by a forced march reached that beleaguered town in three weeks.

The American force at the battle of King's Mountain, which proved a turning point in the war, was composed of Huguenot and Scotch-Irish volunteers. This contest was a forerunner of the surrender of Cornwallis at Yorktown and the cause of his defeat.

Besides those officers already mentioned as fighting in the Continental Army during the Revolutionary War who were of Scotch-Irish extraction, among others may be mentioned: General Henry Knox of Massachusetts, General George Clinton of New York, and Colonel John Eager Howard of Maryland, credited with changing the fortunes of the day at Cowpens; Colonel William Campbell of Virginia, the victor at King's Mountain, and General Andrew Pickens of South Carolina.

Some speak of General Anthony Wayne as Scotch-Irish. His father was born in County Wicklow, Ireland. It is a familiar fact that groups of Anglo-Saxons were scattered over Ireland; the Scotch offshoot generally preferring the north. However there is said to be a tradition in the family that the Waynes are of Welsh extraction. Possibly there was Scotch intermarriage. (See *American Ancestry*, Vol. IV, p. 75.)

General Morgan, the victor of the Cowpens and General Pickens, who made arrangements for the battle, were both Presbyterian elders and their fighting men were collected from Presbyterian settlements (see Craighead's *Scotch and Irish Seeds in American Soil*). The same author states that Wayne was a Presbyterian.

Daniel Boone, sometimes spoken of as a Scotch-Irishman, perhaps because he lived with and associated with people of that race, is said by some to have belonged to English Quaker stock.

The Scotch-Irish gave to Delaware her first Governor, John McKinley. To New Jersey Scotland gave her war Governor, William Livingston. Patrick Henry, war Governor of Virginia as well as civic leader, was of Scotch descent (Patrick Henry was the son of John Henry, a Scotchman, and the grandson of Alexander Henry and Jean Robertson related to William Robertson the historian, and to the maternal parent of Lord Brougham.— *Appleton's Cyclopedia of American Biography*).

Of the four members of Washington's cabinet Knox of Massachusetts was Scotch-Irish, Alexander Hamilton of New York was a Scotch-Frenchman, Thomas Jefferson was of Welsh extraction, and Edmund Randolph claimed as his ancestor the Scotch Earl of Murray, and was thus related to James V of Scotland.

New York has the distinction of having furnished the first Chief Justice of the United States, John Jay, who was a descendant of French Huguenots. The second Chief Justice was John Rutledge, who was Scotch-Irish as were also the justices Nelson and Iredell, who were two of the four original justices; the third Blair was of Scotch descent. Chief Justice John Marshall was of Welsh origin.

Conspicuous among our naval great men is Commodore Oliver Hazard Perry, who victoriously opposed the British hero Nelson, who was compelled to haul down the British flag, and to see Britain lose an entire squadron for the first time since she created a navy. Commodore Perry's mother was Sarah Wallace Alexander of Newry, Ireland. She married the father of Oliver Hazard Perry and was the granddaughter of James Wallace, an officer of the Scotch army as well as a signer of the Scotch League and Covenant. James Wallace fled from Ayrshire, Scotland, in 1660 to Ulster, locating near Belfast. Mrs. Perry became the mother of five sons all of whom were officers in the United States navy. (See "Our Naval Heroes," by D. C. Kelly, in *Fifth Scotch-Irish Congress,* pp. 114-6.)

Mrs. Perry had two daughters, one of whom married Captain George W. Rogers and the other became the wife of Dr. William Butler of the United States navy. Dr. Butler was the father of Senator Matthew Galbraith Butler of South Carolina.

Matthew Galbraith Perry ably assisted Scott as naval commander at Vera Cruz and he afterwards organized and successfully conducted an expedition to Japan.

A distinguished Scotch-Irishman who made arrangements for a number of his fellow countrymen in Ulster to come to the United States was Robert Temple. He was an ancestor of the second President of the United States. Thomas Lindall Winthrop and his son Robert Charles Winthrop stated that Captain Robert Temple came to America in 1717 with a number of Scotch-Irish emigrants.

The government of the United States has been in the hands of a number of men of Scotch-Irish blood and parentage.

Andrew Jackson, seventh President of the United States, was born in Mecklenburg County, N. C., in 1767, the son of Andrew and Elizabeth Hutchinson Jackson. The Jacksons came to America with two sons, Hugh and Robert, from Carrickfergus in 1765. Andrew attended Queen's College, Charlotte, N. C., for a time after leaving the academy. His eldest brother Hugh enrolled in the patriot army and died after one of the battles. Andrew and his brother were captured by the British. His mother had her boys returned with other neighbors by an exchange of prisoners. Both the boys were ill with jaundice and Robert died. Mrs. Jackson carried her two boys on horseback one hundred and sixty miles and nursed them until Andrew recovered, and then Mrs. Jackson set out for Charleston, one hundred and sixty miles, to nurse and care for the starving patriots confined on prison ships, many of them her relatives; here she contracted the ship fever and died, so that Andrew was left an orphan at the age of fourteen years. Jackson became a lawyer and public prosecutor. He was elected to the United States Senate in 1797 and became judge of the Supreme Court in 1798-1804. Was elected major-general of the state militia in 1801. In 1828 he was elected President of the United States. Harvard College conferred on him the honorary degree of LL.D. in 1833. He died in 1845, and an equestrian statue was erected by order of Congress to his memory in Jackson Square, Washington, D. C., the first public statue ever erected by order of Congress to a citizen of the United States.

James Knox Polk, eleventh President of the United States, was born in Mecklenburg County, N. C., in 1795; son of Samuel and Jane Knox Polk; grandson of Ezekiel Polk and of Captain James Knox, an officer in the Continental Army during the Revolutionary War. He was a descendant of Robert Polk or Pollock (the name was shortened to Polk) who came from Donegal, Ireland, to Maryland in 1660. He graduated from the University of North Carolina in 1818, was admitted to the bar in 1820, became a Democratic representative in the State legislature 1823-5, was elected Governor of Tennessee in 1839, and inaugurated President of the United States in 1845. He received the honorary degree of LL.D. from the University of North Carolina in 1845, and died in Nashville in 1849.

James Buchanan, fifteenth President of the United States, was born in 1791, son of James and Elizabeth Speer Buchanan. His mother was the only daughter of James Speer of Scotch Presbyterian ancestry who immigrated to Pennsylvania in 1756. His father was born in County Donegal, Ireland, and came to America in 1783. He graduated from Dickinson College in 1809. He was a Federalist in politics and held conservative views with regard to taxation. In Jackson's struggle with the Whigs he supported Jackson. In 1832 was appointed minister plenipotentiary to St. Petersburg; was elected U. S. senator in 1834, and strongly upheld the doctrine of states' rights.

Because of its strategic position he advocated the acquisition of Cuba. He denied the right of any State to secede from the Union. He published *Buchanan's Administration* during the closing months of his term and was succeeded by Abraham Lincoln. Died 1868.

Andrew Johnson, seventeenth President of the United States, was born in North Carolina in 1808, the son of Jacob and Mary McDonough Johnson. His father was drowned while attempting to rescue another and so the early education of Andrew was neglected. He became a tailor and married a girl of good education when he could scarcely read or write, and his wife educated him; he became alderman and then mayor of his town. He was appointed a trustee of the Rhea academy in 1831, became representative in the State legislature, 1834-7, became State senator in 1841. He was Democratic representative in 1843, and supported the annexation of Texas, elected Governor of Tennessee in 1853. Was member of the United States Senate in 1857. His views were strongly anti-slavery and Lincoln appointed him military governor of Tennessee in 1862. He was inaugurated vice-president in 1865 and following the death of Lincoln automatically became president of the United States. He received the honorary degree of LL.D. from the University of North Carolina in 1866 and died in 1875.

Chester Alan Arthur, twenty-first President of the United States, born in Vermont, 1830, was the son of William and Malvina Stone Arthur. His father was a graduate of Belfast College, Ireland, who came to America and became a Baptist preacher in Vermont. His maternal grandfather was Uriah Stone, a pioneer settler in New Hampshire. He graduated from Union College, Schenectady, in 1848, having taught school part of the time in order to help defray his expenses. Was admitted to the bar in 1848. He held conspicuously anti-slavery views and in a number of suits defended the rights of negroes. He acted as quartermaster general during the Civil War. He was elected Vice President with Garfield in 1888, and became President a year after following Garfield's death. He strongly urged the construction of an inter-oceanic canal across the isthmus of Panama. In 1884, a treaty was made with the republic of Nicaragua which authorized the United States government to build a canal, railroad, and telegraph across the Nicaraguan territory by way of the lake and San José River, but the treaty was rejected by the Senate and was withdrawn by Cleveland in 1885. The National Convention endorsed the Arthur administration as a "wise, conservative, and patriotic—under which the country had been blessed with remarkable prosperity." As Mr. Arthur was a widower, his sister Mrs. McElroy presided over the White House during the Arthur administration, and the taste and elegance of the hospitality under her supervision was widely appreciated and admired. Ex-President Arthur died in 1886.

William McKinley, the twenty-fifth President of the United States, was born in Ohio in 1843. He was the son of William and Nancy Allison McKinley and the grandson of David and Esther McKinley who came from Dervock House, County Antrim, Ireland, in 1743, with three sons and a daughter. He served with great credit in the Civil War and rose to the acting assistantship of adjutant general on the staff of General S. S. Carroll. Was admitted to the Ohio bar in 1867. He served in the legislature, and in politics, was a Republican and supporter of the high protective tariff; he established a reputation as a statesman and orator, and was inaugurated President in 1897.

During this administration occurred the Spanish-American war resulting in the treaty with Spain whereby Spain surrendered Cuba as well as the Philippines and other West Indian islands. In 1898 provision was made for the annexation of Hawaii. On March 4th, the President signed the gold currency act. About this time the Russian and German governments were seeking an opportunity to invade China, and because of the probable danger to American commerce if the integrity of China was destroyed the President promptly and decidedly solved the problem by acting as an ally to the Chinese government, thus preventing its partition. Mr. McKinley was renominated for the Presidency in 1900, receiving every one of the 930 votes of the delegates as the party candidate for President. In November he was reëlected President by the largest popular majority ever given to a party candidate up to that time.

In 1901 while at Buffalo with his wife, and inspecting the Temple of Music at the Pan-American Exposition held there, and while the throng of citizens were greeting their President, he took the hand of one of the men in friendly greeting, when the assassin, using the other hand, shot and mortally wounded the President. The assassin was an avowed anarchist named Leon F. Czolgosz. The public manifestations of grief at the President's death were unprecedented. Unusual honors were paid in foreign capitals. In England, a memorial service was held in Westminster Abbey attended by nearly 3,000 persons. English Government buildings had their flags at half mast and all the exchanges in the country were closed. A memorial service attended by 6,000 people was attended by the Archbishop of Canterbury and fifteen other clergymen in St. Paul's Cathedral. Impressive memorial services were held in other foreign capitals, St. Petersburg, Berlin, Brussels, Vienna, Rome, Paris, Constantinople, Pekin, and Bombay.

The public manifestations of grief at President Mc-
Kinley's death have never been surpassed in the history
of the world. In America the funeral observances were
impressive, solemn, and dignified as they could well be.
The whole nation sincerely and solemnly mourned his
passing. He died September 14, 1901, and was buried
in Ohio.

Thomas Woodrow Wilson, twenty-eighth President of
the United States. The famous war president who sought
to make the world safe for democracy, and initiated the
League of Nations, was born in Virginia, 1856. His
father was the Rev. Joseph Ruggles Wilson, pastor of
a Presbyterian church. The grandfather of President
Wilson was an Ulster immigrant, who married Jessie
Woodrow, the daughter of a line of Scotch clergymen.
The grandfather was named James Wilson and came from
County Down in 1807. He became a printer and then an
editor in Pittsburgh. President Wilson's father learned
the trade of printing and afterwards went to college, and
eventually, like so many Scotchmen, became a Presbyterian minister. Woodrow Wilson was President of
Princeton University, and afterwards Governor of the
State of New Jersey, from which position he went to fill
the presidential chair in Washington.

Woodrow Wilson is considered one of our great Presidents, and he awaits the verdict of posterity.

James Madison, fourth President of the United States,
son of an Orange County planter, was bred in the school
of Presbyterian dissenters under Witherspoon at Princeton. See his motion which figures in the Declaration of
Independence.

Some other presidents have had a strain of Scotch-
Irish blood in their veins, Cleveland, for instance, whose

mother was Ann Neal, daughter of a Scotch-Irishman. Cleveland's own father was a Presbyterian minister.

The Scotch have contributed three presidents to the United States, Monroe, Grant, and Hayes, and the Welsh one, Thomas Jefferson. Holland gave us Van Buren and the Roosevelts.

It may be remarked in passing that the Scotch and the Scotch-Irish are virtually one family. There has been practically no intermarriage with the Celtic Irish and to but a very slight extent ·with Puritans and French Huguenots.

The Scotch-Irish have thus had eight of their race who have filled the presidential chair, a ninth, Grover Cleveland, was Scotch-Irish on his mother's side and while Madison was not a member of this race, he was subjected to their influence and example, and received his training and education from Scotch-Irish Presbyterians.

The late Prof. Macloski at Princeton University states that fourteen men of the Scotch-Irish race signed the Declaration of Independence, and ardent republicans as they were, about one third of the officers of the Revolutionary Army were of Scotch-Irish parentage, and a very large proportion of the soldiers belonged to the same race. The famous Pennsylvania line which bore the brunt of battle from the beginning to the end of the war was Scotch-Irish, indicated not merely by their names, but by the overwhelming testimony of numbers of authorities. At the beginning of the Revolutionary War one third of the whole population of the State of Pennsylvania was of Scotch-Irish origin.

"Almost the entire Pennsylvania line, as it was called were Irish Presbyterians" (from Gamble's *Tours in Ireland,* p. 101).

"It was Ulster Presbyterians, banished from Ireland by laws that worked oppression . . . who gave to the American Revolution its most steadfast councilors, and some of its best generals," so says the late T. P. O'Connor, late Irish legislator and statesman.

Massachusetts was obliged to banish 508 of her people for loyalty to England; Pennsylvania attainted 500; New Hampshire 76; and North Carolina 65. Some were hanged for their offensive partisanship to the enemy.

Charles Thompson, born 1729, Secretary of the Continental Congress during the whole period of its existence, was one of the number of Scotch-Irishmen who signed the Declaration of Independence, which famous document is in his own handwriting. Charles came from Mahera, County Tyrone, Ireland, and was the son of a rackrented farmer. Fifty-six persons in all signed the Declaration, and among the names are George Taylor, James Smith, Matthew Thornton, Edward Rutledge, Thomas McKean, George Reade, William Whipple, all of Scotch-Irish extraction.

Thomas McKean was the only member of the Continental Congress who served from the opening to the close of the Congress and it was to him as President of that body that Washington dispatched a courier to bring the glad tidings of the surrender of Cornwallis which meant that the war was ended. This patriot translated the Bible into the Indian language, and compiled a history of the American Revolution.

Rutledge was an active worker in the cause of independence, with sword and pen, James Smith was captain of the first military company raised in Pennsylvania, while Matthew Thornton and William Whipple were an inspiration to the patriots of New Hampshire and aided in guiding them on their way to freedom from oppression.

George Reade holds a conspicuous place among the patriots of Delaware.

John Dunlap, pioneer printer, born in Strabane, County Tyrone, Ireland, in 1747, came to America when a boy. He lived with his uncle William in Philadelphia, who was also a printer. In 1777 John Dunlap founded the *Pennsylvania Packet* which he published daily after 1783. He was printer to Congress and printed the Declaration of Independence. Was an officer in the American army during the Revolutionary War, and served in the first troop of Philadelphia cavalry which acted as a bodyguard to General Washington at the battles of Trenton and Princeton, and he contributed $20,000 to supply the army with provisions and clothing in 1782. Died in 1812.

Anthony Wayne—Mad Anthony—was of Anglo-Irish descent, born in Pennsylvania in 1745. He was descended from Isaac Wayne, an English army officer, legislator, and farmer who removed to County Wicklow, Ireland, and later emigrated to America. Anthony Wayne's military and other exploits were phenomenal. Washington appointed him General in Chief of the United States army. Died in Pennsylvania in 1796. He was a commander in the Pennsylvania line and prominent member of The Friendly Sons of St. Patrick.

Andrew Pickens was a Huguenot refugee who went from Scotland to Ulster and from thence to Pennsylvania. In 1765 he married Rebecca, daughter of James Calhoun and aunt of John C. Calhoun. He raised a band of militia for the Revolutionary War which he commanded. Became brigadier general and fought under General Nathanael Greene. He held many important and prominent positions.

Matthew Thornton, who signed the Declaration, studied medicine and held the rank of a colonel in the State militia.

He served as a speaker of the General Assembly in 1776. Was appointed a delegate to the Continental Congress, serving until 1778. Also the author of political essays. He was born in Ireland in 1714. He held many important and prominent public positions.

Thomas McKean was born in Londonderry, Penn., the son of William and Letitia Finney, both from Northern Ireland. Thomas was a signer of the Declaration; he studied law and was admitted to the bar in 1754. Was deputy attorney general, 1756-8, of Sussex County, and clerk of the Assembly 1757-8. Received an appointment to codify and print the laws of the State prior to 1752; he was a delegate to the Stamp Act Congress in New York in 1765, and influenced the according of one vote to each state. He was a member of the committee which drew up the memorial to the Lords and Commons. He held other important positions too numerous to mention. Was a delegate to the First Continental Congress, and the only member to hold office continuously to the end. He conducted the negotiations of the secret committee which procured arms and munitions from abroad. It was through his initiative that Delaware declared for independence. He was chairman of the convention of deputies and chairman of the Committee of Safety of Pennsylvania. He was colonel of a regiment of associated militia for the support of Washington at Perth Amboy. He was also a member of the convention that framed the constitution for the State of Delaware. Was chief justice of Pennsylvania 1776-98, and President of the State of Delaware in 1776, thus holding two public offices, one in each State at the same time. He was a member of the Pennsylvania convention of 1787 that ratified the Constitution of the United States. Many public honors were conferred on this prominent man. He was a joint author of the Commentaries on the Constitution (1790) and died in Philadelphia in 1817.

There are a number of McKeans of Scotch or Scotch-Irish extraction who were renowned in both war and peace in the early history of the country. Unfortunately space prevents further details of their history.

John Nixon, who read the Declaration of Independence to the assembled people July 8, 1776, was the son of Richard Nixon who appears to have been an Anglo-Irishman from County Wexford, Ireland. John was a subscriber to the Pennsylvania bank to the amount of $25,000 and held a number of important and prominent positions. The Nixons were a rather numerous family, one branch coming from Enniskillen in Northern Ireland. Another John Nixon was a very active Presbyterian. Others have been editors and public-spirited men.

A number of Maxwells fought in the Revolutionary War, some of them immediately under Washington. John Maxwell became a captain in the army, his brother William a major, and another brother a lieutenant. Somewhat later a brigadiership was conferred upon William. This man fought under General Braddock at Fort Duquesne in 1755, with Amherst at Ticonderoga, and with General Wolfe at Quebec in the same year. Later appointed colonel and attached to the commissary at Mackinaw. In 1773 he resigned from the British service and became chairman of the Committee of Safety of Sussex County. Was representative in first and second provisional congresses of New Jersey in 1775, and commissioned colonel of the New Jersey battalion for continental service, November, 1775. In 1776 he fought in the battle of Three Rivers in Canada and conducted a retreat with merit. In 1776 as brigadier general he took command of militia at Morristown and harassed the British army. The

Jersey line opened the battle at Brandywine, and his brigade had a skirmish at White Horse Tavern and also served as left wing and reserve to Washington's army at Germantown in 1777. In 1778 took part in a battle at Monmouth and in 1780 led his brigade at the battle in Springfield. Died in 1796.

William Henry Maxwell was born near Stewartstown, County Tyrone, Ireland, his father a Presbyterian clergyman. Graduated from Queen's University, Belfast, and became assistant master in the Royal Academy, and Professor of English History in the Collegiate Institute, Belfast, Ireland. Came to New York City in 1872 and became reporter on the New York *Tribune* and *Herald,* and managing editor of the *Brooklyn Times.* Became a lecturer on civics and history and later associate superintendent of public instruction in Brooklyn, and in 1898 was elected city superintendent of schools in New York City. Received honorary degrees. Translated Pope's Homer's *Iliad.* Author of several text-books.

George Taylor, signer of the Declaration, was born in Ireland; he was a delegate to the Provisional Assembly in 1776, also a member of the Committee of Safety, a county judge, and a colonel of militia.

James Robertson, Virginia pioneer in 1742. Father born in Ulster. Joined Daniel Boone's third expedition across the Alleghany Mountains and returning leased land from the Cherokees. A fort was erected here with aid of Captain John Sevier. Appointed Governor of North Carolina. Made a second settlement on site of present Nashville and also erected a fort here against Indians. In an Indian attack he was saved by his wife. Successfully opposed British control of Choctaws and Chickasaws. Appointed brigadier general, United States army by Washington, in 1790, and United States Indian Commissioner. Died in 1810.

John Rodgers, from Londonderry, Ireland, in 1721. Presbyterian minister. Became chaplain of Heath's Brigade. Was chaplain of the New York Provincial Congress and the first State legislature in 1777. Trustee of the College of New Jersey, afterwards Princeton University, 1765-1807. Received degree of D.D. from Edinburgh in 1768; was Moderator of the First General Assembly of the Presbyterian Church at Philadelphia in 1789. Died in 1811.

James Potter, born in 1729, County Tyrone, Ireland, commissioned ensign and lieutenant in Colonel John Armstrong's battalion in 1756. Appointed colonel of the upper battalion of Pennsylvania Patriot Militia in 1776. Promoted brigadier general of Pennsylvania militia in 1777. Served on outposts of Washington's army at Valley Forge. Was vice president of Pennsylvania in 1781. Appointed major general of Pennsylvania militia in 1782.

Francis Potter, born in Virginia in 1740, grandson of John and Elizabeth Patton Preston from Londonderry, Ireland. The father of Francis was surveyor under Washington. Francis became a member of the House of Burgesses in Virginia. Representative in third and fourth congresses. Colonel of volunteers in 1812 and major general in State Militia.

Andrew Porter, born in Pennsylvania in 1743, son of Robert Porter from Londonderry, Ireland, 1720. Appointed captain, major, lieutenant, and lieutenant-colonel and colonel in Revolutionary Army. Was personally commended on the battlefield by General Washington after battle of Germantown.

David Porter, grandson of Alexander Porter of County

Tyrone, Ireland, a Presbyterian minister. Was born in Boston, 1780. In 1796 was impressed on board a British frigate. He refused to serve, jumped overboard, and was rescued by a Danish vessel. He reshipped on another vessel, was again impressed, and again escaped. He was warranted midshipman in 1798, promoted lieutenant, 1799. After numerous incidents when he displayed much force of character and ability he was commissioned master-commandant. He commanded naval forces at New Orleans, capturing three French privateers. After other exploits was appointed consul general at Algiers by President Jackson. Died in Constantinople.

William Patterson, born in Ulster, 1745, came to Philadelphia in 1747. Was deputy to New Jersey Provincial Congress in 1775 and was secretary of that body. Was officer of the Somerset battalion of minute men, in 1776.

The first ancestor of the American Livingstons was named Robert who came to America in 1674. His father was a Scotch divine of rank who, because of his religious convictions, was exiled to Holland. Livingston married into the Schuyler family and became the father of four sons. The first Livingstons who became prominent in the Revolutionary War belonged to the third generation, and at a later period also included members of the fourth. Philip Livingston signed the Declaration of Independence and Peter became president of New York's first Provincial Congress, and William, too, was a Revolutionary leader in the State. Robert Livingston of the fourth generation, helped to draft the Declaration of Independence; he became a member of Congress, and as chancellor of state, administered the oath of office to President-elect Washington. Robert subsequently became United States Secretary of Foreign Affairs and Minister to France. He was also a capitalist who made possible the success of Robert Fulton's steamboat. Peter and Edward of the fourth generation were elected to the lieutenant-governorship of New York State, and their brother Henry was one of Schuyler's aides in the Revolutionary War, and afterwards was created a United States general. Three of this distinguished family were colonels in the Revolutionary War, and one of them, James by name, saved West Point from the treason of Benedict Arnold. In 1808, Robert Livingston secured legislation creating the American Academy of Fine Arts. Robert Livingston, as Secretary of Foreign Affairs, 1781-1783, directed all treaties which our envoys were arranging abroad.

The onset of the Revolutionary War saw many traitors to the cause of independence and freedom, who were known as loyalists. They included most of the prominent and wealthy families, afraid to risk the loss of their privileges and their estates, and unwilling, in spite of the provocation, to take up arms against the mother country. The number, however, did not include, as we have seen, the self-respecting Livingstons and their relations by marriage, the Schuyler family. The Van Rensselaers, too, were loyal to the Revolutionary cause when other wealthy colonists shrank from the struggle.

The Rev. Alexander McWhorter, born in Delaware, 1734. His parents, Hugh and Jane McWhorter, emigrated from Armagh, Ireland, where the senior McWhorter was a linen merchant. The family settled in Delaware in 1730, but later removed to North Carolina. Alexander studied theology under the Rev. William Tennant and was licensed to preach in 1758.

In 1775 appointed by congress to visit west North Carolina and persuade the royalists to join the American cause. In 1776 visited General Washington at Trenton to devise measures for the protection of the State and was present on December 26, 1776, when American troops crossed the Delaware and captured the Hessians. He was chaplain to the brigade of General Knox in 1778. In 1779 became president of Charlotte Academy, North Carolina, but left because of the measures of Lord Cornwallis. Became pastor to the church in Newark, N. J., and declined the presidency of Washington Academy. He was active in arranging the Confession of Faith and forming the constitution of the Presbyterian Church of the United States and was a member of the board of trustees of that church. Assisted in securing funds for rebuilding the college of New Jersey which had burned down. Received degree of D.D. from Yale in 1776. Published literary articles and died in 1807.

Charles McKnight, surgeon, born 1750, grandson of Rev. John McKnight, Presbyterian minister from Ulster. Washington appointed him senior surgeon of the flying hospital of the Middle Department. Served as surgeon general with Washington's army, 1779-82. Professor of anatomy at Columbia College, New York, 1784-87.

John McKinlay, born in Ulster, Ireland, 1721, came to America in 1742. Was brigadier of State militia during Revolutionary War.

Alexander McKim, grandson of John McKim, served in Revolutionary War. A representative of his state.

Charles McDowell emigrated from Ulster in 1730. Enlisted in Revolutionary Army. Member of state senate.

Ephraim McDowell, grandson of Ephraim McDowell, who with brothers James and John came from Ulster. Ephraim, born in 1771, was first surgeon to perform ovariotomy. His patient was of his own race, and her name was Mrs. Jane Todd Crawford. In 1809, this woman underwent this major operation without an anesthetic. Other McDowells were well and favorably known in early American history.

Alexander McCurdy, a descendant of John McCurdy who immigrated to America in 1705, also descended from Governor William Bradford, Edward Doty, and Henry Sampson who came over in the *Mayflower* in 1620. Famous educator. Received many honorary degrees.

James Robinson McCormick, a descendant of Andrew McCormick who emigrated in 1776 from Ulster. Served in Revolutionary War and married daughter of John Adams.

The names of men just given are not a catalogue of those who became prominent during the Revolutionary period; rather they are but a relatively few whose deeds of wisdom, heroism, and military prowess thrust them into notice at that time, and have received special notice because of their Scotch-Irish origin.

However it is noticeable in the general history of the country that persons of Scotch and Scotch-Irish extraction have taken prominent places, sometimes leading places, in the various activities of their period.

Samuel Houston was a descendant of John, of lowland Scotch origin, as most of the Ulster colonists were who had settled in the north of Ireland, who left that country in 1689 and arrived in Philadelphia. The Paxton family came over in their company.

Samuel Houston served in General Morgan's brigade of riflemen in the war of independence, and was assistant inspector general of frontier troops with the rank of major at its close. He died in 1806 and his widow with her nine children crossed the Alleghany Mountains and later settled in Blount County. The educational advantages of the family were slight, but Sam could repeat from

memory almost every line of Pope's translation of the
Iliad.

His youthful life was an active one. He was clerk in
a store, became a sub-chief in the Cherokee tribe and
learned their language. He taught a country school and
was later enlisted as a recruit in the army of 1812. Was
commissioned ensign by President Madison. When
wounded by a barbed arrow he had it pulled out and with
his blood flowing from the wound answered the call for
volunteers to storm a ravine in which the Creeks had
taken refuge. Later two bullets pierced his right arm
and shoulder and he was carried off the field. He did
not die as expected and was promoted to a lieutenancy.

Later on was admitted to the bar. Elected governor
of Tennesssee in 1827. He fought in the Texan war for
independence, and at an election for the president of the
Texas republic he received a large majority of votes.
Texas was recognized by the United States as an independent republic. Houston was reëlected governor in
1841. Died in 1863. About half a dozen other Houstons
have been well and favorably known by the people.

John Stark belongs in the company of Revolutionary
heroes. He was born in Londonderry, N. H., in 1728,
and was the son of Archibald Stark of Glasgow, Scotland.
After the battle of Lexington, he organized a body of one
hundred men and with them joined the army at Cambridge. He was promoted colonel, organized a body of
800 backwoodsmen and took part in the battle of Bunker
Hill, June 17, 1775, where he issued his famous order,
"Aim at their waistbands." After the capture of Ticonderoga, he led an independent force of New Hampshire
troops and routed Baum's army at Bennington. Promoted brigadier general in 1777, received the thanks of
Congress; commanded the northern department in 1778,

and in 1783 retired to his farm and died in Manchester, N. H., 1822.

Patrick Henry, famous orator, statesman, patriot and soldier, was born in Virginia in 1736, the grandson of Alexander and Jean Robertson Henry of Aberdeen, Scotland, who came to Virginia prior to 1730. His father, John Henry, was a member of the Church of England and a classical scholar. His mother was a Presbyterian, a sister of the Rev. William Robertson and related to William Robertson, the Scottish historian. Patrick tried shopkeeping and farming without success. He then studied law. In 1765 he was elected to the House of Burgesses. Here he denied the right of Great Britain to enforce the Stamp Act and carried his resolutions by a majority of one. Jefferson said of Henry's talents as an orator, "They were great indeed, such as I have never heard from any living man." He became the political leader of Virginia at the age of twenty-nine. In 1774 was a delegate to the Virginia convention and a delegate to the Continental Congress. He spoke against the plan of a reconciliation with the king of England and his influence carried the measure thus precipitating the war. He prepared resolutions providing for an immediate organization of the militia, and for placing the colony in a position of defense. On being asked to withdraw his resolutions he gave his immortal oration, closing with the following, "I know not what course others may take, but as for me, give me liberty or give me death." The resolutions were adopted. He afterwards led a volunteer force against Lord Dunmore, the royal Governor, and thus became the leader in resistance by arms to British authority in Virginia.

In 1775 he was made commander of all the Virginia troops and commissioned colonel of the 1st Virginia regiment. In 1776 he was elected first Governor of the State and reëlected in 1777 and 1778, 1784 and 1785 and in 1786 declined reëlection.

In 1777 he sent out the George Rogers Clark expedition which conquered the northwest. In 1795, he declined the position of Secretary of State in President Washington's cabinet. In 1796 declined position of Justice of the United States Supreme Court and the nomination for Governor of Virginia, and in 1797 the mission to France offered by President Adams. His biography has been written by his grandson, William Wirt Henry. He died in Virginia in 1799.

Alexander Hamilton was the son of James Hamilton and the grandson of Alexander Hamilton of the Grange, Scotland. His mother a French woman died in childbirth. He received his education chiefly from the Rev. Hugh Knox, a Presbyterian clergyman, finishing at Columbia College, New York City. In 1776 when scarcely nineteen, he was given command of an artillery company of which he made a model. Commissioned captain at the battles of Long Island and White Plains, and later commissioned lieutenant colonel in the Continental Army. After Yorktown, he was brevetted colonel. Was elected a delegate to the Continental Congress of 1782. He pointed out the danger of bankruptcy in the new state, secured ratification of the Constitution as framed. Was author of essays appearing in *The Federalist*.

In 1789 was appointed first Secretary of the Treasury. He provided a system of internal revenue, a protective tariff, regulated the currency, established a United States mint, provided navigation laws as to coasting, trade and as to the post offices, and provided for the purchase of West Point as a military academy; and laws for management of public lands. In 1795 he returned to New York

and resumed the practice of law and soon became a leader
of the New York bar, yet continuing to be adviser to
President Washington. He continued active in political
life and was killed in a duel with Aaron Burr, 1804. He
married Elizabeth, daughter of General Philip Schuyler.

Hamilton's death was regarded as a public calamity and
Burr was banished from New York City. Hamilton was
buried in Trinity Churchyard, New York.

Richard Montgomery, born at Convoy House, County
Donegal, Ireland, in 1736. Son of a British M.P. Married Margaret Livingston and made his home at Rhinebeck, N. Y., until he joined the Continental Army. Was
delegate to the first Provincial Congress held in New York
City in 1775 and a month after was commissioned one of
the eight brigadier generals in the Continental Army and
second in command to General Philip Schuyler. He was
placed in command of the expedition to Canada. He took
Montreal, for which exploit he was created major general
by Congress. He met with other successes but in an attack
on Quebec while leading his men was killed. General
Carleton, commander of the opposing forces, was a coun-
tryman of Montgomery's, both coming from near the same
place in Ireland.

General Carleton had his military enemy and childhood
friend buried with military honors inside the walls surrounding the powder magazine, where he lay for forty-
two years. His remains were finally removed at the request of the legislature of the State of New York and
interred in St. Paul's chapel churchyard.

The death of Montgomery was deeply felt by all who
knew him, and Congress proclaimed for him "its grateful
remembrance, respect, and high veneration." The city of
New York erected a monument to his memory and a
tablet was erected upon the spot where he fell at Quebec,

by the Sons of the American Revolution in 1901. Died last day of December, 1775.

John Caldwell Calhoun, born 1782, the son of Patrick and Martha Caldwell Calhoun who came from Ireland when their son was six years old. They established the Calhoun settlement in the Abbeville district of South Carolina. The parents of John C. Calhoun on both sides were earnest upholders of the patriot cause, and of active participation in the warfare against the Indians. Both families were of the Presbyterian faith. John C. graduated from Yale with distinction in 1804. Was admitted to the bar in 1807, and to the State legislature in 1808, where his sincere patriotism was acknowledged, and his attitude on the impending war with England appreciated. In 1817 was appointed Secretary of War by President Monroe and later was elected Vice President.

He became the head of the Free Trade Party. In 1828 he embodied the doctrine of States' Rights. In the Senate, of which he had become a member, discussing the tariff question he strongly upheld the theory of duty for revenue only as opposed to a duty for the protection of manufacturers. In 1843 he was named a candidate for the presidency of the United States. In 1844 he was appointed Secretary of State. Three colleges conferred on him the degree of LL.D. Author of a number of political essays and other works. Died in 1850 after a most distinguished career.

David Crockett, son of a Revolutionary soldier of Scotch-Irish descent, born in Tennessee in 1786. Became very friendly with General Andrew Jackson. In 1821-3 was a representative in the State legislature, and in 1826 became a representative in Congress. He possessed a remarkable power as an extemporaneous speaker, and led an active and adventurous life. Died in 1836.

Daniel Boone, the hero of many exploits, was of English extraction on his father's side and of Scotch descent on his mother's whose maiden name was Sarah Morgan.

Robert Pinckney Dunlap, descended from Rev. Robert Dunlap, who left Antrim for America in 1736. Graduated from Bowdoin in 1815, State representative, 1821-22. In 1833 Governor of Maine and reëlected three times. A representative in 28th and 29th congresses. Collector of the port at Portland, 1849. Overseer of Bowdoin College, 1821-30.

Samuel Finlay, nephew of President Finlay of Princeton, joined the Revolutionary Army in 1775 and was promoted to rank of major. Later served under Morgan at battle of Cowpens, where he commanded the artillery, and afterwards major of cavalry in Virginia line. Became one of the founders of the town of Chillicothe, Ohio. Appointed by Washington receiver of public moneys in the northwest territory. In the War of 1812 he raised a regiment and served as a general of militia. Died, 1829. The names of many Finlays appear in important and prominent positions in the history of the country.

William Alexander Graham, grandson of James Graham one of the signers of the Mecklenburg Declaration of Independence, and a descendant of the Scotch-Irish Grahams who left Ulster for Pennsylvania. His father was a revolutionary soldier conspicuous for bravery. W. A. Graham was State representative in 1833-40. Secretary of the Navy in cabinet of President Fillmore. Helped to establish commercial relations with Japan and proposed and fitted out an expedition in 1851 to explore the Amazon in the interests of commerce. Was nominated for Vice President of the United States.

David Graham, distinguished lawyer, helped to revise practice, pleadings, forms, and proceedings of the court of record under the constitution adopted in 1846. Author of *Practice of the Supreme Court of the State of New York*, 1832. *New Trials*, 1834, *Courts of Law and Equity*, etc.

Thomas Lewis, born 1718, grandson of Andrew and Mary Calhoun Lewis, a mathematician. Was associated with George Washington in surveys of Virginia land. Was a delegate to the colonial congress in 1775 that ratified the Federal Constitution.

William Lewis, born 1724, in Donegal, Ireland. In 1753 volunteered for service in French and Indian wars. Commissioned a colonel in the Continental Army of 1776-81. Was an elder in the Presbyterian Church.

Another William Lewis, born 1761, the son of an immigrant from Donegal in 1732, was captain in Revolutionary Army and lieutenant colonel in War of 1812.

William Gaston Lewis, also of Revolutionary stock, fought at Gettysburg. Became a brigadier general.

Thomas Lynch, who signed the Declaration of Independence, was the son of an Austrian. He studied in Eton, Cambridge, and later entered Cambridge University, England.

Samuel McClellan, son of William and Jean Calhoun McClellan and grandson of a Scotch-Irishman, fought in the Revolutionary War and French and Indian wars.

Daniel McCook, son of George and Mary McCormick McCook who emigrated from Ulster in 1780, was active in establishing Jefferson College. He and his nine sons served in Federal army and navy during the Civil War.

Edward Duffield Neill, of Scotch-Irish origin. U. S. consul at Dublin in time of President Grant. Established Macalester College and was professor of history.

Francis Nicholls, born in Enniskillen, Ireland, 1769. He became a captain in the Revolutionary Army; his brother William became a quartermaster. Francis afterwards was promoted to the position of brigadier general. George Nicholls, member of the bodyguard of Washington at Valley Forge, and a soldier throughout the Revolutionary War.

Thomas Polk, born, 1758, in Mecklenburg County, a lieutenant colonel in cavalry. General Washington made him supervisor of internal revenue for North Carolina in 1791. Held many important offices.

James Pollock from Londonderry, Ireland. Became Governor of Pennsylvania. Supervisor of internal revenue for South Carolina, 1791. Held other important offices. The name Pollock was shortened to Polk.

James Smith, a signer of the famous Declaration, was born in Ireland in 1729, worked on his father's farm, studied law, became a manufacturer of iron in York County, Pa. In 1774 raised the first company of volunteers to oppose the British government. A member of a committee of three that prepared instructions for the representatives to the general congress. A member of the State convention of 1776, that met to form a new State government and favored a declaration of independence. Organized a volunteer camp of militia to protect the State; was a member of the State constitutional convention of July 15, 1776; a delegate to the Continental Congress, 1776-78, signing his name to the Declaration of Independence. He was a representative in the General Assembly of Pennsylvania, and in 1780 appointed a judge in the high court of appeals. Was commissioned brigadier general of State militia and was a State councilor in a dispute between Pennsylvania and Connecticut in 1784. Practiced law till 1801. Died, 1806.

Alexander Peter Stewart, born in Tennessee in 1821, was descended from James Stewart of County Tyrone,

Ireland. He was also a descendant of Minion Stewart, a son of James I, King of England and Scotland. A. P. Stewart graduated from the United States Military Academy in 1842 and was promoted to a second lieutenantcy of the third artillery. Taught mathematics at the United States Military Academy, 1843-45, and later in Cumberland University and in Nashville University. Joined Confederate army in 1861 and became major and afterwards brigadier general and finally commander of first division. Received many other promotions. The Army of the Mississippi became known as Stewart's corps. Became known as General Stewart and was Chancellor of the University of Mississippi, 1874-76, and fellow of the Royal Historical Society. Honored by the degree of LL.D. from Cumberland University.

Alexander Turney Stewart, better known as A. T. Stewart, famous American merchant prince and philanthropist, a Scotch-Irish Yankee of the first water, was born in Lisburn, County Antrim, in 1803. Owing to the death of his father was brought up by his grandfather, a linen and lace merchant in affluent circumstances. He first studied theology and later emigrated to America in 1823. He taught a private school and afterwards with a legacy inherited from his grandfather invested in fine laces and linens and established himself in New York at Broadway and Chambers Street. His business prospered and he built a large store of marble at the same site. In 1862 moved to Broadway between Ninth and Tenth streets, at a cost of $3,000,000 and used the Chambers Street store for wholesale trade. He was credited with the largest annual income in the United States. Received honors from the executive government and gave largely to charity. In 1846 following the Irish famine he sent a shipload of provisions to the sufferers. He sent a vessel loaded with flour to France in order to relieve the suffering following the Franco-Prussian War. He planned to provide an inexpensive home for working women at Park Avenue and Thirty-third Street, but died before his wishes were carried out. His wealth was estimated at $40,000,000. His marble mansion on Fifth Avenue was said to be the finest private dwelling in America, and his art gallery, the most extensive in the country, was sold at auction in 1887. Died in 1876; and his body was stolen from St. Mark's graveyard. The body was returned afterwards on the payment of a large sum of money and interred in a crypt in Garden City.

Asa Gray, a botanist of international fame, was a descendant of John Gray who emigrated from Londonderry, Ireland, in 1718. He became interested in botany from reading Brewster's *Edinburgh Encyclopedia*. He created the botanical department of Harvard University. Later became president of the *American Arts and Sciences* in 1873. President of the American Association for the Advancement of Science in 1871 and in 1874 regent of the Smithsonian Institution. A charter member of the National Academy of Sciences. He received degrees from Harvard, Hamilton, McGill, Michigan; and from Cambridge, England, from Edinburgh, and from Oxford. Contributed a large number of scientific articles and was the author of many scientific books. He died in Cambridge, Mass., 1888.

Horace Greeley, journalist, descended from Zaccheus Greeley who with his two brothers emigrated from Ulster, Ireland, and settled near Londonderry, N. H., in 1640. On the maternal side was descended from John Woodman who emigrated from Londonderry, Ireland, in 1718. The Irish emigrants who came to Nutfield changed its name to Londonderry in fond remembrance of their home associations in Londonderry, Ireland. It is said that Mary Greeley, mother of Horace, was a woman of strong brain and great endurance. Horace became a printer and was entrusted with much responsibility and editorial work. He contributed his entire earnings to his parents who were poor. He finally reached New York with a capital of $10. On applying for work he was turned away because of his small size and unattractive appearance. He finally found occupation as an editor and began work on a Greek testament. Was afterwards employed on the *Evening Post, Commercial Advertiser,* and *Spirit of the Times.* Formed a company, established the *New Yorker,* and finally achieved a position among leading journalists. He refused to join James G. Bennett in establishing the New York *Herald.* He published the *Jefferson,* the *Log Cabin* and the *Tribune.* At the national convention of Liberal Republicans, Cincinnati, in 1872, was nominated for President of United States, receiving 482 votes to 187 for Charles Francis Adams. At the Democratic national convention held at Baltimore, received 688 votes out of 726 votes cast. Died in 1872. The printers of the United States marked his grave in Greenwood with a bronze bust. The Tribune Association erected at the entrance to their building a colossal bronze statue and New York City erected a bronze statue to his memory in Greeley Square. Author of many literary works including books, and was the recipient of honorary degrees.

The ancestors of John William Mackay, capitalist, emigrated from Scotland to the north of Ireland and later went to Dublin, where the subject of this sketch was born. The family came to New York City in 1840. He attended the public schools and learned the trade of shipbuilding. In 1849 engaged in mining in California, and in time formed a partnership. In 1872 the Bonanza mines were discovered in the Sierra Nevadas and the owners became extremely wealthy, Mackay owning two fifths of the mines. With partners he founded the Bank of Nevada in San Francisco, and in 1884 formed a partnership with J. G. Bennett of the New York *Herald* and in same year laid two cables across the Atlantic from United States to England and France, Bennett and he constituting the sole owners of the Commercial Cable Company, and Postal Telegraph Company, of which he was president. Was elected a director of the Southern Pacific Railroad in 1899 and in consequence of his initiative the Pacific cable was carried from San Francisco to the Philippines. Died in England in 1902.

Robert Fulton, engineer, born in Pennsylvania in 1765 of Scotch-Irish parentage. A large number of Fultons are living today in the north and northeast of Ulster. The Fultons in America were among the early settlers of the town of Lancaster; and Robert Fulton, Senior, was one of the founders of the Presbyterian church of that place.

Robert showed his engineering tastes and artistic tastes in his early 'teens in the manufacture of toy boats and in painting. He went to England and by means of introductory letters secured the patronage of some of the nobility. Fulton had original ideas on mechanics and engineering. In 1790 he was actively engaged as a civil engineer and the following year was author of a number of useful inventions which he patented. He was employed to do some work in France. Fulton met Robert E. Livingston in Paris, then United States Ambassador. Fulton returned to America and experiments were made on the Hudson with the assistance of Livingston and Nicholas Roosevelt. Specifications for an engine were submitted to Watt in England and approved, and in 1807 was in place on the deck of the *Clermont* and the first Hudson river boat made its way to Albany in thirty-two hours, after which regular trips were made between these cities. It was not long before the boat was fitted for passenger traffic and after the installation of a new boiler, steam navigation was established. There was much and expensive opposition to his plans. Before he died five steamboats were navigating the Hudson, also ferry communication with Brooklyn and New Jersey. He built for the United States navy a steamship of war, the first of its class ever built. This inventor published many works. Died in New York, 1815.

Alexander Graham Bell was a native of Scotland, born in Edinburgh in 1847. His father and grandfather had achieved a reputation in the invention and improvement of methods of instructing persons born deaf and dumb. Alexander's education was ordered to fit him for the same kind of work, and he thus became inventor of the telephone.

Samuel Finlay Breese Morse was the son of Rev. Jedediah Morse and great-grandson of Rev. Samuel Finlay, D.D. a Scotch-Irish president of Princeton College.

He first decided to become an artist and did some painting, having considerable success. Returning from Europe to the United States in 1832 he while on board became interested in the affinity of magnetism and electricity; and impressed with the idea that signs representing figures and letters might be transmitted.

His ideas were perfected, exhibited and improved. In time the invention was sufficiently complete to send the news of Polk's election by wire to Washington. Patents were extended and adopted in European countries and Morse then turned his attention to submarine telegraphy.

He received decorations from various foreign countries. He published poems and a number of articles on science and economics. He died in New York in 1872. Among his writings are *Confessions of a French Catholic Priest* and *Is the Protestant or Papal System Most Favorable to Civil and Religious Liberty* (1841).

Thomas Alva Edison, inventor, was descended on the paternal side from Dutch ancestors. His mother was Nancy Elliot Edison of Scotch-Irish extraction, an able woman of strong character. His numerous electrical inventions are almost breath-taking. He sold his patent for a phonograph in France for $1,000,000. In New Jersey he erected the largest private laboratory in the world. Organized manufacturing plants in three states, and formed an electrical company with a capital stock of $12,000,000. His inventions have added immensely to the comfort and wealth of the world.

Cyrus Hall McCormick, of Scotch descent, son of Robert and Mary McChesney Hall McCormick. His father had invented various labor-saving devices. Cyrus at the age of twenty-two was already inventing. In 1851 he took a reaper to the World's Fair in London which the *Times* of London stated was worth more to the farmers of England than the whole cost of the exposition. The McCormick invention was declared by Reverdy Johnson to be worth $55,000,000 a year to the United States, a statement not disputed. Mr. McCormick has received prizes, diplomas, medals, and the rank of officer of the Legion of Honor. He gave $100,000 to found the Presbyterian Seminary of the Northwest in Chicago in 1850 which became the McCormick Theological Seminary and his gifts to the institution aggregated $300,000. Established the McCormick professorship of natural philosophy in Washington and Lee University. Aided Union Theological Seminary in Virginia to the amount of $30,000. Supported the *Interior,* a religious paper in 1872 which developed into the organ of the Presbyterian Church in the northwest. Became president of the McCormick Harvesting Machine Co. on his father's death. Received many marks of distinction. Died in 1884.

James Robinson McCormick was descended from Andrew and Catherine Adams McCormick who came from Ulster in 1776. Andrew served in the Revolutionary War, and married the daughter of John Adams, who with his sister Catherine, fled from Germany to escape the persecution of the Roman Catholics. James graduated from Memphis Medical College in 1849, was a delegate to the State constitutional convention in 1862, which position he resigned to serve in the Federal army where he became brigadier general. In 1856 elected a State senator and later was Democratic representative in the 40th Congress. Reëlected in 41st and 42nd congresses. Died in 1890.

Other McCormicks of note were: Henry Clay McCormick, representative, and descendant of Hugh McCormick and James McCormick from Londonderry, Ireland, in 1754, who had taken part in the famous siege of Londonderry.

Leander J. McCormick, Scotch-Irish, brother of Cyrus Hall McCormick, invented a number of machines for agricultural use and improved others. His manufacturing business was incorporated under the name of McCormick Harvesting Machine Company. He presented in 1871 to the University of Virginia a twenty-six inch refracting telescope, then the largest refracting lens in the world, and the building in which it was placed was known as the McCormick Observatory.

Richard Cunningham McCormick, a Governor of Arizona, is a descendant of James McCormick of Londonderry, Ireland (1700). Was a war correspondent during Crimean War, 1854-55. Editor of *Young Men's*

Magazine, 1858-59. Connected with the *Evening Post,* 1860-61, and other papers. Secretary of Arizona in 1865 when it was a territory, and in 1866 appointed Governor. Became a delegate in Congress from Arizona. He filled a great many other important public positions and was author of a number of papers. Died in 1901.

Robert McCormick, inventor. Father was Scotch-Irish from Ulster and served in the Revolutionary War. He invented and manufactured labor-saving implements for farm use. In 1809 invented the first grain-cutting instrument, improved by his sons Cyrus Hall and Leander J. From his inventions and those of his sons grew the McCormick Harvesting Machine Company in Chicago, Ill. Also invented a hemp-breaking machine, a number of threshing machines, a blacksmith's bellows, and a machine to supply power by putting water under pressure. Was a student of classical literature and science. Died in 1846.

Samuel Black McCormick, educator and Presbyterian minister. President of Coe College in 1897. Received honorary degree of LL.D.

George Brinton McClellan, Scotch-Irish extraction, soldier, general in the Civil War, engineer, and inventor. Declined the presidency of the University of California in 1868, and of Union College in Schenectady in 1869. Was nominated for Vice President of United States; president of railway companies, Governor of New Jersey, 1878-81, author of military papers. Died in 1885.

James Gillespie Blaine, of Scotch-Irish extraction. His grandfather, Ephraim Blaine, served as a commissary general under Washington. His mother came from Ulster, Ireland. Studied law. Took prominent part in debates on Civil War in Congress. Helped to form an equitable basis for reconstruction of the Union, the 14th Amendment being the embodiment of his ideas. He opposed the proposition to pay the national debt in greenbacks. He was the means of having the Anglo-American treaty of 1870 passed, giving protection to naturalized citizens. Speaker of the House from 1869-76. Opposed the Bland Silver Bill favoring a bimetallic currency. Promoted the shipping industries of the United States. Upheld the purity of the ballot. Favored the exclusion of the Chinese. Unsuccessful candidate for the Presidency in 1880 and 1884. Led a very active, distinguished, and useful life. Died in 1893.

James McCosh, educator, born in Scotland. Studied at the University of Glasgow, and studied theology at University of Edinburgh. In 1838 was in charge of a Presbyterian church at Brechin. Appointed professor of logic and metaphysics in Queen's College, Belfast, Ireland, in 1852. Became president of Princeton University in 1868, where he was also professor of biblical instruction, psychology, and the history of philosophy. During his administration number of students increased from 204 to 603; and new fellowships were founded; number of professors increased from seventeen to forty-one. The standard of scholarship was raised, the number of buildings enlarged, the number of books and apparatus trebled, and the sum of $3,000,000 added to the funds of the institution which he raised to the dignity of a university. Resigned his presidency in 1887. Received innumerable honors and many honorary degrees. Author of many works on psychology, science, philosophy, and Christianity. Died in 1894 and was buried in the presidents' lot in Princeton Cemetery.

Alexander K. McClure, journalist and editor. Was commissioned assistant adjutant general of the United States in 1861. With the assistance of two clerks he had seventeen regiments in the field in two months. Practiced law 1868-1875, wrote biographies and other works of merit. Died at beginning of the century.

William Rainey Harper, educator, born in Ohio, a descendant of William Rainey who came from Ireland in 1831 and of Robert and Jennet Harper coming from Ulster in 1795. Became a professor of Hebrew and the cognate languages in the Baptist Union Theological Seminary, 1879-86. Appointed to the chair of the Semitic languages in Yale, 1886, and chosen Woolsey professor of biblical literature. In 1891 became president of the University of Chicago. Instituted the Hebrew correspondence school and the American Institute of Hebrew, which became the American Institute of Sacred Literature. Received many honors and was an author of unusual standing.

Marcus Alonzo Hanna, Senator, direct descendant of Thomas Hanna from Ulster in 1764 to Pennsylvania; some of his descendants now in Virginia. Republican in politics and close friend of President McKinley.

John Hall, born in County Armagh, Ireland, 1829. Graduated in Belfast College, 1846, and in theology in 1849. Was pastor of the First Presbyterian Church in Armagh, 1852-58. Edited the *Evangelical Witness* and built the Rutland Square Presbyterian Church in Dublin. Was appointed by the viceroy of Ireland commissioner of education and received from Queen Victoria the honorary appointment of commissioner for Ireland. Received a call as pastor to the Fifth Avenue Presbyterian Church, New York, then on Nineteenth Street, which he accepted. He was the means of erecting a new church edifice costing $1,000,000, and established numerous missions and charitable institutions supported by contributions from his parishioners. Was chancellor of the University of the City of New York, a trustee of Princeton Seminary, of

Wells College, and Wellesley College, besides membership in many organizations. Author of a number of published works. He died at Bangor in County Down, Ireland, 1898, and his remains were interred in Woodlawn, New York City.

John Borland Finlay, clergyman, from County Antrim, Ireland. Graduate of Royal College of Belfast and received degree of A.M. from University of Leipzig and Ph.D., 1846. Came to New York in 1848. Became pastor of the Williamsburg Church, King's County, New York. Editor of *The Protestant, The True Freeman,* and contributed to the daily *Times,* taught Latin, Greek, and history in the Collegiate Institute. In 1856 was admitted to the bar. Elected to the Pennsylvania Historical Society. In 1860 admitted as attorney and counselor to the United States Supreme Court. Commissioner to the World's Fair at Paris and in 1873 to the Vienna Exposition. Originator of the Omaha Theological Seminary, also originator and president of the University of Omaha. Died in Omaha, 1897.

Samuel Finlay, educator, born County Armagh, Ireland, in 1715. Received a liberal education in his own country. Came to America with parents and six brothers in 1740, entered the Presbyterian ministry in Philadelphia. Became principal of an academy at Nottingham, Md. In 1761 accepted the presidency of the College of New Jersey and was also a trustee. The university made him an S.T.D. in 1763. Died in Philadelphia in 1766.

James Logan, jurist and educator, born in County Armagh, Ireland, in 1674. Secretary to William Penn, founder of public academy afterwards the University of Pennsylvania. A member of the Society of Friends. Bequeathed the Loganian Library to Philadelphia. Author, Governor of Pennsylvania, etc.

James Venable Logan, educator, a descendant of James Logan of Ulster who settled in Pennsylvania about 1700. Received degrees of D.D. and LL.D. Professor of ethics at Central University, Kentucky. His son Sandford McBrayer Logan also a Presbyterian minister.

John Alexander Logan, statesman and soldier. His father came from Ulster in 1823. A candidate for the nomination for President of the United States. Commander in Chief of Grand Army of Republic. It was owing to his proposal that May 30 was made a national holiday.

Daniel McCook, son of George McCormick McCook, who came from Ulster in 1780. Was active in establishing Jefferson College. Daniel and his nine sons served in the Federal army and navy during the Civil War.

Edward Moody McCook, active in Civil War. Became colonel and brigadier general. Was United States minister to Hawaii and territorial Governor of Colorado.

William Thompson, Lord Kelvin, born in Belfast, June 24, 1814, scientist as modest as he was great. Knighted in 1846. In 1892 was raised to the peerage. Received the Grand Cross of the Victorian Order in 1896. In 1890 elected president of the Royal Society, and his list of honors would fill a page. He introduced accurate methods of measuring the state of the atmosphere and noting variations during thunderstorms and at other times. Famous physicist and scientist.

Sir Robert Hart, a controller of customs in China, was the son of a Scotch-Irish mill worker in Belfast, and was educated under Dr. James McCosh, then president of Queen's College, Belfast, later the president of Princeton University in New Jersey.

Another Ulsterman was the famous Francis Hutchison, born in Ulster in 1694. He published *Letters of Hiber-*

nicus, and founded the school of Scotch philosophy in conjunction with William Reid, Adam Smith, and Dugald Stewart, with other members. Also founded a school in Dublin.

Indeed it is the opinion of the Right Hon. Thomas Sinclair, that the north of Ireland has contributed to the British Imperial Service some of its greatest ornaments. He says England owes to Ulster Governors General like Lord Dufferin and Lord Lawrence; soldiers like John Nicholson and Sir George White; administrators like Sir Henry Lawrence and Sir Robert Montgomery; great judges like Lord Cairns and Lord Macnaghten. This author also said that at one of the Delhi Durbars the king decorated three Ulstermen, one of them being Sir John Jordan, British ambassador at Pekin. The author continues, "Ulster produced Sir Robert Hart, the incomparable Chinese administrator who might have been our ambassador to China had he accepted the position." And these distinguished men came from just one tiny corner of the vast British Empire.

The Scotch-Irish race has shown the same characteristics in Canada where Robert Baldwin and a large number of associates of the same blood did much to secure the establishment of Canada.

James J. Hill, the great railroad builder, who by his energy, initiative, and judgment opened up the great country of the northwest, was born in Ulster, Ireland.

Lord Carson, more familiarly known as Sir Edward Carson, the great Ulster leader and statesman, died at his home on October 22, 1935, at the age of eighty-one. His father was Edward Henry Carson, a civil engineer, and his famous son was born at Dublin in 1854. The mother's maiden name was Isabella Lambert of Castle Ellen, Galway. This Ulster leader possessed mental and moral qualities of a high order. In his legal activities he was quick to detect falsehood and was a past master in the art of cross-examination. His addresses were always clear and concise, and his arguments logical and well balanced. By nature he was simple, honest, and direct and his remarks were instinctively felt to be a reflection of his own nature. His straightforwardness and honesty were above reproach and these qualities made of him an antagonist to be dreaded.

Lord Carson was a bitter antagonist of Home Rule for all Ireland and his activities in Irish affairs took precedence of all other work, so that he was fairly idolized by the Protestants of Ulster and disliked just as much by the Roman Catholic and Nationalist majority, who in spite of their hatred of him could not withhold a feeling of admiration for their irreconcilable foe.

The political career of Lord Carson began in 1892, in which year he became solicitor general for Ireland; then solicitor general of the United Kingdom from 1900 to 1906, and attorney general in 1915. In 1892 he was returned to Parliament as Conservative-Unionist member for Dublin University and held his seat in the House of Commons until 1918, and for the three following years he represented the Duncairn division of Belfast.

He was Queen's Counsel at the Irish bar in 1889, and "took silk" at the English bar in 1894. Was knighted in 1900, entered the British Parliament, and did much to defeat Gladstone's second Home Rule Bill. For the succeeding twenty years most of his attention was given to the practice of law, in which he was exceptionally successful, appearing in many famous trials.

Sir Edward approved the threats of armed opposition against Home Rule in Ulster, and organized a local volunteer force which soon assumed vast proportions, increasing to 100,000 men, and the leader urged peace but with preparation. The situation was changed by the World War but aggressive measures were resumed when that war was over.

Carson is remembered best as an unequaled cross-examiner. In the House of Lords Lord Chancellor Hailsham said, "Lord Carson was a great man in every sense of the word. His courage, sincerity, and deep patriotism marked him out as one of the great figures of his generation." And Sir Gerald Hurst, K.C., in behalf of the bar, associated its members in the Lord Chancellor's tribute. Lord Chief Justice Hewart had this to say of the dead: "He was without doubt one of the most illustrious advocates and one of the bravest and strongest statesmen the world has ever known." Ulster will never forget the heroic efforts of this friend in need in one of her darkest hours.

James, Lord Bryce, who acted as Ambassador to Washington some years ago, was the son of another Bryce, a Presbyterian clergyman, who lost his life while obtaining some geological specimens. An ancestor of Ambassador Bryce was also a James Bryce, who went to Ulster, Ireland, leaving his home at Dechmont Hill in Lanarkshire, where the Bryce family resided in 1659.

James Bryce the Ambassador was born in Ireland in 1838 so that he was nearly eighty-four years old at the time of his death.

The ancestor of Bryce was the younger son of Bruce, the laird of Auth, who obtained his degree from the University of Edinburgh, became a Presbyterian minister to a parish near his home, where he met his wife. To escape the persecution raging in Scotland against persons of his faith he fled to Ireland, locating at Aghadoey, where he ministered for fifty years.

Ambassador Bryce liked to be remembered for the improvement he effected in Anglo-American relations during his term at Washington.

When only twenty years old, he published *The Holy Roman Empire,* and in his more mature years he prepared *The American Commonwealth,* used in schools and colleges throughout the country since 1888, and regarded as one of the foremost works of its kind. A later work was entitled *Modern Democracies.*

Ambassador Bryce was considered one of the leading scholars in politics and governmental work throughout the world. He served Great Britain for six years in this country, from 1907 to 1912. As a linguist and translator he was above the average, and besides a cultured English spoke fluently six other languages. He was also a mountain climber, as well as author, traveler, explorer, lawyer, statesman, and diplomat.

The Ambassador received his education at the University of Glasgow, and later was a student at Trinity College, Oxford.

Lord Bryce was an advocate of the League of Nations, and headed the commission which investigated and presented the evidence of atrocities committed by Germany in Belgium. He criticized the Treaty of Versailles, saying it contained the seeds of future wars. He stated, while lecturing at Williams College, that he favored a World's Court, a Code of Law, and disarmament. More than thirty universities in all parts of the world recognized his scholarship and public service by awarding him honorary degrees.

Lack of space forbids further addition to the list of notables of the Scotch-Irish race who have taken an important part in building up the commonwealth of the United States. To make a mere list of names without mentioning achievements would occupy much more space than remains at disposal, but the relatively small number given is sufficiently large to show the caliber of the men and the nature of the service they had the honor to render. And they have combined a marked intellectuality with high moral principles, integrity, and a strong love of education.

Parker has said: "These Scotch Calvinists breathed the spirit of John Knox, and always fervently contended that the final regulation of political action belongs to the people." They were always rigid upholders of the separation of church and state, and the democratic form of their church government had fostered democratic ideals of government among their people spread over a large part of the country. It is not therefore surprising that the Scotch-Irish Presbyterians of Carolina, of New York, New Jersey, and Pennsylvania, were some of them the very first and others among the first to declare for American independence. No wonder Bancroft, speaking of the Presbyterians of Maryland and other colonies where Scotch-Irish prevailed, said, "They rose as one man for the rights and liberties of America."

The race under discussion had also aided in the nurture of republican sentiment in the states for they had contributed the principal schoolmasters in all the American provinces south of New York, prior to the Revolution, so that a large number of the leaders in the war of independence, as well as the youth in the lower, middle, and southern states, had received their instruction from the Scotch-Irish race, and it has been unequivocally stated that "From them [these schoolmasters] the people undoubtedly caught that ardent love of liberty, and gained an increased glow of patriotism from the association."

Thus in war and peace the members of the Scotch-Irish race have proved themselves doers rather than talkers and dreamers. They have given direction to the common-wealth, and proved the very backbone of the Republic. In this the country of their adoption they do not herd together in political or other associations but blend with their fellow countrymen, but if they disappear as a racial entity they remain loyal, patriotic citizens of the greatest, freest country in the world.

INDEX

Agriculture, methods poor, better understood in north, 218-220

Anne, the Queen, gave rein to prelates of Established Church, 127

Army, Continental, mostly Protestant, 281-282

Bancroft, the historian, opinions on Presbyterian support of Revolutionary War, 290-291

Belfast, metropolis of the north, and industries, 124-126, 157

Bell, Alexander Graham, inventor of telephone, 328

Black and Tans, difficulty in obtaining for police work because of frequent murders, 236-239

Blair, James, Scottish Episcopal clergyman, established College of William and Mary in Virginia, 260-261

Boone, Daniel, his exploits, 297

Boyne, battle of the, sweeping victory, and results, 101-103

Brehon Laws, of Celts, any crime might be compensated in money, 32, 36

Brutality, atrocities committed in the United States during Revolutionary War by the English, 271-275

Bryce, Edward, historian, scientist, diplomatist, 338-339

Carrickfergus Bay, near Belfast, 55, 149

Carson, Sir Edward, signs Solemn League and Covenant, 244

Catholic religion proscribed, 136

Catholics allowed to re-arm, 147-148

Cavendish, Sir Frederick, murdered by Invincibles who were Fenians, 221-222

Celtic characteristics, as depicted by Macaulay, Froude, O'Connor, Nassau Senior, 167-172

Censorship of press and literature, 229-230

Charles I, favors Catholics, 53

Charles II, penal laws in abeyance under, 82

Church, the Established, in Maryland, desires special privileges, 256

Clark, George Rogers, exploits in Virginia remarkable and valuable, 278

Coercion Acts, imposed really to suppress crime, did not interfere with liberties of peaceful citizens, 224-225

Colleges, established by Scotch-Irish, 268-271

Communism is favored by De Valera, 240

Cookstown, the Presbyterian church here torn down by order of Anglican prelates in eighteenth century, 105

Cornbury, Lord, related to the Queen, intolerant to Dissenters and very friendly to Anglicans, 257

Corruption, Parliamentary, very marked and widely known, 178-180

Crommelin brothers, supervise linen industry in north and south, 123

Cromwell, Oliver, punishes assassins who loudly complain of measures less severe than their own, 66-71

Dale, Mrs., murdered by Catholic women and boys, 205

Defeat, Huck's, many Scotch-Irish participated, 293

343

www.ingramcontent.com/pod-product-compliance
Lightning Source LLC
Chambersburg PA
CBHW070551270326
41926CB00013B/2280